KANT'S
THEORY OF
JUSTICE

KANT'S
THEORY OF
JUSTICE

Allen D. Rosen

CORNELL UNIVERSITY PRESS

ITHACA AND LONDON

First published 1993 by Cornell University Press.
First printing, Cornell Paperbacks, 1996.

International Standard Book Number 0-8014-2757-6 (cloth)
International Standard Book Number 0-8014-8038-8 (paper)
Library of Congress Catalog Card Number 93-25807
Printed in the United States of America
Librarians: Library of Congress cataloging information appears
on the last page of the book.

Contents

Preface

OVER THE PAST TWO OR THREE DECADES THERE HAS BEEN A
marked revival of interest in Kant's political philosophy. In part
this revival is a reflection of the increased interest in Kant's
philosophy generally. In part it is a result of the broad resur-
gence of interest in liberalism and the philosophical roots of
liberal political thought, some of which are distinctly Kantian.
Whatever the reason, it represents a welcome turn of events.
Kant is one of the founders of classical liberalism and it is all to
the good that his political philosophy is now receiving the attention it has deserved all along.

I have tried to write this account of Kant's political philosophy at a level that will engage the interest of Kant specialists
without leaving the general reader or undergraduate philosophy
major in a fog. I have therefore avoided technical jargon wherever possible and explained it when avoidance was not viable.

I have also tried to steer a middle course between two errors
that are widespread in the literature on Kant's political philosophy. One consists in uncritically and slavishly accepting at
face value everything—or nearly everything—Kant happens to
say. From works of this kind we can learn little. The other

consists in rejecting Kant's political philosophy out of hand as
the tired ideas of a once great thinker well past his prime. From
works of this kind, rarer now than twenty years ago, we can
learn even less. It has been my objective to approach Kant sym-
pathetically, as befits one of the great thinkers in the history of
philosophy. But I am also keenly aware of his limitations as a
writer and political philosopher, and so I have also attempted to
maintain a critical distance from his arguments and assumptions. When it has seemed to me possible to present his beliefs
in a plausible light, I have endeavored to do so; when they have
struck me as manifestly indefensible, I have said so.

I owe a debt of thanks to several people and organizations in
connection with this book. To Allen Wood at Cornell University, I owe the largest debt of gratitude. I learned a great deal
from Allen, more than from any other teacher I have had. He
has always been generous with his time, wise and prudent with
his advice, and encouraging at just the right moments. My
wife, Catherine, also deserves special thanks—for providing
moral support as I struggled through this project. In addition I
express my appreciation to a small group of friends and teach-
ers for their help and encouragement: David Lyons, Terence Irwin, Michael Alexander, Richard Moran, Susan Bruce, Alan
Sidelle, Steven Sullivan, Dana Hays, Teresa Lowe, and Betty
Wall. Not to be omitted from the list of those who helped this
book along, and made it better than it otherwise would have
been, are Roger Haydon, my extremely patient, good-humored,
helpful editor at Cornell University Press, and Thomas Pogge,
whose incisive and constructive comments on an earlier draft
led to many revisions, which, I hope, improved the final product. Last, I express my thanks to two organizations whose fi-
nancial assistance made this book possible: the Social Sciences
and Humanities Research Council of Canada, from which I received generous support throughout my years as a graduate
student, and the Woodrow Wilson National Fellowship Foundation, whose award of a Charlotte Newcombe Doctoral Dis-

sertation Fellowship allowed me to finish my dissertation in a timely fashion without suffering the embarrassment of being evicted from my modest student apartment for nonpayment of rent.

A. R.

Toronto

Abbreviations

Abbreviations and page numbers directly after abbreviations refer to works in *Kants Gesammelte Schriften*, herausgegeben
von der Deutschen [formerly Königlichen Preussischen] *Akad-
emie der Wissenschaften*, 29 vols. (Berlin: Walter de Gruyter
[and predecessors], 1902–). The volume number of each work
cited in the Prussian Academy edition is given below. Page
numbers after a back slash (\) refer to English translations cited
below. The page numbers of English translations are cited only
when the translation does not also contain the Prussian Academy pagination.

APH   *Anthropologie in pragmatischer Hinsicht*, 1798. Ak VII.
      Anthropology from a Pragmatic Point of View. Translated
      by Victor Dowdell. Carbondale: Southern Illinois Univer-
      sity Press, 1978.
G   *Grundlegung zur Metaphysik der Sitten*, 1785. Ak IV.
      Foundations of the Metaphysics of Morals. Translated by
      L. W. Beck. Indianapolis: Bobbs-Merrill, 1976.
IAG   *Idee zu einer allgemeinen Geschichte in weltbürgerlicher
      Absicht*, 1784. Ak VIII.

"Idea for a Universal History with a Cosmopolitan Purpose." In *Kant's Political Writings*. Translated by H. B. Nisbet. Edited by Hans Reiss. Cambridge: Cambridge University Press, 1985. [Cited below as "Reiss 1985."]

KPV   *Kritik der praktischen Vernunft*, 1788. Ak V.
Critique of Practical Reason. Translated by L. W. Beck. Indianapolis: Bobbs-Merrill, 1982.

KRV   *Kritik der reinen Vernunft*, 1781/1787. Ak III, IV.
Critique of Pure Reason. Translated by Norman Kemp Smith. New York: Macmillan, 1965.

KU   *Kritik der Urtheilskraft*, 1790. Ak V.
Critique of Judgment. Translated by J. C. Meredith. Oxford: Oxford University Press, 1982.

MA   *Mutmasslicher Anfang der Menschengeschichte*, 1786. Ak VIII.
"Conjectural Beginning of Human History." In *Kant on History*. Edited by L. W. Beck. Indianapolis: Bobbs-Merrill, 1984.

PAD   *Pädagogik*, 1803. Ak IX.
Education. Translated by Annette Churton. Ann Arbor: University of Michigan Press, 1986.

REL   *Religion innerhalb der Grenzen der blossen Vernunft*, 1793–94. Ak VI.
Religion within the Limits of Reason Alone. Translated by T. M. Greene and H. H. Hudson. New York: Open Court, 1960.

RL   *Rechtslehre*. First part of *Die Metaphysik der Sitten*, 1797. Ak VI.
Metaphysical Elements of Justice. Translated by John Ladd. Indianapolis: Bobbs-Merrill, 1965.

SF   *Der Streit der Fakultäten*, 1798. Ak VII.
Part of this essay has been translated and published as "The Contest of Faculties." In Reiss 1985.

TL   *Tugendlehre*. Second part of *Die Metaphysik der Sitten*, 1797. Ak VI.
The Doctrine of Virtue. Translated by Mary Gregor. Philadelphia: University of Pennsylvania Press, 1964.

TP   *Über den Gemeinspruch: Das mag in der Theorie richtig sein, taugt aber nicht für die Praxis,* 1793. Ak VIII.
"On the Common Saying: This May Be True in Theory, But It Does Not Apply in Practice." In Reiss 1985. Cited as "Theory and Practice."

VE   *Eine Vorlesung Kants über Ethik,* 1780. Edited by Paul Menzer. Berlin: Rolf Heise, 1924.
Immanuel Kant: Lectures on Ethics. Translated by Louis Infield. Gloucester, Mass.: Peter Smith, 1978.

WIA   *Beantwortung der Frage: Was ist Aufklärung?,* 1784. Ak VIII.
"An Answer to the Question: What Is Enlightenment?" In Reiss 1985.

ZEF   *Zum ewigen Frieden,* 1795. Ak VIII.
"Perpetual Peace." In Reiss 1985.

KANT'S
THEORY OF
JUSTICE

Kant as a Political Philosopher

For a long time it was fashionable to regard Kant's political writings as minor works, not simply because they are relatively brief but also, according to this judgment, because they are intellectually substandard, at least when measured against the exceptionally high standards of other Kantian texts. Hannah Arendt, one of the best-known exponents of this view, went so far as to claim that even Kant himself did not take his political writings "seriously," which was probably a good thing from her point of view, since she regarded them as products of a mind fast approaching senile incompetence.[1] It will become apparent that I do not share this assessment. Kant was a notoriously late bloomer, having written his first great work, the *Critique of Pure Reason*, when he was in his late fifties. The fact that his political essays were products of his later years does not, therefore, count against them. But the low esteem in which Kant's political writings were held for a considerable period does serve to explain why, until recently, they received so little attention, as well as why the attention they did receive

[1] Arendt 1982, 7–9.

was often not of the sort Kant (or any other author) might
have wanted.

Fortunately, that has begun to change in the last decade or so
with the publication of a few informed but not uncritical books
on Kant's political philosophy.[2] Kant is finally beginning to be
taken seriously as a political philosopher. My hope is that the
present study will contribute in some measure to the continu-
ation of that trend. It is not my goal, however, to explicate in
this brief book the whole of Kant's political philosophy. What is
usually called "Kant's political philosophy" is an extended discourse on *Recht*, a term rendered most idiomatically in English
as *justice*.[3] Kant's views concerning justice range over many issues, only some of which I discuss here. The two most salient
topics I omit are penal justice and international law, both of
which would have to be dealt with by any work purporting to
provide a complete account of Kant's political philosophy.[4] I by-
pass them not because they are uninteresting or unimportant
topics, but because they are tangential to the primary task of
understanding, first, the basic elements and principles of
Kant's theory of justice and, second, how these influence
Kant's conception of the legitimate state.

---

[2] The most notable example is Williams 1983. Although I take issue with
Williams on some points, his presentation of Kant's political philosophy is
on the whole fair and accurate.

[3] John Ladd's introduction to his translation of the *Rechtslehre* contains
a useful discussion of the difficulties involved in translating *Recht* into English. See Abbreviations, above.

[4] With a few exceptions, I have also not discussed the historical context
and background of Kant's political philosophy. The reader who is interested
in this topic should consult the following sources. For useful discussions of
eighteenth-century Prussian society and the intellectual environment in
which Kant wrote his political works, see Cassirer 1981, chap. 7; Vorländer,
b. 4, 210–38; Holborn 1982, chap. 9–13; Gay 1969, 98–108. On the important issue of Kant's relation to the French revolution, see Burg 1974 for an
extended analysis and Williams 1983, 208–13, for a briefer account. The
crucial influence of Rousseau on Kant's moral and political philosophy is
discussed in Cassirer 1945b, 1–60.

I deal with the basic elements and principles of Kant's theory of justice in the initial three chapters, leaving until the last two chapters the question of how they shape his view of the state. Chapters 1 and 2 focus on the relation between justice and freedom. As is natural for a liberal, Kant's theory of justice revolves around the idea of individual freedom. Kant's main principles of justice are meant to regulate and safeguard individual liberty. Yet despite the fact that these principles form the foundations of Kant's theory of justice, they have been given only cursory attention by most interpreters. To rectify this oversight, I examine them at length and attempt to explain their origins in other parts of Kant's moral philosophy. Chapter 1 focusses on the practical ramifications of these principles, on the kinds of rights and liberties they permit and prohibit, while Chapter 2 traces their genealogy back to more familiar rules in Kant's ethical theory, particularly the principles of universal law, autonomy, and humanity.

Chapter 3 shifts from Kant's principles of justice to the problem of how Kant separates the domain of justice from that of ethics, as well as how he differentiates between various types of rights, duties, and laws within the sphere of justice. For example, Kant distinguishes "ethical" rights and duties from rights and duties of "justice," "wide" rights and duties from "narrow" rights and duties, "perfect" duties from "imperfect" duties, and "natural" laws from "positive" laws. Most of these distinctions are problematic for one reason or another—usually because Kant either neglects to define them adequately or fails to apply them consistently. They are, nonetheless, central to his conception of justice. These distinctions demarcate the domain of justice and separate it from the realm of ethics by establishing—among other things—that rights, duties, and laws of justice are coercive, enforceable, and require the performance or omission of actions, in contrast with ethical rights, duties, and laws, which are noncoercive, unenforceable, and require the adoption of ends. I further argue in this chapter that some of

Kant's distinctions, especially the one between perfect and imperfect duties, have commonly been misconstrued and stand in need of reexamination.

Chapter 4 is concerned with the specifically political dimensions of Kant's theory of justice, that is, with his understanding of the just state, the nature of sovereignty, political legitimacy, the obligations of citizens to obey laws, and the moral status of rebellion. I claim that there is a deep-seated dualism, characterized by alternating strands of liberalism and conservatism, in Kant's attitude toward political authority. This dualism, I suggest, is most apparent in the juxtaposition of Kant's emphasis on individual rights and liberties with his absolutist conception of sovereign authority, in his tendency to legitimize all existing governments, and in his unwillingness to recognize the moral acceptability of rebellion under any circumstances.

I also argue in this chapter that Kant's dualism is a product of his attempt to combine a liberal commitment to individual rights and liberties with three other beliefs. The first, rooted in his philosophy of history, is that a just state can develop only after a prolonged period of political injustice, and that since unjust states are therefore historically necessary precursors of just states, they must be accorded a degree of legitimacy. The second is that the logic of sovereignty precludes all legal restrictions on the authority of the sovereign, so that the power of the sovereign can never be anything other than absolute and illimitable. The third is that a theory of justice must take the form of an ideal theory of law—which is to say, a theory of the rights, duties, and laws that can and should be enforced by legal systems—and that, because a right of rebellion would be legally unenforceable, there can be no such right of justice. I argue, however, that Kant's second belief rests on a confused understanding of the logic of sovereignty, and is moreover incompatible with his own constitutional republicanism. I further suggest that although Kant is correct in holding that there can be no legal right of rebellion, the proper response is not to con-

clude, as he does, that there can never be any right of justice to
rebel against oppressive governments, but that a theory of justice must be understood more broadly than as a theory of the
rights, duties, and laws that can and should be enforced by legal
systems. I claim, in other words, that two of the beliefs that in-
spire Kant's conservatism with respect to political authority
are ill-advised and unnecessary.

Chapter 5 turns to Kant's view of the relation between justice
and human welfare. I mentioned before that Kant's principles
of justice are intended to regulate individual freedom. They
prohibit us from interfering with each other's legitimate liberty. But that, according to Kant, is *all* they do. Kant believes
that justice has nothing to do with human needs or desires. Justice, as he understands it, does not require the state to provide
for the material needs of its subjects. Concern for human welfare is a matter of benevolence, and benevolence, Kant insists,
lies in the province of ethics, not of justice. For a number of reasons, but chiefly because Kant believes that justice demands no
more than noninterference with individual freedom and therefore does not require the state to provide for the needs of its subjects, most interpreters have regarded Kant as a defender of the
night watchman state. I argue against this view. It is true that
justice does not, in Kant's estimation, require the state to concern itself with matters of social welfare. On the interpretation
I propose, though, Kant believes that the state has a moral responsibility to go beyond the requirements of strict justice in
order to ensure the material well-being of its subjects. Therefore, Kant is not, I argue, an advocate of the night watchman
state. On the contrary, he believes governments should take active steps to ensure the material well-being of their subjects.

CHAPTER ONE

The Limits of Freedom

A WELL-KNOWN PASSAGE OF THE *Critique of Practical Reason* describes the concept of freedom as the "keystone" of the entire critical philosophy.[1] I will not venture an opinion as to how apt this may be as a characterization of Kant's metaphysics and epistemology, but it is certainly true of his moral or practical philosophy.[2] Freedom, however, is a complex concept through-

---

[1] KPV 3.

[2] Kant usually treats the term *practical* (*praktisch*) as interchangeable with *moral* (*moralisch*), and for convenience I propose to follow suit. This requires some explanation, though, because Kant sometimes also uses *moral* and *practical* in nonequivalent ways. Strictly speaking, the latter has a broader meaning than the former in the Kantian scheme of things. Kant says that "practical principles contain a general determination of the will" and therefore include subjective "maxims" as well as objective, universally valid moral "laws" (KPV 19–20; cf. G 389, 400n, 420–21n). Practical principles, in other words, are simply general rules that regulate action. Some practical rules are moral, namely categorical imperatives, and some are nonmoral, e.g., subjective maxims and hypothetical imperatives. This is Kant's official distinction between *practical* and *moral*, but he often ignores it (e.g., KU 171), and no harm will come from doing the same as long as we keep in mind that he occasionally also uses *practical* in the broader sense just mentioned.

out Kant's philosophy. Within Kant's moral theory there are two main types of freedom: inner freedom and outer freedom.[3] Inner freedom is the primary subject of Kant's ethical theory, while external freedom is the primary subject of Kant's theory of justice. External freedom in the most general sense is independence of constraints imposed by others,[4] but from a normative perspective it is divided into two further categories: "rightful" external freedom, which is freedom of action circumscribed by laws of justice, and "lawless" or "wild" external freedom, which is the unrestrained, anarchic liberty of the state of nature.[5] The purpose of a theory of justice, for Kant, is to distinguish rightful from lawless external freedom, and to determine the conditions that make rightful freedom possible.

Principles of External Freedom

In the Introduction to the *Rechtslehre*, Kant asserts that the concept of justice has three essential characteristics.[6] First, it applies only to external relations between individuals insofar as their actions may affect each other "directly or "indirectly." Second, it is not concerned with the "wishes or desires" of individuals, but solely with the "relationship of a will to another person's will." Third, it deals only with the "form of the relationship between the wills insofar as they are regarded as free." Synthesizing these three characteristics, Kant defines justice as "the aggregate of those conditions under which the will of one person can be conjoined with the will of another in accordance with a universal law of freedom."[7]

---

[3] TL 213.
[4] RL 237.
[5] RL 316; ZEF 350n.
[6] RL 230.
[7] RL 230.

What Kant means is not too difficult to understand. Principles of justice are moral principles and all such principles, according to Kant, are "formal" rather than "material." To say that a principle is formal instead of material is to say, inter alia, that it is independent of the shifting content of individual wills, namely, changeable desires, wishes, intentions, needs.[8] Moral principles, for Kant, do not depend on what we may or may not happen contingently to desire, wish, intend, or need. They are categorical imperatives, which means they are unconditionally and universally binding commands that obligate all "finite rational beings" who, like ourselves, are capable of responding to the call of duty, but who may also allow themselves to be drawn away from the path of duty by the countervailing influence of inclinations.[9] Beings who are thus capable of determining their wills in accordance with the demands of duty, yet who also experience and can succumb to the temptations of inclination, possess free choice (*frei Willkür*).[10] Because moral laws regulate free choice, they are called "laws of freedom." Unlike ethical laws, though, laws of justice restrict only the external manifestations of free choice instead of the internal determining grounds of the will. Bringing these different ideas together, we may say that justice is the sum total of those formal conditions, whatever they may be, that regulate free choice so as to make possible a consistent system of external freedom by means of universally binding laws.

The same underlying conception of justice is present in all of Kant's laws and principles of justice. The "universal law of jus-

---

[8] This should not be taken to imply that Kantian moral principles cannot have any "content" or that they must be "empty," as critics down through the ages have continually, and erroneously, alleged. A moral principle is not made "formal" by eliminating all contents or ends. It is formal if it ignores all merely "subjective ends." Moral principles can and do provide definite ends or goals of action, but these must be "objective" and "universally valid" ends determined by reason alone, not by changeable inclinations (G 427).

[9] G 412–14; KPV 79–80.

[10] RL 213.

tice" in the *Rechtslehre*, for instance, commands us to "act externally in such a way that the free use of your will can be compatible with the freedom of everyone else according to a universal law."[11] Employing much the same language, the "principle of innate freedom" in the *Rechtslehre* asserts that "freedom (independence from the constraint of another's will) insofar as it is compatible with the freedom of everyone else in accordance with a universal law, is the sole and original right that belongs to each human being by virtue of his humanity."[12] Again, in *Theory and Practice* Kant defines justice as "the restriction of each individual's freedom so that it harmonizes with the freedom of everyone else (insofar as it is possible within the terms of a universal law)."[13] All of these principles, laws, and definitions express essentially the same thought: that justice is a condition in which each individual's external freedom is restricted so as to make it consistent with the freedom of all others in the framework of a common law or system of laws.

This condition is rightful or lawful external freedom. As I noted earlier, it contrasts with the "wild" freedom of the state of nature in which there are no legal restraints on external liberty.[14] The state of nature, in Kant's view, exists wherever there is no established judicial system capable of enforcing laws to protect individual rights.[15] The state of nature is therefore historically real for Kant, not simply a heuristic device: it exists in all prepolitical societies and whenever systems of public legal justice break down (for example, during political revolutions or in dictatorships that abandon the rule of law).[16] Like Hobbes, Kant regards the state of nature as a condition of war. He does not suppose that it must be full of actual violence, any

[11] RL 231.
[12] RL 237.
[13] TP 289–90\71.
[14] RL 316; IAG 22\46; *Reflexion* 7649, Ak XIX, 477.
[15] RL 306.
[16] TP 301\82.

more than does Hobbes, merely that it contains a constant threat of violence due to the absence of an alternative method of adjudicating disputes between individuals.[17] According to Kant, justice requires a guarantee that personal rights and liberties will be protected, and because there is no impartial method of settling quarrels in the state of nature, such an assurance is impossible there. The state of nature is consequently unjust in the sense that it is always devoid of justice, even if it is not always a condition of active injustice.[18]

It is worth stressing that the state of nature is not unjust as a result of any evil in human nature. There may be plenty of human wickedness in the state of nature, as there is in political society, but that is not what makes the state of nature unjust. It is unjust for the more basic, more *structural* reason that justice can exist only when there is some systematic means of protecting individual rights, and insofar as the state of nature contains no mechanism of this kind it is by hypothesis lacking in justice. It follows that even if men were "ever so good natured" the state of nature would still be a condition of injustice; for in the event of a dispute between individuals about their respective rights, no impartial system of adjudication could ensure a nonarbitrary settlement.[19]

The remedy for this structural deficiency is civil society, which alone can provide a set of institutional arrangements, namely, a legal system, capable of impartially protecting individual rights and liberties. Political society is thus a sine qua non of justice.[20] Accordingly, because there is an obligation to promote justice and prevent injustice, there is also an obligation to quit the state of nature and enter civil society.[21] But of

---

[17] REL 97n\89n.
[18] RL 312; ZEF 348–49\98.
[19] RL 312.
[20] Kant's justification of civil society is discussed in more detail in Chapter 4.
[21] RL 307.

course not every political society is entirely or even partially just. The primary requirement of a just civil state, Kant says, is that it have a just constitution, one that allows the "greatest freedom" for each individual along with "the most precise specification and preservation of the limits of this freedom so that it can coexist with the freedom of others."[22] Justice is consequently more than a condition in which external freedom is guaranteed to all through a system of coercive laws: it is a condition of *maximum* liberty for all.

These are broad and general ideas, comparable in spirit to many other expressions of eighteenth-century liberalism.[23] What, we may wonder, do they mean in practice? Is there a single system of laws capable of ensuring maximum individual liberty or many such systems? Similar questions arise in connection with Kant's other abstract principles of justice, for instance, the universal law of justice. Do they determine any specific constraints on external freedom? Is there only one system of laws capable of making the freedom of each person compatible with the freedom of all others? It might be argued that there are as many ways of maximizing individual liberty as there are of interpreting the idea of liberty, and as many systems of law capable of making the freedom of one individual compatible with the freedom of all others as there are ways of understanding the idea of compatibility. It is possible,

[22] IAG 22\45–46; cf. KRV A316\B373.

[23] Note the similarities, for instance, between Kant's view of a just constitution—as one assuring as much freedom for each individual as can coexist under universal laws with a like liberty for all others—and Article IV of the French Declaration of the Rights of Man of 1789: "Liberty consists in the power to do anything that does not injure others; thus, the natural rights of every man have only such limits as assure to other members of society the enjoyment of the same rights. These limits can only be determined by law" (Quoted in Hobhouse 1964, 35). There are also striking similarities between Kant's general view of justice and Adam Smith's, whose writings Kant knew and admired (Smith, *Moral Sentiments*, 82; *Reflexion* 1355, Ak XV; RL 289).

therefore, that there is a measure of indeterminacy in Kant's formulations of his abstract principles of justice.[24] This creates no insuperable difficulties, however; for whatever indeterminacy there may be in Kant's more abstract principles of justice largely disappears once we realize that Kant *intends* them to be interpreted in quite definite ways.

Consider, in particular, the central principle of Kant's theory of justice: the universal law of justice. The universal law of justice is derived from Kant's supreme principle of morality, the categorical imperative. More specifically, it is a transformation of Kant's ethical principle of universal law, the first and most "rigorous" formulation of the categorical imperative in the *Groundwork*.[25] The principle of universal law commands us to "Act only on that maxim by which you can at the same time will that it should be a universal law."[26] As their names make explicit, the ethical principle of universal law and the universal law of justice both emphasize the concept of universal law (*allgemein Gesetz*). The major difference between them is that the principle of universal law is an ethical principle requiring maxims to be capable of being willed as universal laws, whereas the universal law of justice places a parallel restriction on external actions.[27] The difference between these principles

[24] On this issue see Pogge 1988, especially 408–15. See also Chapter 2, where I argue that there is less indeterminacy than one might suppose in Kant's universal law of justice.

[25] G 436.

[26] G 421.

[27] Maxims are "subjective" principles of action and are distinguished from "objective" principles of action (G 420–21n; cf. 427). The moral law or categorical imperative is an objective principle because it is "valid for every rational being." Maxims are subjective principles because they depend on subjective choices and desires. A merchant, for instance, might adopt the maxim "Buy low, sell high" in order to optimize profits. Such a rule is subjective insofar as it depends on the goal of optimizing profits, which other persons may or may not share, and which they are not morally obligated to share. The rule that one should not make false promises, on the other hand, is an objective principle, because it is one that all rational beings ought to comply with even if they do not wish to do so (G 422).

can therefore be summarized by saying that the universal law of justice is an *externalized* version of the ethical principle of universal law.

Kant holds that in order to understand the implications of the categorical imperative in its several different formulations we must have "principles of application" to translate it into more readily usable rules and policies.[28] The categorical imperative enters the realm of justice by a transformation of the ethical principle of universal law into the universal law of justice, which is in turn the core principle of Kant's theory of justice.[29] In order to apply this very abstract principle of justice to the empirical world, Kant translates it into three intuitively clearer principles designed to show how, in practice, the external freedom of each individual can be made compatible with the external freedom of all other individuals within a system of coercive laws. These principles appear in slightly varying forms in many of Kant's political writings, including the *Rechtslehre, Perpetual Peace,* and *Theory and Practice.*[30] They represent Kant's intended interpretation of the universal principle of justice. Their function is to provide the basic constitutional principles for every possible "lawful state."

The first of these constitutional principles is a rule of civil liberty, described by Kant as the principle of the *"freedom* of every member of society as a *human being."*[31] The purpose of this rule is to define an area of personal liberty within which individuals are free to act as they wish. Kant's use of the predicate human (*menschlich*) serves two purposes. *Humanity* is defined in the *Tugendlehre* as the "power to set ends," that is, the power of free choice.[32] In Kant's view, therefore, human beings are essentially choice-making beings. To be free *as* a

---

[28] RL 217.

[29] Versions of this principle can be found in the *Religion* and the *Critique of Pure Reason,* as well as in the *Rechtslehre* (REL 98\90; KRV A752\B780).

[30] RL 237–38; TP 290\74; ZEF 349–50\99.

[31] TP 290\74.

[32] TL 392.

human being is to possess freedom of choice. But the principle of civil liberty is a principle of justice, and justice is concerned only with external freedom, so the freedom of choice required by this principle must be external freedom of choice. Moreover, since all members of society are equally human, in the sense that all share equally in the capacity for free choice, Kant evidently means that external freedom of choice must be distributed equally among all individuals.

The second constitutional principle is a rule of legal equality that Kant calls the principle of the *"equality* of each with all others as a *subject."*[33] The main function of this principle is to make explicit what is only implicit in the first constitutional principle, that justice demands an equal distribution of civil freedom. As subjects of the state, all individuals must, this principle suggests, be treated equally "before the law." None may have any legal advantage over others.[34] The law, in short, must not be biased, must not be a respecter of persons or of classes.

The third constitutional principle is a rule of political freedom that Kant characterizes as the principle of the *"independence* of each member of a commonwealth as a *citizen."*[35] According to this principle, citizens are authorized to be "co-legislators" of the laws they are required to obey. Not all citizens, however, are allowed this privilege. Only "active" citizens, who must satisfy special property qualifications, should be enfranchised, Kant believes. "Passive" citizens should enjoy full civil rights and legal equality, Kant maintains, but should not be allowed to vote. Kant does not, therefore, believe that political freedom, as opposed to civil freedom and legal equality, should be distributed equally among all subjects of the state.[36]

[33] TP 290\74.
[34] TP 292, 294\75, 77.
[35] TP 290\74.
[36] RL 314–15.

Each of these principles has its own complexities and obscurities, and each requires detailed analysis before it can be understood properly.

Civil Freedom

No one can compel me to be happy in accordance with his conception of the welfare of others, for each may seek his happiness in whatever way he sees fit, so long as he does not infringe upon the freedom of others to pursue a similar end which can be reconciled with the freedom of everyone else within a workable general law.[37]

This passage from *Theory and Practice* represents Kant's clearest articulation of the principle of civil freedom.[38] Notice, however, that it actually contains two different rules. The first is an antipaternalistic principle to the effect that no one should be forced to live by someone else's conception of the good. Kant's main target is paternalistic governments that operate on the "principle of benevolence."[39] A government of this sort is one that forces a particular conception of the good on its subjects. Such a government, in Kant's view, produces the "greatest conceivable *despotism*" because it "suspends the entire freedom of its subjects, who henceforth have no rights whatsoever."[40] At first glance, this language seems too extreme. Kant's point is nevertheless sound. When all rights are subject to revocation in the name of public utility or the

---

[37] TP 290\74.
[38] It also bears a close resemblance, in spirit at least, to Mill's principle of liberty (Mill, *On Liberty*, 68).
[39] TP 290\74.
[40] TP 290–91\74–75.

common good, as calculated by the current administration, every individual liberty may be swallowed up by the state. Then there can be no permanent, constitutionally assured rights, no liberties on which citizens can depend. In this sense, paternalistic governments leave their subjects with "no rights whatsoever," for unrestricted state paternalism is inconsistent with constitutionally assured individual rights.[41]

Although Kant's rule of antipaternalism prohibits certain justifications for restricting individual liberty, it does not by itself define any particular sphere of civil freedom. The proper limits of civil freedom are specified not by this rule, but by the second part of the quoted passage, which asserts that each individual should be free to pursue his own happiness as long as he does not infringe the liberty of his fellow subjects to pursue their own ends.[42] Emphasizing individual freedom as it does, this is a characteristically liberal view of civil freedom. The main difficulty lies in determining exactly what counts as an infringement of the rightful liberty of others. Remarkably, Kant never addressed this issue directly. His view, though, is fairly clear. An action qualifies as an unjust infringement of the freedom of others if it satisfies one of two criteria. First, provided that I am not "hindering" others in their pursuit of their own ends, my legitimate liberty is infringed whenever another person "violates" my freedom by means of an "external action."[43] Put differently, an action is unjust if it forcibly prevents someone from doing something that does not itself constitute forcible interference with the liberty of others. Second, an action is unjust if it is fraudulent. I do nothing unjust if I deceive or lie to someone without intending to detract from any of his rights or property.[44] But if I lie with the intent to "deprive him of

[41] On this point see also Kersting 1984, 233–35.
[42] Cf. VE 255\201.
[43] RL 231.
[44] RL 238.

what is his (*falsiloquium dolosum*) [deceitful falsehood]," I then act unjustly.[45]

Force and fraud are thus Kant's two criteria of injustice. Presumably, actions that fit neither of these categories qualify as just. But Kant also has a positive criterion of just acts: the Roman law maxim "*volenti non fit injuria* [to one who has consented no wrong is done]."[46] For mentally competent adults consent rules out injustice.[47] However much an action may harm someone or run contrary to her objective interests, the volenti maxim implies that if she consents to the way she is affected by the action there can be no injustice.

Kant's acceptance of the volenti maxim explains why he holds that the concept of justice applies only to relations between different individuals, and why he believes it is impossible for an individual to commit an injustice against himself.[48] I cannot commit an injustice against myself because "whatever I do to myself I do as a consenting party."[49] All acts of injustice must therefore occur between at least two different persons. The consequences of restricting justice to relations between different individuals may not, however, be what they first appear. Granting that nothing an individual does to himself ever qualifies as an injustice *to himself*, it does not follow that what he does to himself may not count as an injustice *to others*. Justice is concerned with actions that affect others both "directly" and "indirectly."[50] If I commit suicide, for instance, I do no injustice to myself; yet my suicide may count as an injustice to

[45] RL 238n.
[46] RL 313; cf. TP 294–95\77. This maxim still serves as the basis of some liberal conceptions of civil freedom. See Feinberg 1984, 115–25; 1983, 4–6. It also survives in modern tort law in the form of the rule that someone who voluntarily assumes a risk cannot recover damages arising from that risk.
[47] TL 454.
[48] RL 230.
[49] VE 145–46\117.
[50] RL 230.

others—to members of my family perhaps, or to those with whom I have contractual obligations. It is not, consequently, always unjust to prevent someone from harming himself. Such interference is unjust only when self-inflicted harm does not also infringe the rights of others.

We can now summarize Kant's view of civil freedom in four rules, which I will refer to collectively as Kant's *Principle of Civil Freedom:*

1. Each individual has the right to pursue her own happiness as she sees fit, provided that she does not fraudulently or violently interfere with the liberty of others to pursue their own happiness.
2. No one may abridge this right in the name of promoting the good of others.
3. All consensual interactions are just. No person does an injustice to others if they consent to the manner in which her actions affect them.
4. Nothing an individual may do to herself counts as an injustice to herself.

These are the general and rather abstract rules of civil freedom to which Kant is committed. I turn now to the question of how well these rules harmonize with the specific rights and liberties that Kant believes ought to be protected by law.

As one would expect, freedom of expression ranks high on Kant's list of protected freedoms. In *Theory and Practice*, Kant advocates "freedom of the pen" and in *What Is Enlightenment?* he supports the right to make "public use" of one's reason.[51] The public use of reason contrasts with its "private" use.[52] An

[51] WIA 36–38\55–56.
[52] Valuable discussions of Kant's distinction between the public and private use of reason can be found in Habermas, "Publizität," especially 177–81, and O'Neill 1986.

individual uses her reason privately, according to Kant, when she employs it in her capacity as an official of some sort. Reason is used publicly, on the other hand, when it is employed—principally by scholars—to address the "reading public."[53] The public use of reason must be unrestricted, but not its private use. When a person is acting in her capacity as a civil servant, for instance, she is not entitled publicly to criticize the government. She is paid to be its *instrument,* and *as such* she is not permitted to voice complaints publicly.[54] Yet, in her capacity as a scholar the same individual must be free to criticize the government and to address those criticisms to the general public. For *as* a scholar she is entitled to make *independent* use of her reason, without being under any obligation to employ it in the *service* of her employer.

As we have already seen, Kant regards freedom of action as another fundamental right. Each individual must be at liberty to pursue her own ends as she pleases, so long as she does not violently or fraudulently infringe on the rights of others to do the same. There is no doubt that, to a large extent, Kant sees this freedom as the liberty to compete for personal advancement in the context of a free-market economy. Individuals must be free, he argues, to use their "talent," "industry" and "good fortune" to promote their own social and economic welfare.[55] Freedom of this kind is thus, to a considerable degree, freedom to compete (successfully or unsuccessfully) in the marketplace of skills and talents.

Not surprisingly, this liberty is linked with the right to private property. Kant's argument for a right to private property is a practical reductio ad absurdum of the hypothesis that private property is impossible. He begins with the premise that an external object is "a thing I have the physical power to

[53] WIA 37\55.
[54] WIA 37–38\56.
[55] TP 292\75.

use."[56] He then claims that if it were not possible to own an external object, "freedom would be robbing itself of the use of its will . . . inasmuch as it would be placing usable objects outside all possibility of being used."[57] From a "practical point of view," Kant concludes, "that would turn an external object into a *res nullius* [thing belonging to no one]."[58] Putting this argument into ordinary language, Kant's contention is that for practical purposes there would be a contradiction in the idea of an external object that could not be owned by someone, because such a thing would be both a usable object and an object that could not be used. But that is impossible, hence private property is necessary.[59]

Kant often defends the preceding rights and liberties, all of which are consistent with the principle of civil freedom, even if not all are entailed by it. Kant's view of the proper limits of individual liberty is not, however, reconciled so easily with the principle of civil freedom. An especially problematic area concerns sexual offenses. Kant assumes, as do most of us, that rape and pederasty (taking the latter in the strict sense of adult sodomy with a boy) should be legally prohibited. Behavior of this sort is clearly not protected by the principle of civil freedom and poses no threat to Kant's

[56] RL 246.
[57] RL 246.
[58] RL 246.
[59] There are at least two serious weaknesses in this reasoning. It seems, first, to trade on a confusion between rights of ownership and rights of usufruct. Having a right to use an object need not entail ownership rights. Property rights are a special class of rights to the use of objects. Contrary to Kant's assumption, rejecting property rights does not therefore require rejecting all rights of usufruct. (On the distinction between property rights and rights of usufruct see Nicholas 1988, 110–11, 138; Watson 1968, 205–16; Tuck 1978, 10–17; Pound 1954, 110–12.) Second, even if we assume that property rights of *some* kind are necessary, Kant does not provide any reason to believe that *private* property rights, as opposed to communal, corporate, or state property rights, are necessary. (For a discussion of these different forms of property see Macpherson 1978.)

prohibitions.[60] But these cases are easy; others are much harder. Consider, for example, prostitution and bestiality. Kant holds that both should be legally prohibited.[61] The trouble with doing so is that both appear to be protected by the principle of civil freedom. Prostitution is a consensual activity and bestiality, no matter how morally offensive it may be, does not appear to qualify as an injustice by Kant's standards. It is therefore difficult to see any plausible Kantian justification for prohibiting these activities. The same applies to other problematic cases such as public begging and voluntary slavery, which Kant also believes should be legally prohibited.[62] Again, our initial assumption, pending evidence to the contrary, must be that public begging and voluntary slavery fall within the domain of the principle of civil freedom insofar as they do not seem to violate any of its constituent rules.

For the most part, Kant is exceedingly casual about justifying these prohibitions. Bestiality is proscribed on the grounds that it is a "crime against humanity in general."[63] What this means is never made clear. Kant nowhere argues that humanity "in general" possesses any rights. Indeed, Kant's taxonomy of rights appears to include only differing kinds of individual rights. Since Kant does not argue that bestiality infringes any individual rights, it is not obvious what he means by describing it is a crime against humanity.[64]

Kant's reasons for prohibiting prostitution are similarly dubious. He calls it an offense against "public decency," and claims that it violates the "moral sensibilities" of mankind.[65] But he fails to explain why these considerations should count as compelling—or even marginally adequate—reasons for

---

[60] RL 366.
[61] RL 325, 366.
[62] RL 325, 330.
[63] RL 366.
[64] RL 241.
[65] RL 325\92.

prohibiting actions that would otherwise be protected by the principle of civil freedom. In fact, Kant never argues that immoral actions should in general be legally prohibited, unless they are unjust, and prostitution does appear to fit Kant's understanding of injustice. Kant probably did not give much thought to these problems, but unreflectingly assumed that those actions that offended both his own moral sensibilities and those of his middle-class Prussian contemporaries would be restricted by his rule of civil liberty.

On the question of voluntary slavery, Kant at least provides an argument. A contract of voluntary slavery, he alleges, would be logically incoherent: "A contract by which one party would renounce its entire freedom for the profit of another would be self-contradictory, that is, null and void, since by it one party would cease to be a person and so would have no duty to keep the contract but would recognize only force."[66] This argument is less than overpowering. Consider an analogy. A will is not legally void when the testator dies and therefore ceases to be a person; its provisions, on the contrary, come into force *only* at that time. The right of a legatee to an inheritance depends only on whether the testator is legally competent when the will is signed. It matters not in the slightest what may happen to him afterwards. By the same token, there is no reason why the fact that someone might cease to be a legal person after signing a slavery contract should mean either that he could not have a right to sell himself in the first place, or that his would-be purchaser could not have a legal right to have the contract enforced. On the assumption that a slave is not a legal person, and that he consequently could not be the subject of legal rights or duties, it would follow that he could have no legal duty to comply with the provisions of a slavery contract. By itself, however, the absence of a legal duty on the part of the slave to comply with a slavery contract would not entail either that the pur-

[66] RL 283.

chaser could not have a right to enforce the contract or that the would-be slave was not entitled to sell himself.

The central problem in all of these cases is that Kant wishes to hold (A) that consent is sufficient to prevent injustice, (B) that laws should prohibit only unjust actions, and (C) that there are some activities that ought to be legally prohibited despite being consensual. Minimally, Kant is in the grip of some apparent contradictions. At least one possible solution is available. The primary concept of consent in Kant's moral philosophy is not *empirical* consent (e.g., a contractual agreement), but *rational* consent.[67] When Kant describes the categorical imperative as a test of maxims that can be willed as universal laws, for instance, he means that it is a test of maxims that can be willed or consented to by fully rational beings. Similarly, when he says in connection with his social contract theory that a law is just if an "entire people could agree to such a law," he is not referring to empirical consent.[68] Rather, he means that a law is just if an entire people could rationally consent to it. He holds that many laws cannot be consented to rationally even though they can be consented to empirically.[69]

One might suppose, then, that the problems we have encountered could be resolved by concluding that the notion of consent operative in Kant's principle of civil freedom is rational instead of empirical consent. Prostitution, bestiality, and voluntary slavery might then be prohibited on the grounds that fully rational beings cannot consent to them. But this approach has its own problems. Suppose we interpret Kant as holding that only rational consent is sufficient to eliminate injustice. In that case, Rule 3 of the principle of civil freedom should be construed as permitting only actions one might consent to rationally. Then, however, Rule 3 would

[67] E.g., G 429–30.
[68] TP 299\81.
[69] WIA 39–40\57; TP 297\79, 302\83; RL 329.

conflict with Rule 4, which claims that there can be no self-inflicted injustice. The conflict develops in the following way. Recall that, for Kant, the reason why it is impossible to do an injustice to oneself is that one always consents to all of one's actions. Although Kant never elaborates on this claim, he presumably means that all actions that can properly be ascribed to an agent are in some fairly ordinary sense *voluntary* actions. Understood in this way, it is correct (if slightly awkward) to say that an individual *consents* to all of his own actions. But the kind of consent at stake here can only be empirical, not rational, consent. From the fact that an action is voluntary, it may follow that the agent has consented to it empirically, yet it does not follow that the action satisfies the minimal requirements of rationality.

Therefore, if the concept of consent operative in the principle of civil freedom is rational consent, Kant has no justification for claiming that one always consents to all of one's actions. But that was Kant's only reason for concluding that no one can do an injustice to himself. Accordingly, if we take Kant's concept of consent to be rational consent, there is no reason to suppose that self-inflicted injustice is impossible. Rule 4 of Kant's principle of civil freedom would then have to be eliminated, or another justification would have to be found. This would also mean that Kant would no longer have any reason to insist that justice and injustice are concerned only with relations between different individuals.

The end result is that Kant faces a dilemma. If the type of consent relevant to his principle of civil freedom is empirical consent (voluntariness understood in the usual way), it is hard to see how some of the restrictions he wishes to place on individual freedom can be justified consistently with his own principle of civil freedom. If, on the other hand, the type of consent in question is rational consent, then revisions must be made to some of the premises of Kant's theory of justice, in particular his assumption that there can be no self-inflicted injustices, and that the concept of justice is therefore concerned exclusively with relations between different individuals.

All things considered, the second horn of this dilemma is preferable to the first. Nothing of consequence is lost by accepting the possibility of self-inflicted injustice. Inasmuch as an injustice can occur only when a right has been violated, allowing the possibility of self-inflicted injustice entails acknowledging that a person may have rights that it would be unjust for her to give up, and that she should not therefore be allowed by law to trade away. But this is hardly a radical idea: it means only that there are *some* limits to what a person should be allowed to do to herself, or to allow others to do to her, and such limitations are both commonsensical and well-entrenched in most contemporary legal systems.[70]

The other alternative would be to interpret Kant as holding that empirical consent is sufficient to eliminate injustice. Doing so would enable us to retain his claim that self-inflicted injustice is impossible, but would be inconsistent with the fact that he usually understands consent as rational consent. More importantly, perhaps, it would also leave an irresolvable contradiction between his principle of civil freedom and his belief that some consensual or voluntary activities should be prohibited by law. Since this is a far less acceptable result than permitting a relatively minor revision to Kant's assumptions about the domain of justice and injustice, it is the least palatable choice.

The remaining problem is to give some content to the idea of rational consent. I will not discuss this issue any further at this point. I will return to it, however, in Chapters 4 and 5. In the meantime, it seems reasonable to conclude that Kant's principle of civil freedom requires some rational limitations on the actions to which an individual may consent. These limitations need not involve any drastic alterations to the principle of civil

---

[70] On this general issue see Feinberg 1983, 3–4; also Dahl 1983, 261–71.

freedom. The moving idea of the principle of civil freedom is that consent is sufficient to ensure justice, and it is certainly Kant's belief that in *most* circumstances *empirical* consent is sufficient for that purpose. Only at the margins, in extreme cases such as bestiality and voluntary slavery, is there any need for rational restrictions on consent. Only in cases of this sort does empirical consent fail to meet minimal requirements of rationality. On the whole, there is no irresolvable conflict between rational and empirical consent.

Legal Equality

I noted earlier that Kant's principle of legal equality is not completely distinct from his principle of civil freedom. The right to civil freedom belongs to "every member of society as a *human being.*"[71] Because all members of society are equally human, all are entitled to an equal share in the distribution of civil freedom. In substance, this is what Kant means when he claims that all persons are equal "before the law."[72]

Historically, the idea of legal equality has been neither transparently clear nor unambiguous. As encapsulated in the slogan that "like cases should be treated alike"—both legislatively and in the courts—it is doubtless a salutary notion. Of course, *every* case is like every other case in *some* respects. If the recommendation to treat like cases alike is to be of any use, it must therefore be supplemented by a detailed account of which similarities (and differences) between cases are judicially and legislatively pertinent. For instance, the race or ethnic background of a thief ought not to affect the way he is treated by the courts, but mental incompetence is obviously a relevant matter.

[71] TP 290\74.
[72] TP 292\75.

Parallel considerations suggest that the ideal of legal equality cannot demand the elimination of *all* legal differences between different individuals or groups. Pensioners and handicapped persons receive special legal benefits in many countries; soldiers are usually drafted from particular age groups; only certain individuals are eligible for workers' compensation, welfare, and veterans' benefits. These differential entitlements establish legal inequalities, yet it is rarely claimed that they are for that reason unjust.[73] Examples of this kind suggest that it is pointless to suppose that all legal benefits and liabilities should be distributed equally—which in effect would mean indiscriminately—among an entire population. Such examples indicate further that the ideal of legal equality is more than a little elusive.

Kant's understanding of legal equality is not altogether free of these difficulties and ambiguities. He writes, for instance, that justice does not allow an individual's "fellow subjects" to "have any advantage over him," and that an "unequal distribution of burdens can never be considered just."[74] Without further elaboration, which Kant does not provide, these statements are not very helpful. What, after all, is an "unequal burden"? Is a poor person burdened unequally if she is required to pay the same rate or amount of tax as a rich person? Or conversely: is a rich person burdened unequally if she is required to pay a higher rate or amount of tax than a poor person? Questions of this sort appear never to have occurred to Kant.

Nonetheless, if there is a degree of vagueness in Kant's position, his main point is clear enough. When he claims that legal equality demands the elimination of special benefits and burdens, he means primarily that legally sanctioned class privileges, especially hereditary ones, are unjust. The *"birthright of each individual . . . is absolutely equal"* with respect to his rights as a "subject of the state":

[73] See, e.g., Sidgwick 1981, 267–68.
[74] TP 293–94, 297n\77, 79n.

> Thus no member of the commonwealth can have a hereditary privilege as against his fellow subjects; and no one can hand down to his descendants the privileges attached to the rank he occupies in the commonwealth, nor act as if he were qualified as a ruler by birth and forcibly prevent others from reaching the higher levels of the hierarchy . . . through their own merit.[75]

The point of these remarks could not have been missed by anyone living under the semi-feudal social conditions and class structures of eighteenth-century Prussia. Kant's rejection of hereditary privileges was directed toward the entrenched system of class preferences maintained by the Prussian state—above all to the continued existence of legally sanctioned classes of nobles and serfs, whether serfdom took the form of strict ownership, or as was increasingly the case, of hereditary subjection to the land. Even as late as the end of the eighteenth century the Prussian nobility enjoyed a large number of state sponsored privileges: a near monopoly on higher positions in the military and civil service, exemption from taxation, exclusive rights to purchase "noble lands," and, among other benefits, the right to entail their estates, thereby preventing members of other classes from purchasing much of the available land.[76] Kant argued that all privileges of this sort were unjust. He objected in particular to allowing an "arbitrarily selected class" of "feudal landowners" to entail their estates and decried the widespread practice of reserving official positions for members of special classes.[77]

Kant's larger target was the class structure itself rather than specific class privileges. A "hereditary nobility is a class of persons who acquire their rank before they have merited it."[78] Be-

---

[75] TP 292–93\76.
[76] See Hertz 1975, 20–21; Holborn 1982, 375–78; Ritter 1974, 159–64.
[77] TP 295–96\78.
[78] RL 329.

cause Kant regarded unmerited legal advantages as unjust, he considered the existence of a class of hereditary nobles an affront to justice. Naturally, he also viewed serfdom in the same light: by depriving an individual of his legal "personality" it unjustly relegated him to the status of a "domestic animal to be employed in any given capacity without his consent."[79]

On the issue of class-based privileges and restrictions Kant stated his views openly. Indeed he had little reason to camouflage them, for criticisms of serfdom and the nobility had by then become common and widely accepted, especially among the intelligentsia. Kant was more circumspect, however, and recognized the need to act more "prudently" in expressing publicly opinions that might still have been seen as "dangerous" by the "powers that be."[80] So it is not surprising that he was cautious in drawing attention to the fact that although his principle of legal equality was not incompatible with an elective monarchy, it was plainly inconsistent with the system of hereditary monarchy under which he lived. Kant was never bold enough to say so openly; yet there can be little doubt that he meant to imply as much when he insisted that all "hereditary prerogatives or privileges" are unjust, and consequently that "no one" is "qualified as a ruler by birth."[81]

As far as it goes, Kant's view of legal equality is fully defensible. The problem is that it does not go far enough. For Kant the main purpose of legal equality is to eliminate class-based legal privileges. Kant's legal equality is formal, not material.[82] It requires the dismantling of legally enforced class barriers, the removal of formal class benefits and burdens. But it is compatible, Kant believes, with great material inequalities. "This uniform equality of human beings as subjects of the state is . . .

---

[79] TP 293\76; RL 241.
[80] Letter to Beister, April 10, 1794 (Ak XI, 477–78); Letter to Friedrich Schiller, March 30, 1795 (Ak XII, 10–12).
[81] TP 292–93\75–76.
[82] TP 292\75.

perfectly consistent with the utmost inequalities in the mass and degree of their possessions."[83] Kant holds that every individual "must be entitled to reach any degree of rank which a subject can earn through his talent, his industry, his good fortune."[84] However, this right of meritocratic advancement is as far as Kant's legal equality extends. No one has any grounds for complaint "so long as he is aware that, if he does not reach the same level as others, the fault lies with himself (i.e. through lack of ability or serious endeavor) or with circumstances for which he cannot blame others."[85] The interests of justice thus are not, in Kant's view, damaged by material inequalities resulting from differences in merit, talent, or luck.

There is much in these sentiments with which one might take issue, especially the assumption that material inequalities can be justified as long as they flow from differences in natural talents and abilities. The natural lottery, as John Rawls points out, is morally random.[86] As the sun shines upon good and bad alike, so also are talents distributed without regard to moral merit. Natural talents and abilities are no more products of choice than are height or hair color (though of course one can sometimes choose whether to develop one's talents). Like all accidents of birth, natural talents and abilities are morally undeserved consequences of factors beyond the control of the individuals concerned. They cannot, accordingly, provide any grounds for praise, blame, or ascriptions of responsibility; nor, for the same reasons, can they provide any moral basis for material inequalities.

This line of argument is not new. It has been developed in detail by Rawls,[87] and poses a substantial threat to Kant's concep-

---

[83] TP 291–92\75.
[84] TP 292\75.
[85] TP 293\76–77.
[86] Rawls 1971, 72–75.
[87] Rawls 1971, 101–4.

tion of legal equality. But there is a more serious objection to Kant's understanding of legal equality. I leave aside for now the problem of inequalities across a single generation caused by meritocratic competition—or even by luck. Perhaps these can be justified, perhaps not. There remains the problem of cross-generational inequalities produced by the unlimited rights of inheritance Kant favors. According to Kant, a person should be permitted to "hand down everything . . . so long as it is material and not pertaining to his person [that is, not a class privilege or title]."[88] Kant recognizes that over a "series of generations," unrestricted rights of inheritance will inevitably "create considerable inequalities in wealth among members of the commonwealth (the employee and the employer, the landowner and the agricultural servants, etc.)."[89] Nevertheless, these widening inequalities are fully consistent, Kant believes, with justice and the demands of legal equality.

The trouble with Kant's tolerance for massive inequalities deriving from unrestricted rights of inheritance is that it clashes, indirectly at any rate, with his support for the ideal of a meritocratic social and economic order. Again and again Kant insists that every individual must be allowed to reach whatever position in the social and economic sphere she can attain through her own talent and industry.[90] What Kant appears not to have understood is that the ideal of a meritocratic social and economic order contains the further ideal of a level playing field, and that the ideal of a level playing field is inconsistent with unlimited rights of inheritance.

The relation between a meritocracy and a level playing field is all too obvious: the latter is a necessary condition of the former. Superior talent and industry will regularly win out over inferior talent and industry only when competition is on equal

[88] TP 293\76.
[89] TP 293\76.
[90] TP 291–94\74–77.

terms, only when all gains and losses arise solely from differences in talent and industry. A level playing field is consequently a presupposition of the development of a genuine meritocracy. Just as clearly, though, the ideal of a level playing field is undermined in practice by inequalities resulting from unlimited rights of inheritance. The considerable economic inequalities Kant recognizes as inevitable consequences of unrestricted rights of inheritance produce decisive advantages for the affluent and their children—in access to education, to capital, to resources, and to the reins of power, both economic and political. Not surprisingly, there are corresponding disadvantages for the lower classes and their children—in diminished educational options, shrunken horizons of personal opportunity, and little or no access to economic resources, or political power.

A playing field of this kind is hardly level. It is steeply graded, to the detriment of some and the benefit of others. Kant's legal equality, as long as it is conjoined with unlimited rights of inheritance, will undermine the meritocratic ideals it is meant to foster. It serves not so much to destroy class barriers as to replace *de jure* class structures with *de facto* ones, and the formal domination of one class with the informal domination of another.

This aspect of Kant's view of legal equality has not escaped the attention of critics, including Marx, who argued that the formal legal equality championed by Kant and other liberal philosophers is an ideological tool through which the bourgeoisie exercise control over other classes by masking their narrow class interests under an illusory "form of universality" and presenting them as "the only rational universally valid ones."[91] It is difficult to acquit Kant of this charge. His legal equality presents itself as a rule of neutrality prohibiting the state from conferring advantages on particular classes or groups. But, as

[91] Marx, *German Ideology*, 64–66, 97–99.

Marx suggests, this is an ideological "illusion."[92] The actual effect of Kant's legal equality, when tied to unlimited rights of inheritance, is to protect the interests of whatever class is most adept at accumulating property and maintaining its wealth through devises and bequests to its own members. Equality of this sort is anything but neutral between classes.

Political Freedom

The point of departure for Kant's view of political freedom is Rousseau's statement that liberty consists in obedience to self-prescribed laws.[93] In political societies where many persons must abide by the same rules, it is not possible for each citizen to create his own laws. Kant therefore argues that political freedom must consist in the right to participate with others in determining the laws to which all are equally subject.[94] And since, as Kant further believes, this freedom is morally necessary, all legislative authority must reside in the "united will of the people."[95]

Following Montesquieu, Kant additionally claims that justice requires separating the legislative, executive, and judicial functions of government. This division in Kant's view, is the primary characteristic of a "republican" state. He argues that any state lacking a separation of powers system of government is "despotic," for if the entire authority of the state is concentrated in the hands of a single individual or group there can be no effective restrictions on the arbitrary exercise of power.[96]

[92] Marx, *German Ideology*, 65.
[93] Rousseau, *Social Contract*, 1:8.
[94] RL 223; TP 296\78–79.
[95] RL 313.
[96] RL 316–17; ZEF 352\100–101.

The idea of a republic is nowadays barely distinguishable from that of a democracy. For Kant, however, the two are very different. A pure democracy is not, as he understands it, comparable to a modern liberal democracy. It permits no separation of powers, but is instead a form of government in which the people make laws, and assume executive and judicial authority without intermediaries or representatives. Kant views this as a version of mob rule, merely another kind of despotism.[97] He envisions pure democracy as a system in which all political questions are settled directly, without any constitutional restrictions, by a majority vote in a citizens' assembly. Such an assembly also has the power to punish individuals whether or not they have committed a wrong under existing laws.[98] In Kant's view, a direct democracy of this sort subjects the individual to the whims of the majority and, because it contains no constitutional safeguards against the tyranny of the majority, cannot protect personal rights.[99]

Kant's distaste for pure democracy highlights one of the main features of his theory of justice: the belief that political and civil freedom must be evenly balanced, each limiting and complementing the other.[100] Justice demands that a people be given the right to make its own laws. But that right must be constrained by constitutionally guaranteed civil liberties. Political freedom alone does not ensure civil freedom. The majority may fail to respect the rights of the minority—indeed, they may well act as tyrannically as any individual dictator. Hence political freedom must be supplemented by constitutionally guaranteed civil liberties; otherwise it leads only to despotism.

Political freedom must be restricted in still another way, according to Kant. Legislative authority should be placed in the hands of a representative assembly, whose members are to be

[97] ZEF 352\101.
[98] *Reflexion* 8054, Ak XIX, 595.
[99] ZEF 352\100–101.
[100] TP 290\74.

elected by a majority (or plurality) of voters in each district.[101]
But Kant's franchise is restrictive. He assumes, as was common
in his own time, that it should extend only to adult males who
"have some property."[102] These persons alone qualify as "active" citizens; the rest are merely "passive," and while they
must be assured the same civil rights and legal equality as everyone else, they should not be allowed to vote.[103]

Kant's property qualification, however, is not what one
might expect. Property qualifications have often been used to
limit the electoral franchise to taxpayers or owners of real property. This is not, at least not entirely, Kant's intention. If it
were, Alan Ryan would be right to suggest that Kant attempts
to confine "political activity to the propertied."[104] Ryan's assertion is bound to mislead, though, for it fosters the false impression that Kant wishes to restrict the franchise to those who
possess property in the ordinary, contemporary sense. Kant's
conception of property differs from the present-day conception.
Property, for Kant, includes not just external objects, land, and
vendible commodities of all kinds; it includes in addition any
"skill, trade, fine art or science."[105] Ownership of property in
any of these forms is sufficient for Kant's franchise.

No doubt, this class of property owners will coincide largely
with a more conventionally defined class of property owners.
Yet the distinction should still not be ignored. To ignore it is to
make Kant appear excessively conservative. In principle, Kant's
property qualification is not meant to restrict the franchise to
propertied classes in the contemporary sense. Its explicit purpose is to limit the right to vote to those who are economically

[101] TP 296\78–79.
[102] TP 295\78.
[103] RL 314–15. Gunther Bien argues that Kant's distinction between active and passive citizenship derives ultimately from Aristotle, although it
was transformed by later philosophers. See Bien 1976, 77–81.
[104] Ryan 1984, 73; cf. Pateman 1985, 115.
[105] TP 295\78.

independent, to those who are their "own masters."[106] Any adult male able to earn a living without depending on the will of another satisfies this requirement, and Kant intends this group to include all independent tradesmen, merchants, estate owners, and artisans, as well as anyone who possesses a private income.[107] Also included in this category is anyone "who does a piece of work which belongs to him until he is paid for it"— which is to say, anyone who owns the raw materials and means of production from which he derives his livelihood.[108] Among those not included in this category are laborers, domestic servants, shop assistants, and in general all who are economically dependent on "arrangements by others."[109] Kant holds that such persons should not be given the franchise. The line between economic dependence and independence is sometimes hard to draw, as Kant understands. "I do admit," he says, "that it is somewhat difficult to define the qualifications that entitle anyone to claim the status of being his own master."[110] Notwithstanding this problem, Kant believes that economic independence is the appropriate test for active citizenship.

Kant's property qualification is without question a product of patterns of thought that now seem quaint at best, dangerously backward at worst. While it would be pointless to bludgeon Kant for failing to shake off the prejudices of his own age, there are more appropriate grounds for criticizing his property qualification, most notably that it violates the spirit of his own conception of justice. In the *Critique of Pure Reason*, Kant argues that a just constitution must permit the "greatest possible human freedom in accordance with laws which ensure that the freedom of each can co-exist with the freedom of all

[106] TP 295\78.
[107] RL 314–15.
[108] TP 295n\78n.
[109] RL 314–15.
[110] TP 295n\78n.

the others."[111] As I noted before, Kant defines *humanity* as the power to set ends (that is, the power of free choice). Human freedom must therefore be understood as freedom of choice.[112] It follows that the greatest possible human freedom is the greatest possible human freedom of choice. It seems plain, also, that the amount of freedom of choice increases in direct proportion to the number of people who are allowed to exercise freedom of choice. Because voting is a way of exercising freedom of choice, and because a just constitution requires the greatest possible freedom of choice, a just constitution must surely extend the electoral franchise to the greatest possible number. By Kant's own standards, therefore, only compelling reasons can justify excluding anyone from the franchise, for every restriction on electoral freedom diminishes the sum total of human freedom. To arrive at a convincing justification of Kant's property qualification, it would be necessary to show that extending the franchise to economically dependent classes would make it impossible for the freedom of each subject to co-exist with the freedom of all others. Kant offers no such argument; nor is it likely that a plausible one could ever be found. Even within Kant's own theory of justice, therefore, his property qualification lacks support or justification.

There is a second reason for scepticism about Kant's property qualification. In an effort to tailor it so that it excludes only the groups Kant intends to exclude, he engages in some blatant gerrymandering. An individual is not his "own master," Kant says, if his livelihood depends "not on his own industry, but on arrangements by others."[113] Persons of this sort lack the "civil personality" which Kant regards as a prerequisite of the right to vote.[114] The economic category this description applies to is

[111] KRV A317\B373.
[112] TL 391.
[113] RL 314.
[114] RL 314–15.

that of the *employee*. One would consequently expect Kant to exclude *all* employees from the franchise. Not so. Employees of the state, presumably including university professors in Germany, are eligible for Kant's franchise. For unexplained reasons, an exception is made for them; somehow, *their* economic dependence is not objectionable.[115] The incompatibility of Kant's property qualification with his conception of justice is thus compounded by his arbitrary application of it.

A peculiarity of Kant's property qualification is that the reasons for it are never made clear. Perhaps its merits seemed too obvious to Kant, but if we wish to understand what may have motivated him to adopt it, the following considerations may be of some help. There have traditionally been three justifications for property qualifications. The first, used by Edmund Burke, is that they keep the franchise out of the hands of persons engaged in "servile" and "dishonourable" occupations, in effect the lower classes.[116] The second, employed at one time by Condorcet, is that those without property have no "interest" in the welfare of the nation and consequently should not be given a voice in shaping its policies.[117] The third, which differs significantly from both of the others, played a part in the Putney Debates of the English civil war. Giving voice to this last justification, one participant in those debates, Maximillian Petty, argued thus: "I conceive that the reason why we should exclude apprentices, or servants, or those that take alms, is because they depend on the will of other men and should be afraid to displease them."[118]

---

[115] RL 314–15.

[116] Burke 1973, 62–63.

[117] Baker 1975, 253.

[118] Wootton 1985, 315. The Putney Debates were discussions held in 1647, during the second English Civil War, at St. Mary's Church, Putney. The participants were officers and soldiers of Cromwell's new Model Army and the focus of the debates was on whether the army should support the demands of Levellers for radical changes in English society.

Kant's view is more akin to Petty's than to Burke's or Condorcet's. He does not argue that the laboring classes should be excluded from the franchise on the grounds that their occupations are servile or dishonourable; nor because they are unable to take an interest in the well-being of the commonwealth. He claims instead, with Petty, that they should not be given the franchise because they depend for their subsistence on the "will" of others.[119] Kant does not explain *why* this should be sufficient to exclude those who are economically dependent, but in the absence of any other explanation it seems reasonable to suppose that he may have been thinking along the same lines as Petty. He may have believed, in other words, that those who depend on others for their livelihoods would either be too eager to please their masters or too susceptible to pressure, particularly in an open ballot system, for their votes to be truly their own.

[119] RL 314–15.

CHAPTER TWO

The Justification

of Freedom

THUS FAR, I HAVE EXAMINED KANT'S PRINCIPLES OF CIVIL liberty, political freedom, and legal equality with a view to understanding both how Kant intended them to be interpreted and what sorts of practical implications they may have. Except in connection with the principle of legal equality, whose merits have already been considered, I have said little about Kant's method of justifying these principles. The basic question we have not yet confronted, and which I shall address in this chapter, is why external freedom, including both civil and political freedom, is the primary value in Kant's theory of justice.

One possible answer must be rejected at the beginning. Discussing the place of freedom in Kant's political philosophy, Jeffrie Murphy writes: "Kant quite clearly believes that freedom does not stand in need of any positive justification, for it is a good in itself."[1] What Murphy means is not entirely clear. Kant never describes freedom as a good in itself. The only thing he describes in that way is a good will, a will that constantly

---

[1] Murphy 1970, 109.

strives to perform duties purely from the motive of duty.[2] Murphy's assertion is in fact demonstrably wrong. Presumably, Murphy is referring to *external* freedom, since that is the kind of freedom with which Kant's political philosophy is concerned. But it is incorrect to suppose that Kant regards external freedom as a good in itself, at least if that is taken to mean, as it is by Murphy, that further justification is unnecessary. In connection with external freedom Kant's attitude is decidedly mixed, as is shown by his repeated claim that the unbridled freedom of the state of nature is destructive and must be replaced by the controlled freedom of civil society.[3] Kant does not, therefore, regard external freedom as an unqualified good requiring no justification. As much as any other political philosopher, Kant recognizes the dangers of unrestricted freedom and the harm it may produce.

There are additional reasons for skepticism with regard to Murphy's view. For one thing, contrary to his suggestion, Kant does attempt to justify external freedom, as I will explain shortly. For another, it sidesteps the question of justification to declare that Kant regards freedom as a good in itself. In no way does the contention that freedom is a good in itself eliminate the need for justification. Such a claim merely shifts the burden of justification to another plane; for even if freedom is a good in itself, we still need to know *why*. This question persists even if we accept Murphy's suggestion that Kant regards freedom as a good in itself. Murphy's claim therefore serves only to postpone, not to resolve, the problem of justification.

Kant's attitude toward freedom, inner as well as outer, is complex and ambivalent. He distinguishes two types of inner freedom, one "negative," the other "positive." Both are presuppositions of the possibility of morality. Negative freedom is a capacity of the will, possessed by human beings but lacking in

[2] G 393, 396–97.
[3] IAG 22–4\46–48.

animals, to resist determination by sensible impulses and the laws of nature that govern them.[4] Positive freedom is the ability of pure reason to be practical, to determine the will apart from the influence of sensibility.[5] It is, in other words, the capacity for purely rational action, untinged by desire or inclination. Kant believes that if human beings did not have a capacity for negative freedom, there could be no duty to obey the moral law; for the moral law requires us to subordinate our sensible impulses to the demands of duty, and if we did not possess negative freedom we could not satisfy that demand.[6] Neither could the idea of duty influence human action if we did not possess positive freedom. To act in a morally worthy way is to perform one's duties from the motive of duty, which is the same as determining one's choices through pure practical reason. But positive freedom is the capacity to determine one's will by pure practical reason; so the impossibility of positive freedom would be tantamount to the impossibility of morally worthy action.[7]

Because positive and negative freedom are crucial to the possibility of moral action, and because Kant believes that humanity's "absolute" value consists in its moral capacities, he argues that freedom "constitutes man's worth" and is the "inner value of the world."[8] There is, however, a less exalted side to human freedom: it is the source of "all evil in the world."[9] Insofar as external freedom can be used to violate the rights of others, one can easily understand how it may be a source of evil. What is more difficult to comprehend is how inner freedom could also be a cause of evil. Positive freedom, after all, is just the capacity to obey the moral law from an awareness of duty, and negative freedom is simply the will's ability to resist

---

[4] G 446; RL 213–14; KPV 29.

[5] RL 213–14; G 446. For a more detailed discussion of positive and negative freedom see Allison 1983, chap. 15.

[6] REL 44\40.

[7] KPV 29; G 448–49.

[8] VE 151–52, 313–14\122, 249; TL 434; KU 442–44.

[9] VE 153\123; cf. MA 115\60.

the influence of inclinations, desires, and passions, which are the source of all temptations to disobey the moral law.[10]

It seems paradoxical therefore to suppose that inner freedom could be a cause of evil. There is, nevertheless, a straightforward way of understanding this idea. Because positive freedom is the capacity to obey the moral law for its own sake, the moral law would be incapable of imposing duties on human beings if there were no positive freedom; for there can be no duties where there is no capacity to respond to the demands of duty, and without positive freedom there could be no such capacity. The concept of duty would then be empty and void of meaning for human beings. Without duties, in turn, there could be no actions or choices contrary to duty. Finally, without actions or choices contrary to duty there could be no evil. Inner freedom accordingly introduces the possibility of evil into the world.[11] In the absence of inner freedom there would be no moral evil, nor of course any moral good.[12]

It should now be apparent that inner and outer freedom are justified differently. Inner freedom is required for the possibility of moral action; therein lies its justification. The same is not true of outer freedom. The complete absence of external freedom would not diminish positive or negative freedom in the slightest. A person does all that morality demands of her so long as she determines her choices in accordance with the moral law, even if, due to external impediments, she is unable to fulfill any of the outer requirements of duty.[13] The justification of external freedom cannot, consequently, be derived from the moral necessity of inner freedom. We must look elsewhere for its moral underpinnings.

---

[10] G 424.

[11] Allen Wood has pointed out to me that this reasoning is similar to Paul's argument in his letter to the Romans that "the law" provokes us to sin (Rom. 5:20, 7:5, 7:12).

[12] On the general issue of the relation between inner freedom and evil see Allen Wood's paper "Kant's Compatibilism" (Wood 1984).

[13] G 394.

Justice and Ethics: Preliminary Connections

Let us begin to examine the justification of external freedom by considering a few of the parallels between Kant's view of external freedom and his ethical theory. This will provide a glimpse of the unity and continuity between Kant's theory of justice and his ethical theory, making it easier to see how, as will become clear in later sections, Kant's ethical theory provides normative moorings for his principles of civil and political freedom.

The first parallel is that civil and political freedom are the analogues in Kant's theory of justice of negative and positive freedom in Kant's ethical theory. Negative freedom allows the "inner exercise of choice" to be independent of determination by sensible impulses.[14] In a comparable way, properly circumscribed civil freedom defines an area within which each person's "outer exercise of choice" can and should be protected against interference by other individuals or invasive public laws.

Corresponding to the parallel between negative and civil freedom is another between positive and political freedom. Positive freedom, as I have indicated, is the will's ability to determine itself by pure reason, and because reason always operates in accordance with laws it follows that positive freedom is the capacity of the will to determine itself through laws of reason. This explains why Kant equates positive freedom with the principle of autonomy, described in the *Groundwork* as "the idea of the will of every rational being as making universal law."[15] Autonomy of the will is the same as positive freedom: both are the will's capacity for purely rational self-determination.[16] In addition to the idea of rational self-determination present in the

[14] RL 213–14.
[15] G 431.
[16] KPV 33; G 446–47.

concept of positive freedom, the principle of autonomy adds—
or rather makes explicit—that this self-determination must be
law-governed.

The kinship between autonomy or positive freedom and political freedom should now be plain. Political freedom is an externalized form of autonomy or positive freedom. Political
freedom is the capacity to create laws governing external acts of
choice, just as autonomy or positive freedom is the capacity to
create laws governing inner acts of choice. Still, there is an important difference between these two capacities: unlike autonomy or positive freedom, political freedom need not always
express itself rationally. Positive freedom cannot be exercised
wrongly, except in the sense that one might elect not to use it
at all. A people, however, can misuse its political freedom to
create irrational and unjust laws.

As the last remark suggests, there are limits to the analogy
between positive freedom or autonomy and political freedom.
There are limits, as well, to the parallel between negative and
civil freedom. Civil freedom provides an area of personal liberty that should not be transgressed either by other individuals
or by public laws. But civil freedom also depends on public laws
for its preservation, and here the analogy with negative freedom breaks down, for it does not depend in any comparable way
on natural laws. A more significant limitation to the analogies
between civil and political freedom on the one hand, and positive and negative freedom on the other, is that the first two are
logically independent of the second two. Neither political nor
civil freedom entail positive or negative freedom. A society
with civil and political freedom can exist even if, as many people believe, inner freedom is purely mythical.

Although the *existence* of civil and political freedom does
not, strictly speaking, entail inner freedom, Kant's manner of
justifying them does. If human beings have a right to civil and
political freedom, they must *a fortiori* be capable of having
rights. But a right, according to Kant, is a moral capacity "to

obligate others to a duty."[17] Every right therefore corresponds to a duty. Consequently, there can be no rights without duties. Remember also that there can be no moral duties without inner freedom. For without inner freedom there would be no capacity to subordinate sensible impulses to the demands of duty; and without such a capacity there would be no ability to respond to the demands of duty; and without an ability to respond to the demands of duty the concept of duty would be empty and meaningless. In the absence of inner freedom, therefore, moral duties would be impossible, and because there can be no rights without corresponding duties, the impossibility of inner freedom would also spell the impossibility of moral rights. Given Kant's view of the nature of moral rights and duties, therefore, possessing a right to civil or political freedom entails possessing inner freedom.[18]

External Freedom and the Categorical Imperative

None of the above discussion explains why civil and political freedom are necessary or desirable. Part of Kant's justification of political freedom is found in the *Rechtslehre:*

> When someone decides for another, it is always possible that he thereby does the other an injustice, but this is never possible with respect to what he decides for himself (for *volenti non fit injuria*). Hence, only the united and consenting Will of all—that is, a general united Will of the people by which each decides the same for all and all decide the same for each—can legislate.[19]

---

[17] RL 239.

[18] For an extended analysis of the place of inner freedom in Kant's political philosophy see Kersting 1984, Teil A, especially 16–35.

[19] RL 313–14.

This argument should have a familiar ring. It is based on the *volenti* maxim that figures prominently, as we saw earlier, in Kant's principle of civil freedom. The most natural interpretation of Kant's argument is as follows. Voluntary consent precludes injustice. Therefore, whenever an individual makes a decision for herself, there can be no injustice. Whenever one person makes a decision for another without her consent, however, there may be injustice. Consequently, every individual whose actions are governed by laws must give her consent to those laws.[20] Only so is it possible to ensure that all laws are just. The power to legislate must, accordingly, be vested in the entire people—in the united general Will of the people.

The conclusion of this argument appears to be that justice requires the unanimous consent of all citizens to all legislation. But that is a recipe for stalemate, since unanimity cannot plausibly be expected when thousands or millions of individuals are involved in any decision-making process. Rousseau's solution to this dilemma is to settle for a majority vote on legislation in a citizens' assembly.[21] A direct democracy of this sort has the advantage of ensuring the active participation of citizens in the law-making process. As Rousseau is aware, however, it does not provide a practical system of legislation in large nations.[22]

Kant is more concerned than Rousseau with the pragmatic question of combining the principle of popular sovereignty with the existence of large national states. For this and other reasons, he rejects Rousseau's direct democracy, preferring instead Montesquieu's conclusion that although the power of legislation belongs by right to the people as a whole, they must delegate it to elected representatives in large nations due to the practical impossibility of assembling great numbers of citizens for protracted periods of time to discuss, deliberate, and vote on

[20] Obviously this claim must be qualified in various ways, e.g., that it applies only to adults and to citizens.

[21] Rousseau, *Social Contract*, 4:2.

[22] Rousseau, *Social Contract*, 3:15.

legislative proposals.[23] In *Theory and Practice* Kant explains why he accepts the need for a representative, and majoritarian, legislative system:

> An entire people . . . cannot be expected to reach unanimity, but only to show a majority of votes (and not even of direct votes, but simply of the votes of those delegated in a large nation to represent the people). Thus the principle of accepting majority decisions must be accepted unanimously and embodied in a contract; and this is the ultimate basis on which a civil constitution is established.[24]

Kant's claim is that participants in a rational social contract, recognizing the pragmatic impossibility of achieving unanimous agreement on every law in large states, would unanimously consent to the principle of majority rule. More specifically, they would consent to the principle that a majority of representatives in an elected legislative assembly should have the power to create laws that are binding on all subjects. Practical exigencies thus transform the pure principle of popular sovereignty (the principle that each citizen must consent directly to every law he is required to obey) into the pragmatic rule that the power to legislate must reside in a popularly elected majoritarian representative assembly.

There is, however, a problem with this pragmatic compromise. Kant's argument in the *Rechtslehre* depends on the premise that since self-imposed decisions are never unjust, a law cannot be unjust if it is consented to by the entire body of citizens. True enough, perhaps. But when Kant concludes that, owing to the practical impossibility of reaching unanimous agreement on every legislative decision in large states, it is necessary for participants in a rational social contract to consent

[23] Montesquieu, *Spirit of the Laws*, 2:6.
[24] TP 296\79.

unanimously to a majoritarian representative legislature as a vehicle of popular sovereignty, the prospect of injustice surfaces once again. It may be true that laws can never be unjust if they are freely and directly accepted by those to whom they apply, but it does not follow that laws imposed by elected representatives in a majoritarian legislative system can never be unjust. In the first place, representatives of the majority may pass oppressive laws against minorities. In the second place, elected representatives may become corrupt, as Rousseau warns, and promote their own interests rather than those of their constituents.[25] Therefore, even if Kant is right to conclude that popular sovereignty can in practice only imply a right to elect representatives in a majoritarian legislative system, such an arrangement offers little protection against injustice, especially for the minority, but also for the majority.

Where does this leave Kant's justification of political freedom? Political freedom is the right of citizens to participate in determining the laws by which they are governed. Kant bases this right on the principle that injustice can be prevented only if all citizens consent to the laws they are required to obey. But this protection against injustice disappears, I have suggested, as soon as Kant argues that citizens' consent to legislation can in practice consist only in the right to vote for representatives in a majoritarian legislative system. The question, then, is whether this pragmatic compromise of Kant's undermines his own justification of political freedom and popular sovereignty.

The answer is partly yes and partly no. As in our earlier discussion of civil freedom, it is necessary to remember that consent for Kant, particularly in a normative context, usually means rational consent. Both the *Rechtslehre* passage and the text from *Theory and Practice* must be interpreted in this light if we are to make sense of them. Kant's view is not that a majoritarian representative legislature is incapable of creating

[25] Rousseau, *Social Contract*, 3:15.

unjust laws. Indeed, he knows full well that elected representatives may become corrupt and that majorities sometimes op-
press minorities.[26] After all, that is why Kant insists a just
constitution must guarantee not only political freedom but
also civil freedom and legal equality. The latter two requirements are rational constraints on the principle of popular sovereignty and on the legitimizing potential of popular consent.
They ensure that political freedom—when it takes the only
form Kant believes is pragmatically feasible: a right to vote for
representatives in a majoritarian legislative system—does not
lead to injustice.

These considerations may serve to establish that Kant's
principle of political freedom provides a guarantee against injustice. That is not, however, an altogether satisfactory conclusion, for political freedom, within the framework of Kant's
political theory, provides an assurance against injustice only
when it is conjoined with civil freedom and legal equality. Political freedom alone affords no protection against injustice. We
have therefore not yet arrived at a convincing justification of
political freedom. What needs to be shown is that political
freedom is morally necessary, not merely that it is consistent
with the demands of justice when it is constrained by other political principles.

Kant holds that all moral principles can be derived, directly
or indirectly, from one "supreme principle" of morality: the
categorical imperative.[27] Our task, consequently, is to deter-

[26] ZEF 352\101; SF 90n\186n.
[27] G 421, 424. I shall follow Kant's practice of referring sometimes to
"the categorical imperative," as though there were only one, and sometimes to "categorical imperatives" in the plural, as though there were several. This usage can produce confusion, but it represents a necessary
distinction. When Kant speaks of categorical imperatives in the plural he is
referring to particular moral commands, for instance, "Do not steal," "Do
not make false promises," or "Do not commit suicide." When he speaks of
the categorical imperative in the singular, he is referring to the supreme
principle of morality from which, he believes, all particular moral com-

mine how the moral justification of political freedom can be traced back to the supreme principle of morality. The simplest way to approach this problem is to begin with Kant's own attempt in the *Groundwork* to discover the supreme principle of morality by analysing the ordinary concept of morality or moral duty.[28]

Kant notes in the *Groundwork* that, according to our ordinary understanding of morality, duties are expressed by means of imperatives ("You *ought* to do thus and so"). He also notes that there are two basic types of imperatives: one hypothetical, the other categorical.[29] Hypothetical imperatives tell us that we ought to do one thing as a means of achieving some other objective or end. Thus the hypothetical imperative "If you wish to wake up early, you ought to set the alarm" tells us that we should set the alarm, provided we want to wake up early. Because hypothetical imperatives always refer to subjective ends or objectives, Kant describes them as both "material" and "conditional."[30] They are material because the ends to which they refer are drawn from the material contents of the will— from subjective desires, wishes, and ends. They are conditional because their imperatival force ("You *should* set the alarm") is conditional upon having the relevant desire or end (here, waking up early). The fact that hypothetical imperatives are material and conditional therefore means that they provide valid

---

mands can be "derived" (G 421–22). The supreme principle of morality can be formulated in different ways—as the formula of universal law, the formula of autonomy, the formula of humanity, the formula of the law of nature, and the formula of the kingdom of ends. The different formulations of the supreme principle of morality are not, however, different moral principles. Kant regards them simply as alternative characterizations of the same principle.

[28] The reasoning I set out below is only one of several lines of argument in the first two chapters of the *Groundwork*.

[29] G 415–16.

[30] G 416.

rules of action only for those who share the objectives they are intended to promote. So, for instance, the hypothetical imperative about setting the alarm provides a valid rule of action only for those who wish to wake up early.

Hypothetical imperatives can never, Kant insists, be moral imperatives. What makes them unsuitable as principles of morality is that they are dependent on shifting and variable material contents of the will. One person may wish for this, another for that; one may desire to wake up early, another to sleep in. Since hypothetical imperatives are always dependent on contingent and variable desires, wishes, and ends, they cannot provide universally valid rules of action for all rational beings. Kant believes, however, that the proper function of moral principles is to provide universally valid rules of action for all rational beings.[31] The moral command not to commit murder, for instance, applies to all individuals without regard to whether they do or do not wish to kill others. Like all moral imperatives, this command is unconditional. It does not say that we should avoid murder only if, for example, we do not wish to go to jail. On the contrary, it asserts unconditionally and categorically: Do not commit murder, whatever your personal wishes or desires.

As this indicates, moral imperatives must be categorical rather than hypothetical, which means, to summarize, that they must be unconditionally valid rules of action for all rational beings without regard to their subjective wishes and desires, not merely conditionally valid rules of action for some rational beings who happen to share the same wishes and desires. This explains why Kant says that moral principles must be "formal" and must be able to serve as "universal laws."[32] They must be formal in the sense that they must be independent of all contingent desires, wishes, and other material con-

[31] G 408, 416.
[32] G 421n, 427.

tents of the will. They must be capable of serving as universal laws in the sense that they must be fit to qualify as rules of action for all rational beings.

All of this Kant claims to have discovered in the *Groundwork* through an analysis of our everyday understanding of morality.[33] Reduced to essentials, what Kant has discovered is (1) that moral principles must be categorical imperatives, and (2) that the concept of a categorical imperative is, as I have just indicated, the idea of an *unconditional command that ought to serve as a universal law of action for all rational beings without regard to their subjective wishes, desires or ends.* This conception of the nature of categorical imperatives brings us close to uncovering Kant's supreme principle of morality. Indeed, it tacitly contains the supreme principle of morality. For reasons noted above, all moral principles must be categorical imperatives. The supreme principle of morality must consequently be a categorical imperative. Kant therefore suggests that we can discover the supreme principle of morality by examining the concept of a categorical imperative.[34] But the concept of a categorical imperative is purely formal insofar as it excludes all material ends and objectives. In fact, Kant claims, it contains nothing except what we have already encountered: the idea of an unconditional command that ought to serve as a universal law of action for all rational beings.[35] Because this idea provides the sole content of the concept of a categorical imperative, it alone can supply the content of the supreme principle of morality.

If we now ask what the supreme principle of morality is, the answer should be plain. The supreme principle of morality must draw its content from the concept of a categorical imperative. But it must also take the form of a categorical imperative. To discover the supreme principle of morality, we therefore

[33] G 389, 392, 403.
[34] G 420.
[35] G 402, 420–21; cf. RL 222.

need to transform the *content* of the concept of a categorical imperative into the *form* of a categorical imperative.[36] The result of this transformation is that the concept of a command that ought to serve as a universal law of action for all rational beings becomes a command to *ensure that your actions conform to rules that can serve as universal laws for all rational beings.* This command is the underlying principle in all of Kant's formulations of the supreme principle of morality,[37] though it differs somewhat from each of his characterizations of that principle. It is evident, for instance, in the *Groundwork* when Kant first formulates the supreme principle of morality as the principle of universal law: "Act only according to that maxim by which you can at the same time will that it should become a universal law."[38] Absent from this version of the supreme principle of morality, but present in others, is the further specification that the "universal laws" to which our maxims must conform are laws for "all rational beings."[39]

We have now seen, briefly at least, how Kant arrives at the supreme principle of morality in the *Groundwork*. What remains to be shown is how the principle of political freedom can be derived from this supreme principle of morality. I noted in Chapter 1 that the supreme principle of morality enters the domain of justice through a metamorphosis of the ethical principle of universal law in the *Groundwork* into the universal law of justice in the *Rechtslehre*. The principle of universal law is

---

[36] G 421–22.

[37] Consider, e.g., a passage from Kant's early lectures on ethics, predating yet capturing the essence of all Kant's later formulations of the categorical imperative in the *Groundwork* and elsewhere: "Morality is the harmony of actions with the universally valid law of the free will. . . . In all our actions what is called moral is regular. . . . It conforms to a rule. . . . If we make it the foundation of our conduct that our actions shall be consistent with a universal rule, which is valid at all times and for everyone, then our actions have their source in the principle of morality" (VE 42).

[38] G 421.

[39] G 438.

an ethical rule that regulates our inner freedom by command-
ing us to ensure that our maxims of action are capable of serving as universal laws for all rational beings. The universal law
of justice externalizes this command by requiring us to "act externally in such a way that the free use of your will can be compatible with the freedom of everyone else according to a
universal law."[40]

The supreme principle of morality, in the form of the ethical
principle of universal law, therefore leads directly to the universal law of justice. If we can derive Kant's principle of political
freedom from the universal law of justice, we will have succeeded in showing how political freedom can be traced back
to the supreme principle of morality. My suggestion is that
Kant's principle of political freedom can be derived from the
universal law of justice by considering more closely Kant's
analysis of the concept of justice in the *Rechtslehre*, along with
his claim that the universal law of justice commands us to ensure that our external actions "can be compatible" (*zusammen
bestehen könne*) with the external freedom of all other rational
beings under universal laws.

As with all moral principles, the universal law of justice is a
categorical imperative. It must consequently be formal in the
sense that it cannot depend on contingent desires, wishes,
ends, or other material contents of the will. The compatibility
referred to by the universal law of justice must therefore be formal inasmuch as it cannot rely on contingent desires, ends, or
objectives. Accordingly, the requisite compatibility cannot be
predicated on any assumption that laws ought to have this or
that contingent content, or that they should promote this or
that contingent objective. Any such compatibility would be
material, not formal.

The same conclusion emerges from Kant's analysis of the
concept of justice in the *Rechtslehre*. Recall Kant's claim,

[40] RL 231.

discussed in Chapter 1, that the "concept of justice does not take into account the matter of the will," but is concerned only with the "form of the relation between wills insofar as they are free, and whether the action of one can be reconciled (*zusammen vereinigen lasse*) with the freedom of the other in accordance with a universal law."[41] The reconciliation Kant alludes to here, no less than the compatibility mentioned in the universal law of justice, must be formal, having nothing to do with shared "wishes, desires . . . or even . . . needs."[42]

How, then, it is possible to achieve this "reconciliation" of the external freedom of all rational beings under universal laws, or to ensure that the external freedom of each rational being can be made compatible with the external freedom of all other rational beings under universal laws? The answer lies in Kant's remark that the concept of justice is concerned only with "the form of the relationship between wills insofar as they are considered free." There are two possible forms or types of relationship between individuals: one is based on compulsion or force, the other on consent or free choice. If an individual is compelled to act contrary to his own will, he is not treated as free. Compulsion is the antithesis of freedom. An individual is treated as free only when he freely chooses or consents to his relations with others. Consequently, the only form of relation between individuals that properly acknowledges their status as free beings is a relation of consent. The only way in which the freedom of every individual can be reconciled or made compatible with the freedom of every other individual is thus by means of the principle of consent.

The question raised by the universal law of justice—"How is it possible to make the external freedom of each individual compatible with the external freedom of all other individuals under universal laws?"—now has an answer: by ensuring that

[41] RL 230.
[42] RL 230.

everyone consents to the laws governing their external freedom. The universal law of justice therefore requires that individuals consent to the laws they are required to obey. It follows that the principle of political freedom, that individuals have a right to participate in determining the laws that regulate their external freedom, is contained in the universal law of justice; which in turn is derived from the supreme principle of morality in the form of the ethical principle of universal law; which in turn is derived from the concept of a categorical imperative; which in turn is shown by an analysis of our ordinary concept of morality to be the sole carrier of moral duties. In this way, the principle of political freedom can be traced back to the supreme principle of morality, and ultimately to our ordinary concept of moral duty, via the universal law of justice and the ethical principle of universal law. The principle of political freedom is thus a corollary of the supreme principle of morality.

For reasons already explained, however, Kant believes that political freedom must, in the modern world, take the restricted form of a right to vote for representatives in a majoritarian legislative assembly. Recall Kant's argument once again. Only consent provides a guarantee against injustice; so external laws must be based on the principle of consent. But in large nations it is not possible to obtain the consent of every citizen to every law. Practical exigencies therefore make it necessary to accept the principle of majority rule. Yet even the principle of majority rule must be qualified, for it is not possible in large states to have all citizens vote directly on all laws. In practice, the right to create laws must be restricted to a small group of elected representatives of the people. In practice, therefore, political freedom implies no more than a right to vote for representatives in a majoritarian representative assembly. In this way, we are led from the supreme principle of morality to the necessity of political freedom in the only form Kant considers pragmatically feasible.

External Freedom and the Principle of Autonomy

The principle of political freedom can be derived from the supreme principle of morality in another way as well. One of Kant's formulations of the supreme principle of morality is the principle of autonomy,[43] according to which "The will is . . . not merely subject to the law but is subject in such a way that it must also be regarded as self-legislative and only for this reason as being subject to the law (of which it can regard itself as the author)."[44] Kant is referring, in the first instance, to the moral law, the categorical imperative. But his claim is also perfectly general, applying to all practical laws, positive laws no less than moral laws, that govern the actions of rational beings. Irrespective of the nature or content of a law, the principle of autonomy implies that we are obligated to obey it only if we can regard it as freely self-imposed, as a law to which we are able to give our consent.[45]

The core idea of the principle of autonomy is that rational beings have a right to self-government, whether moral or political. The principle of autonomy therefore leads to the idea of political freedom. To see precisely how it provides a normative foundation for political freedom, however, we must examine in some detail the reasoning that leads Kant to the principle of autonomy. Kant arrives at this principle by distinguishing an autonomous or self-determining will from a heteronomous will that is determined by external forces.[46] Whenever laws are heteronomously imposed on rational beings there must be an "interest as a stimulus or compulsion to obedience."[47] Part of

---

[43] Stated as an imperative, the principle of autonomy is the command to "so act that your will can regard itself at the same time as making universal law through its maxim" (G 434).

[44] G 431.

[45] RL 313–14.

[46] G 433, 440–41; KPV 33.

[47] G 432–33.

what Kant means is that if a law is not self-imposed, rational beings must always have a reason or incentive for obeying it, more specifically an expectation that some benefit will accrue from obedience or a fear that disobedience will yield some disagreeable result. Contrary to the view of some interpreters, this does not entail that Kant believes there must always be a *selfish* motivation for obeying heteronomous laws.[48] Indeed, Kant says explicitly that a person may be motivated to obey a heteronomous law either by "his own interest or that of another."[49] Kant's view is therefore not that obedience to heteronomous laws must be motivated by *self*-interest, but rather that there must always be *some* interest or motive, selfish or altruistic, to explain why a rational being would obey such a law.

Kant also claims that the reasons and interests, wishes and fears that motivate compliance with heteronomous laws cannot provide any basis for a moral obligation of obedience. Imperatives that command obedience to heteronomous laws can only be "conditional."[50] They are conditional because, when a law is imposed on a rational being without his consent by someone else, he will always, to the extent that he is rational, require a reason for obedience. The reason, if it is to provide a plausible incentive for obedience, must refer to some good (for himself or others) that he may expect to result from compliance, or some evil (for himself or others) that he may expect to result from noncompliance. Insofar as a rational being's compliance with heteronomous laws is thus dependent on the results of obedience or disobedience, the only imperatives that can require him to obey heteronomous laws are conditional or hypothetical imperatives, for example, "You ought to obey this law if you do not want to be punished" or "You should obey this law because doing so will promote respect for the rule of

[48] See Ross 1954, 59–60.
[49] G 433.
[50] G 433.

law." But hypothetical imperatives can never, as we have already seen, be moral imperatives; for moral imperatives are unconditionally valid rules of action that apply categorically to all rational beings without regard to contingent wishes, desires, goals, or objectives of any kind.[51] It follows that because all moral duties are based on categorical imperatives, and because there can be no categorical imperative to obey all heteronomous laws, there can be no general moral duty to obey all heteronomous laws.

I am not suggesting that Kant believes there are never moral duties to obey specific heteronomous laws. The point is that Kant believes there is no *generic* duty to obey heteronomous laws considered as a special class of laws. It would be untenable to claim that there are no moral duties to obey any heteronomous laws. There is, for instance, a duty to obey laws that prohibit murder, whether they are heteronomous or autonomous. In the case of a heteronomous law against murder, however, the duty of obedience operates *despite* the law being heteronomous. There is no duty, according to Kant, to obey heteronomous laws *as such*. Yet there is obviously a duty not to commit murder, so there is also a duty to obey laws of any sort that prohibit murder. The same applies to all other heteronomous laws that seek to enforce compliance with duties of justice: they ought to be obeyed, but despite rather than because they are heteronomous.

The situation is different with autonomous laws. Kant says that the principle of autonomy is "unconditional."[52] Although Kant does not bother to explain his meaning, it is nonetheless passably clear. Rational beings, insofar as they are rational, always have reasons for actions and choices. To the extent they

[51] It is not Kant's view that categorical imperatives are indifferent to *all* objectives or ends, only to contingent, subjective, or material ends (G 427). Although this is an important distinction in Kant's moral theory, it does not affect the present argument, so I shall not pursue it further.
[52] G 432.

are rational, they consequently have reasons for imposing laws on themselves. Once a rational being has decided to impose a law on himself, however, he does not need *additional* reasons for obeying such a law. The reasons he has for choosing to impose the law on himself are ipso facto reasons for obeying it. Choosing to impose a law on oneself entails choosing to obey it. That is part of the concept of "imposing a law on oneself." Indeed, the proposition "I choose to impose a law on myself, but I also choose at the same time not to obey it" is self-contradictory, given that "I choose to impose a law on myself" means "I choose to require myself to act in accordance with a law."

The principle of autonomy is therefore *unconditional* because it rests ultimately on the law of noncontradiction, which, like all rules of logic, is unconditionally valid, as both a theoretical and practical norm, for all rational beings.[53] Since it rests on an unconditionally valid rule of action, the principle of autonomy is also an unconditionally valid rule of action. But a rule of action that is unconditionally valid for all rational beings, regardless of their subjective wishes, desires, or ends, is a categorical imperative (for finite rational beings). The principle of autonomy is consequently a categorical imperative.

We can now see how the principle of autonomy provides a normative foundation for political freedom. A fully legitimate system of laws is one that merits the obedience of those who are subject to it, and a system of laws merits the obedience of those who are subject to it only if it is rational to obey the rules it contains. The legitimacy of a system of laws is thus dependent on whether or not it is rational to comply with the rules it contains. Individual laws, though, may be good or bad, just or unjust, worthy or not worthy of obedience. The legitimacy of

---

[53] Readers familiar with Kant's ethical theory may notice that this argument, which bases the principle of autonomy on the law of noncontradiction, is similar to Kant's contradiction in conception test in the *Groundwork*.

laws is thus always contingent, always subject to doubt, as long as we are concerned only with their individual content or matter. But there are some laws, distinguished by source rather than content, that are always legitimate in the sense that those to whom the laws apply invariably have reason to obey them. Autonomous, self-imposed laws alone possess this degree of legitimacy; for obedience to self-imposed laws alone rests on a principle, the principle of non-contradiction, which is unconditionally valid for all rational beings. This point applies to autonomously imposed external-political laws as well as to autonomously imposed internal-ethical laws. Therefore, political freedom is a presupposition of any fully legitimate system of external laws, of any system of laws that merits the complete obedience and allegiance of those who are subject to it.

External Freedom and the Principle of Humanity

Political freedom has still another connection with the supreme principle of morality, this time by means of Kant's principle of humanity, one of five formulations of the categorical imperative in the *Groundwork*.[54] According to the principle of humanity, we are each required "to treat humanity, whether in your own person or in that of another, always as an end and never as a means only."[55] Treating a person as an end-in-himself implies respecting the ends he sets for himself, his objectives, goals, and projects. The principle of humanity is thus a rule of respect for human choices. Considered in relation to political freedom, the consequences are obvious. Kant says that treating a citizen "not just as a means, but also as an end"

[54] The present discussion of the principle of humanity will be relatively brief. For an extended analysis see Korsgaard 1987.
[55] G 429.

requires making him a "co-legislative member of the state."[56]
The point here is that since the principle of humanity requires
respect for human choices, it suggests that laws ought not to
restrict personal freedom without the consent of the governed.
Whenever this rule is not observed, whenever laws are imposed
without popular consent, citizens are treated merely as means
to whatever ends rulers wish to promote. Even if this end is the
"common good" or some other exemplary goal, suppressing political freedom means failing to respect the right of individuals
to determine their own ends.

The principle of humanity also has a bearing on the justification of civil freedom. Respecting human choices, in Kant's
view, involves not interfering with the "freedom," "property,"
"rights," or "happiness" of others.[57] Kant is not recommending
the complete abolition of all restrictions on individual freedom. The principle of humanity is not intended as a recipe for
anarchy. Kant means only that each person should be free to
pursue her own ends as long as doing so does not violate anyone
else's rights.[58] Applying this rule to everyday cases naturally
presents difficulties, for its practical implications are by no
means always clear. But the underlying thought, that each individual should be permitted to pursue her own ends as long as
they are consistent with the rights of others, is the same idea
that motivates Kant's principle of civil freedom. The principle
of civil freedom is in fact best understood as a rule for *applying*
the principle of humanity to the task of determining the proper
limits of civil freedom.

This discussion may convey an impression of illicit boot-
strapping. I have suggested that Kant's principles of civil and
political freedom can be justified by reference to the principle of
humanity. But what justifies *that* principle? In virtue of *what*

[56] RL 345.
[57] G 430.
[58] RL 231.

is a person entitled to be treated as an end-in-himself? *Why* should we respect human choices? Unless a plausible answer can be given to these questions, we will not have progressed far in explaining why Kant believes that civil and political freedom are made necessary by the principle of humanity.

The principle of humanity asserts that human beings are ends-in-themselves and the "ground" of this principle, Kant says, is that "rational nature exists as an end in itself."[59] The status of a human being as an end-in-herself is thus tied to her rational nature. But "rational nature," in this context, does not refer to theoretical rationality.[60] Kant instead asserts that rational nature "is distinguished from others in that it proposes an end to itself."[61] Setting ends is a function of the will, so Kant is identifying rational nature and what makes a human being an end-in-herself with her possession of a will. Having a will is therefore the basis of a human being's "absolute," "unconditional," "intrinsic" value as an end-in-herself.[62] This claim, however, is a little misleading. The absolute value of a human being lies not *simply* in the fact that she possesses *a* will. Animals, too, have wills, yet Kant does not accord them absolute value. What gives a human being absolute value is that, in contrast with an animal will (*arbitrium brutum*), which is causally determined by inclinations, a human will (*arbitrium liberum*) is "affected" by sensible impulses without being causally determined by them, and always remains capable of setting its ends by reference to pure practical reason.[63] A will of this kind is a potentially good will, and this potentiality is what gives every human being unconditional worth and raises him

[59] G 429.
[60] KU 443–44.
[61] G 437.
[62] G 428–29.
[63] RL 213.

in value "above mere animality."[64] A human being is consequently an end-in-himself in virtue of possessing a potentially good will.

The "absolute" value of rational or human nature stands opposed, in Kant's view, to the merely "relative" value of everything else.[65] All objects in the world possess whatever value they have solely because they are "means" to the attainment of some human goal, or because they are chosen as "good for" something by a human being.[66] This is why Kant says that the "being of everything in the world gets it worth" from "human beings."[67] For an object to be of value is for it to be an object of human choice. Human beings alone are ends-in-themselves; everything else is an end-for-human-beings.

These considerations make it easier to see why the principle of humanity requires respect for human choices, as well as how civil and political freedom may be justified through this principle. Apart from the absolute worth of human beings, all value, all moral good, is created by human choice. Human choices are "value conferring."[68] Suppressing human choices therefore means suppressing not only the creation of specific instrumental goods but also the source of all value in the world. The act of choice consequently merits respect as the source of all value, and all restrictions on its exercise accordingly require justification. This amounts to an argument for a prima facie right to the fullest possible human freedom of choice, and because this freedom would be incomplete if it did not include civil and political freedom, there is also a prima facie right to these freedoms.

[64] KPV 61; KU 443.
[65] G 428.
[66] KPV 59; G 428.
[67] KU 442–43.
[68] Korsgaard 1987, 196.

Human Nature and Happiness

Kant often insists that moral laws apply to all rational beings without depending at all on knowledge of the particular nature of human beings.[69] Moral laws are laws of rational nature generally, not of human nature in particular.[70] This is true even of the principle of humanity, for Kant believes that, despite its name, it applies quite generally to all rational beings, each of whom is entitled to be treated as an end-in-itself.[71] Human beings, though, are the only rational beings with whom we have or are ever likely to have any acquaintance, so one might wonder whether Kant is not laboring a moot point when he insists that moral laws apply to all rational beings. The point is not moot, however; it serves a definite purpose. Kant wants to avoid "indulgent moral laws" that make concessions to human weaknesses.[72] Morality must be kept pure, must not bargain with vice, nor take its principles from observations of human nature. To do so would reduce morality to anthropology, and transform what human beings ought to do to what they have been observed to do. Hence Kant's concern that morality avoid any dependence on knowledge of human nature, lest it thereby compromise its own principles.

All the same, it is a mistake to exaggerate the degree to which Kantian morality is, or could be, indifferent to the facts of human nature.[73] Moral principles must be applied to human beings, which means that they must take into account the "special nature of man," at least to the extent of not requiring the impossible of human beings.[74] Morality must therefore acknowledge the limits of human nature. One of these is of par-

---

[69] E.g., G 389–90.
[70] RL 216.
[71] G 428–29.
[72] RL 217.
[73] This theme is usefully explored in Wood 1991.
[74] RL 217.

ticular relevance to the issue of civil freedom, and provides a justification of civil freedom over and above those we have thus far considered. In the *Groundwork*, Kant claims that happiness is an end that by a "necessity of nature" no person can avoid having.[75] Because it is a necessary end for all human beings, it is also an end that forms part of the "essence" of human nature.[76] Kant does not mean just that every individual inevitably desires happiness. An "end" is not just a desire; it is an "object" of the will, something one chooses as a goal of action, though not always with the self-conscious awareness that one has so chosen it.[77] When Kant calls happiness a necessary human end he implies more than that human beings necessarily desire or wish for their own happiness. He implies that it is a necessary *goal* of human *action*.[78]

It is far from self-evident that happiness is a necessary human end. Indeed, at first glance such an assertion appears to fly in the face of experience. History and everyday experience combine to suggest that self-ruination is as much a goal of human action as happiness. Nevertheless, once we understand Kant's assumptions his view is not unreasonable. Kant distinguishes between "subjective" and "objective" ends. An end is objective just in case it is determined by morally practical reason. An end of this kind is one that all persons ought to adopt, regardless of whether they do so or not.[79] An end is subjective, in contrast, if it is determined by individual desires and inclinations, which may or may not be shared by others. A person may fail to adopt any objective ends, for he may eschew morality altogether. But

---

[75] G 415; cf. KPV 25; TP 278\64; TL 387.

[76] G 415–16.

[77] TL 380.

[78] This does not, of course, mean that Kant is a psychological egoist or hedonist. He believes that happiness is *a* necessary human end, not that it is the *only* end men ever can or do pursue. Happiness is one end among others, even if it is a necessary end, and, as with all nonmoral ends, Kant believes that it must always be subordinated to moral ends.

[79] TL 385; G 427.

no human being can avoid having subjective ends. As a partly sensible, partly rational, creature, a human being is a "being of needs."[80] So long as a person continues to exist, he continues to have needs and desires. Since he cannot continue to live without attending to the demands of his sensible nature, he cannot avoid having subjective ends directed toward the satisfaction of his needs and desires.[81] Survival requires as much.

Happiness, though, is the satisfaction of the "sum total" of an individual's subjective ends, or of as many of them as can be fashioned into a consistent whole.[82] Having one's own happiness as one of one's ends is therefore simply having a nonempty set of subjective ends.[83] Because every individual must have some subjective ends, it follows that every individual must have his own happiness as an end.[84] A human being's "own finite nature as a being of needs" thus ensures that he must strive after his own happiness.[85] This need not be something of which the person concerned is either fully or partially aware. Just as we may act without reflecting on our motives, and

[80] KPV 61.

[81] KPV 25.

[82] The "satisfaction" of "all inclinations taken together . . . that can be brought into a fairly tolerable system" is "called happiness" (KPV 73); "happiness . . . is merely the general name for subjective determining grounds" of the will (KPV 25); "happiness consists in the satisfaction of all our inclinations" (VE 46\38); "all inclinations are summed up" in the "idea" of happiness (G 399); happiness is "the sum of all inclinations" (KU 434n); happiness is the "unity" of all the "incentives of inclination" (REL 36–37\32); see also TP 282–83\67–68; TL 386.

[83] This conception of happiness is, in my opinion, the one that dominated Kant's thinking during the critical period, but it is not the only one Kant ever entertained. In a fragment that Schilpp dates from around the mid-seventies, Kant rejects the subjectivistic view he later came to accept, namely that happiness is just the "greatest sum of enjoyment" (Schilpp 1938, 127–29). There is evidence in this fragment of a more rationalistic conception of happiness, in particular of a tendency to regard virtue as a "means" to the attainment of happiness. This view, however, is one Kant later condemned and abandoned in the *Critique of Practical Reason* (Schilpp 1938, chap. 9; KPV 110–19).

[84] KPV 25.

[85] KPV 25.

hence without being aware of them, so too is it possible to adopt ends without being reflectively conscious of having done so. To say that happiness is a necessary human end is not, accordingly, to say that all human beings have a deliberate policy of pursuing their own happiness. It is to say only that all persons have a totality of ends, and that as they attempt to achieve each of their separate ends they also, consciously or unconsciously, attempt to achieve the totality.

The remaining question is how the *fact* that human beings necessarily pursue their own happiness is connected with a *right* to do so in civil society. Staying within the framework of Kant's understanding of happiness, this is-ought gap can be easily bridged. Kant, as I have just indicated, has a subjectivistic conception of happiness. An individual's happiness consists in the satisfaction of the largest consistent set of his personal ends. There is for Kant no objective, intersubjectively valid criterion of happiness—no Aristotelian basket of goods capable of providing normative standards for correct ascriptions of happiness. Whatever subjective ends an individual may have, those and those alone determine what will make him happy. But subjective ends are infinitely variable; so happiness too varies indefinitely as it tracks personal preferences and desires.[86] Just as crucially, only the person concerned is equipped to decide what his own ends may be, and so only he is in a position to know what will make him happy.

These thoughts provide us with the first two premises of an argument for civil freedom:

1. Every human being necessarily tries to achieve his own happiness.
2. Only the individual himself can know his own ends, and therefore only he can decide what will make him happy. No one else can decide this for him.

---

[86] TP 298\80; KPV 25–26.

Two more premises, both of which can be found in Kant's writings, are needed:

3. Morality cannot require the impossible of human beings.[87]
4. If it is wrong forcibly to prevent someone from doing something, he has a right to do it.[88]

These premises jointly entail, or at least strongly support, the conclusion that each person has *some* right to pursue his own happiness, which is the substance of Kant's view of civil freedom.[89] The reasoning is fairly straightforward. If every individual necessarily attempts to achieve his own happiness, and if (by Premises 3 and 4) it is wrong to prevent him from do-

---

[87] TP 278\64; G 445.

[88] This type of right is what I will call a "right of justice" or a "juridical right." In the *Tugendlehre,* Kant distinguishes between "rights to exercise compulsion" and rights that do not allow the use of coercion (TL 383). Neither type of right is given a name by Kant. He says, however, that coercive rights correspond to duties of justice, which is why I call them "rights of justice"; and he asserts that noncoercive rights correspond to ethical duties, which is why I call them "ethical rights." (See Chapter 3.) The expression "rights of justice" will seem odd, even perverse, to German speakers; for the word I have been translating as "justice," namely *Recht,* also means a "right." Thus, a "right of justice" may sound as though it were a right to a right. Nonetheless, I propose to retain this usage because it has the merit of conveying clearly in English the fact that Kant recognizes two types of rights: those corresponding to duties of justice and those corresponding to ethical duties.

With particular reference to Premise 4, it is virtually analytic for Kant that if it is wrong forcibly to prevent someone from doing something, then he has a right (of justice) to do it (RL 232\36–37). Understood in this way, there can be rights to act wrongly. The case of nonfraudulent lying discussed earlier provides one example of a right of this kind. Kant believes that lying is always morally wrong, but he also thinks that as long as a lie is not intended to deprive someone of her rights or property it should not be prohibited by law. Such lies are protected by the principle of civil freedom, and there is consequently a right of justice, though not an ethical right, to engage in this kind of lying.

[89] TP 290\74. This right is what I later describe as a "strong" right. See Chapter 4 below.

ing so, then he has a right to attempt to achieve his own happiness. And because (by Premise 2) no one else can decide what will make him happy, his right to pursue his own happiness cannot be usurped by a self-appointed proxy (for example, a paternalistic government), but must instead be exercised by the individual concerned. Clearly, this right cannot be unqualified or absolute. One person's pursuit of his own happiness may interfere with another's pursuit of his happiness. So if there is a right to pursue one's own happiness, it can only be a prima facie right that is subject to whatever limitations are required to ensure that it can be distributed equally among an entire population.

All of the premises of this argument are traceable directly to Kant. So, although it is not an argument Kant ever explicitly formulates, it is nonetheless a Kantian argument. What it serves to show is that a principle of civil freedom of the sort Kant believes is necessary for any just political society can be derived from Kant's own understanding of happiness and the partly sensible character of human nature.

History, Progress, and Reason

Kant believes that the intrinsic value and dignity of human beings lie in their rational capacities—principally, if not exclusively in their capacity for morally practical reason. But these capacities, Kant also holds, are not yet fully developed, with the result that the unconditional value of human nature is still only partially realized. This brings us to another and in some respects the most important reason for Kant's emphasis on external freedom: it is necessary for the complete development of human rational capacities and hence for the attainment of humankind's complete value. Kant's argument, which takes the form of a speculative history of human society, attempts to show that the development of practical and theoretical rationality follow causally from the emergence of increasingly rational social structures.[90]

The starting point of Kant's speculative history of human society is the original human moral condition in the state of nature. Human beings, according to Kant, are "by nature" neither good nor bad, for by nature they are not "moral" beings at all.[91] A moral being must first of all be able to grasp moral concepts, so as to understand the difference between good and evil. Initially, human beings have no such developed capacity, but are entirely instinctual creatures, much like other animals.[92] They subsequently become moral beings when their reason has developed sufficiently to enable them to understand the concepts of "duty and the law."[93] This is not to suggest, however, that human beings do not originally have good or evil "propensities." They have both, because even before their reason has developed to any appreciable extent they possess opposing tendencies to allow their inclinations to overpower their rational capacities and to bring their inclinations under the control of reason.[94] The existence of these differing tendencies represents a conflict between humankind's "animality" and "humanity."[95] Animality is manifest in humankind's sensuous nature, more specifically in its inclinations, while humanity is present in its will, that is, in its practical reason, which exercises control over inclinations, even if in the early stages of human development this control is directed only toward bringing inclinations into an orderly system to ensure that they can be satisfied in a rational way.

[90] My discussion of Kant's philosophy of history in this section will of necessity be both brief and partial. For a more thorough analysis see Yovel 1980 and van der Linden 1988, chaps. 3, 4, and 5.
[91] PAD 492\108.
[92] MA 111\55.
[93] PAD 492\108.
[94] APH 324–25, 329\241–44, 246; REL 26–28\21–23.
[95] REL 26\31; APH 325\241–42.

From their animal natures, human beings inherit unsociable tendencies toward greed, selfishness, and aggression, as well as a desire to exercise power over others.[96] But inasmuch as they feel themselves to be human only by measuring themselves against and competing with other humans there is also a natural human desire to associate with others of their kind.[97] The result of these opposing drives is humankind's "unsocial sociability."[98] Human beings crave the company of other humans, for they desire "rank" and "honour" among their peers, yet their selfishness, egoism, and lust for power inevitably lead them into conflict with each other.[99]

In the state of nature, these conflicts are continuous and unresolvable, for there are no means of adjudicating disputes or preventing them from degenerating into violence. General insecurity, and the desire to find a more satisfactory way of providing for their needs, therefore drive human beings toward civil society where they can be protected against each other's encroachments.[100] But cooperation is at a minimum and distrust at a maximum in the state of nature, so that although human beings are forced in the direction of civil society by their need for security, "violence" must still be used to compel them to accept it.[101] Civil society is for this reason originally founded on conquest instead of consent.

The transition to civil society is crucial for Kant. Nature's "highest purpose" for humankind is the development of its "natural capacities," "skills," "talents," and "abilities"; in a word, its theoretical, instrumental, and moral rationality.[102]

---

[96] IAG 20–22\44–46; REL 93–94\85.
[97] IAG 20–21\44–45.
[98] IAG 20\44.
[99] IAG 21–23\15–16.
[100] IAG 23\45–46.
[101] ZEF 371\117; RL 339.
[102] IAG 18–22\42–46.

But Kant believes this can occur only in civil society.[103] Two conditions are necessary for the complete development of human rationality. First, there must be a natural egoism that fosters competitiveness and the desire for personal advantage. Second, there must be enough social stability to ensure that competitiveness and egoism do not degenerate into lawless destruction.[104] In the state of nature only the first condition is satisfied, so it is a state of war. Political society alone is able to ensure that both conditions are met, for in civil society lawless freedom is restrained, while at the same time "self-seeking energies" are channeled into noncoercive forms of competition that generate the skills needed to acquire social position and advantage.[105]

Evidently, this picture of constrained freedom operating to produce the development of natural human abilities presupposes not merely a law-governed political society but also a particular economic structure: a system of free market capitalism, or something very much like it. Competition and its attendant inequality, rather than civil society considered generically, as Kant is prone to suggest, are the incubators of human rationality.[106]

This picture also illustrates a recurring theme in Kant's political and historical thought: good develops out of evil, and cannot do otherwise.[107] If human beings were not full of "selfish pretensions," if they did not wish to exercise power over each other, and if they did not prefer their own interests to those of others, they might live side by side in an arcadian paradise of "concord, contentment and mutual affection."[108] Many natural human capacities would then never be developed, and human

---

[103] KU 432.
[104] IAG 21–23\44–47.
[105] IAG 25–26\49.
[106] MA 117–19\62–64; KU 430–34.
[107] ZEF 366, 379\112–13, 124; IAG 22–23\46–47; TP 312\91.
[108] IAG 21\45.

beings would be no better than sheep. So antagonism, selfishness, and conflict are necessary for the development of human rationality. Although these qualities are destructive in the state of nature, they produce an "essentially healthy hostility" in civil society, a hostility that takes the form, not of overt violence, but of disciplined competition for economic and social advantage.[109] Therefore, notwithstanding the fact that these qualities are inherently evil, they are beneficial once they have been properly tamed.[110] Civilization itself, Kant believes, is the product of this controlled antagonism. The same egoistic impulses that make it impossible for human beings to coexist peacefully in the state of nature become the driving force of economic and cultural progress once they are properly harnessed. "All culture, art which adorns mankind, and all the finest social order are fruits of man's unsociableness, which forces it to discipline itself, and so, by a contrived art, to develop the natural seeds to perfection."[111]

A force akin to Adam Smith's invisible hand is evident throughout this line of argument. Private greed is transformed into social benefits. Conflicting individual passions and interests are channeled so that they become the mainsprings of progress. These ideas were not new in Kant's time. In varying forms they had already found expression in the writings of Vico, Mandeville, Turgot, Smith, and others.[112] What holds them together in Kant's thinking is chiefly the idea of individual freedom. Human beings must be permitted to pursue their own private ends, no matter how self-serving they may be, for the pursuit of these selfish aims, when properly constrained by public laws, produces the development of individual talents, rationality, and culture in general. Animality thus gradually

---

[109] IAG 26\49.

[110] TP 312\91.

[111] IAG 22\46.

[112] See Vico, *New Science*, 1:2:7; Hirschman 1977, chap. 1; Nisbet 1980, chap. 6; Smith, *The Wealth of Nations*, 184; Gay 1969, chap. 7.

yields to humanity, but only by controlling it through the imposition of external social and economic structures, not by attempting to eradicate it.

Nonetheless, Kant recognizes that relying on market competition to stimulate human rational capacities brings mixed blessings. Besides being responsible for the growth of art, culture, industry, and science, free markets generate material deprivation and gross inequality. The "great majority" must subsist in a state of overworked "oppression" with few opportunities for enjoyment.[113] Culture and progress may therefore seem to produce only so much "splendid misery." Kant understands this, while insisting that it is the unavoidable price of developing humankind's natural abilities to the fullest possible degree.[114] Even so, he acknowledges that it is open to question whether the benefits are worth the cost. Rousseau's "preference for the state of savagery does not appear so very mistaken," he admits, unless we leave out of consideration the "last stage which our species still has to surmount."[115] This final stage, the one that justifies all the preceding misery, is the growth of human moral capacities. But this can occur only if economic competition, civil society, and culture have first brought discipline to unruly sensible impulses; hence, Kant believes, these are necessary for the development of morality among human beings.[116]

From this it should not be inferred that Kant believes the direct purpose of political society is to make individuals good. The truth is quite otherwise. Kant holds that moral goodness requires a virtuous attitude of will, and such an attitude cannot be produced by the mechanism of behavioral control available to the state.[117] The purpose of the state is not to make individ-

[113] KU 432.
[114] MA 117–18n\62n; KU 432–33.
[115] IAG 26\49.
[116] REL 92–93\86.
[117] REL 95–96\87.

uals good, but to enforce laws of justice. Nonetheless, Kant believes that political society is a training ground for inner morality. By accustoming individuals to obey laws that regulate their external relations, it imposes an outer discipline that prepares the way for the inner discipline of morality. In this way the state makes it easier for the "capacities of human beings to develop into an immediate respect for right," and even though this is not yet a "moral step," it is nonetheless a definite step "toward morality."[118] Culture has a similar effect. The arts, sciences, and commerce do not directly make individuals good, but their civilizing influence promotes the development of rationality and helps to release human beings from the "tyranny of sense," thereby preparing humankind for "higher purposes."[119]

To summarize Kant's argument: the moving force behind the progressive development of human reason—from the lowest technical-instrumental forms, in which it is little more than a slave of the passions, to the highest level in morally practical reason—is the conjunction of (1) external freedom, (2) the enforced discipline of civil society and culture, and (3) human "unsociableness" (namely, selfishness, love of power, and the desire for personal aggrandizement). Together, these eventually lead to the growth of inner morality:

> All man's talents are now gradually developed, his taste cultivated, and by a continued process of enlightenment, a beginning is made toward establishing a way of thinking which can with time transform the primitive capacity for moral discrimination into definite practical principles; and thus a *pathologically* enforced social union is transformed into a *moral whole.*[120]

[118] ZEF 376n\121n.
[119] KU 433.
[120] IAG 21\44–45.

The line of argument culminating in this passage is open to any number of objections. I shall discuss two. The first is that Kant offers little evidence to support his belief, surely a controversial one, that rationality can *best* be developed through antagonistic or competitive social and economic relations. Still less does he demonstrate that this is the *only* way human abilities can be made to flourish. Whether more cooperative forms of economic and social organization might serve the same purpose just as well, perhaps even better, is something Kant fails to consider. Neither does he entertain the possibility that more cooperative forms of organization, even supposing that they are less efficient means of developing man's rational capacities than the competitive struggle Kant favors, would still be preferable insofar as their reduced efficiency might be more than offset by a corresponding reduction in misery, deprivation, and suffering.[121]

Kant is not entirely immune to the charge that he neglects to take account of alternative means of developing human rationality. But his position is more understandable, and more defensible, than it may initially appear. Part of the explanation for his willingness to assume that only antagonistic economic and social relations can lead to the development of human reason was probably that other thinkers with whom he was familiar, Mandeville for one, had already expressed similar thoughts.[122] Kant may have believed that the case for this view had already been made persuasively enough by others.

Whatever part of Kant's view cannot be explained in this way can be accounted for by his philosophical psychology. Kant believes, as I said before, that in the early stages of human history humanity's animal nature dominates its still primitive rational capacities. Because it consists largely of egoistic inclinations and self-serving instincts, this animal nature precludes the

[121] I owe this suggestion to Allen Wood.
[122] Nisbet 1980, 188; KPV 40.

possibility of unselfish or farsighted motivations for the development of individual abilities. This in turn seems to ensure that human beings will develop their natural abilities only in a competitive framework where each struggles for advantage over the other. Such are Kant's psychological assumptions. Though not terribly appealing, even today Kant's picture of human beings as predominantly competitive, selfish, and acquisitive creatures will strike hardly anyone as implausible. Kant's psychological assumptions seem eminently reasonable, and so too do his views concerning the development of human rationality.

The second objection runs somewhat deeper, and concerns Kant's understanding of the transition from civil society and culture to inner morality. One may reasonably doubt whether there is any connection of the sort Kant envisages between political society and culture on the one hand, and inner morality on the other. Kant alleges that the former are productive of the latter, that a "pathologically enforced" social union can transform itself into a "moral" one.[123] But why is it not just as plausible to believe, along with Rousseau in his darker moments, that there is an inverse relation between morality and political society together with advanced culture, a relation such that the increasing sophistication of the state and general culture tend to produce declining rather than rising moral standards?[124] As much can be said for this pessimistic assessment as for Kant's more optimistic one.

Kant is not entirely unworried by this question. On occasion, his confidence that cultural progress and the external discipline of civil society can aid in the production of inner morality appears to dissipate, as when he suggests in *The Contest of the Faculties* that the "profit which will accrue to the human race as it works its way forward will not be an ever increasing quantity of *morality* in attitudes. Instead, the *legality*

---

[123] ZEF 376n\121n; KU 432–33; APH 321–22\238.
[124] See the "Discourse on the Sciences and Arts" in Rousseau 1986, 1–27.

of its attitudes will produce an increasing number of actions governed by duty, whatever the particular motives behind these actions may be."[125] Here the linkage between culture, the state, and inner morality disappears. But this text is an exception. Generally speaking, Kant remained confident that the connection was genuine.

I have already suggested that Kant's ideas often seem more reasonable when his tacit assumptions are brought into the open. That is especially true in the present case. Kant pictures a two-stage process in the development of human rationality. In the beginning, external freedom, economic and social competition, cultural progress, and the discipline of civil society jointly produce increasing amounts of theoretical rationality. Afterwards, the same process leads to the development of morally practical reason. Evidently, what appears dubious here is more the second step than the first. It seems peculiar, if not perverse, to suppose that increasing levels of instrumental-theoretical rationality inevitably transform themselves by a kind of moral alchemy into increasing amounts of moral virtue.

This is a natural reaction to Kant's views, yet it depends on an assumption about the relation between rationality and morality that Kant does not accept. It depends, specifically, on the idea that morality and rationality are distinct from or even opposed to each other. Although this view is now common, it is an egregious error from Kant's perspective. Morality requires sacrifice, of course, and one may ask whether it pays to be moral, but Kant is committed to the view that there can ultimately be no conflict between rationality and morality. For Kant, moral laws *are* laws of reason, and despite the fact that they are laws of practical rather than theoretical reason, there is no dichotomy between them. Reason is always "one and the same."[126] It may take practical or theoretical forms, but

[125] SF 91\187–88.
[126] KPV 121.

these are merely different applications or uses of an always identical faculty of reason.[127] No doubt, this is a controversial conception of rationality and morality. It makes clear, however, why Kant believes that the development of theoretical rationality ought to translate, sooner or later, into a corresponding development of inner morality. If theoretical and morally practical reason are ultimately one and the same, then the development of one should eventually lead to the development of the other.

[127] G 391.

CHAPTER THREE

Types of Rights,
Duties, and Laws

Kant divides moral philosophy into two parts: ethics and the theory of justice.[1] Each is composed of different sets of rights, duties, and laws. The theory of (strict) justice contains "external," "enforceable," "coercive," "narrow," and "perfect" rights and duties. Ethics in contrast contains "internal," "unenforceable," "voluntary," "wide," and (mostly) "imperfect" rights and duties. As this comparison indicates, rights and duties of justice are closely connected with ethical rights and duties. Juridical rights and duties are logical correlates of ethical rights and duties. Both types of rights and duties are defined in relation to each other, and therefore can be understood only in relation to each other. To understand what Kant means when he refers to "narrow" duties, for instance, it is necessary to understand the nature of correlative "wide" duties, and to understand what Kant means when he refers to "perfect" duties it is necessary to understand the nature of correlative "imperfect" duties. The objective of the present chapter is to explain how Kant's several types of rights, duties, and laws of justice fit to-

---

[1] TL 406–7.

gether into a formal system of justice. For the reasons just given, however, it will also be necessary to examine how, within Kant's moral theory, rights and duties of justice are distinguished from ethical rights and duties. Indeed, understanding how Kant separates ethics from justice is one of the most important steps in understanding his theory of justice.

Distinguishing Justice from Ethics

Kant holds that laws and duties of justice are external and enforceable, as opposed to ethical laws and duties, which are internal and unenforceable. What "essentially" distinguishes ethical duties or duties of virtue from juridical ones, Kant points out in the *Tugendlehre,* is that "external compulsion to a juridical duty is morally possible, whereas a duty of virtue is based on free self-constraint."[2] Enforceability through coercion is therefore the essence of a juridical duty or law. The externality of justice follows from its enforceability. Because only external actions—never motives, intentions, or other states of mind—can be controlled through the use of coercion, all juridical legislation must be oriented toward the regulation of external conduct.[3] Ethical legislation in contrast, because it is based on free self-constraint and allows no "incentive other than the Idea of duty," is always "inner" legislation.[4]

Some scholars have seen Kant's emphasis on the external and enforceable nature of justice as his most significant contribution to jurisprudence. It enabled him, or so this line of thought suggests, to draw more clearly than had hitherto been possible a firm and definite line between ethics and law—between un-

[2] TL 383.
[3] RL 219–20; TL 381.
[4] RL 219.

enforceable inner laws and duties and enforceable external ones.[5] Although this contrast between the inner, voluntary nature of ethics and the external, coercive character of justice is indeed an essential component of Kant's moral theory, it has more often than not been exaggerated and misunderstood. We should therefore examine closely how, in Kant's view, the externality and enforceability of justice distinguish it from the internality and voluntariness of ethics.

The Externality of Justice

Justice, Kant claims, "has as its object only what is external in actions."[6] On the basis of remarks of this sort a number of writers have concluded that Kant believes justice has nothing whatsoever to do with inner, psychological states. Ernst Cassirer, for one, interprets Kant as holding that justice or "law" "abstracts from every consideration of [subjective maxims and motives], so as to judge action as such merely with respect to its objective circumstances and execution. It is sheer agreement or disagreement of an action with the laws, without respect to its motives, that constitutes its legality."[7] A very similar view is developed by H. L. A. Hart, who interprets Kant as having originated the "famous" though "profoundly misleading" theory that the difference between justice and ethics, or "legal rules" and "morals," is that "while legal rules only require "external" behaviour and are indifferent to motives, intentions, or other "internal" accompaniments of conduct, mor-

[5] D'Entrèves 1952, 87, 94, 121–22.
[6] RL 232.
[7] Cassirer 1981, 398.

als on the other hand do not require any specific external actions but only a good will or proper intentions or motive."[8]

These readings of Kant are close enough to the truth to be initially plausible, yet far enough off the mark to be seriously misleading. In one sense it is perfectly correct to hold that Kant believes justice or law should be indifferent to inner states; but in another sense nothing could be farther from the truth. Kant regards justice as purely external in the limited sense that the sole purpose of juridical laws is to regulate external conduct. However, this does not mean that justice has no interest in inner states. As is evident from the long history of the legal concept of *mens rea* [a guilty mind], as well as from recurring debates in the legal community about the role of intentions and motives in the criminal law, jurists have traditionally supposed that mental states are of concern to the law.[9] Kant shares this assumption and in at least three respects regards inner states as vital to justice and jurisprudence.

First, even though juridical laws do not *require* any special motives, they nonetheless *provide* a motive for compliance: fear of coercion or punishment.[10] All that is strictly necessary for the performance of a juridical duty is the external action itself, but in order to ensure external compliance the law supplies an "incentive" or motive to induce compliance by threatening to punish noncompliance.[11] Kant's view is therefore

---

[8] Hart 1984, 168, 252.

[9] See, e.g., Hart 1982, chaps. 2, 5, and 6; Edwards 1955, chap. 11; Denning 1961; Stephen 1890, 68–71; Salmond, *First Principles of Jurisprudence*, 203–5.

[10] RL 219.

[11] To avoid confusion, I should make clear that Kant's position is not that the law can directly compel the adoption of particular motives or the formation of specific intentions. He holds the opposite view that intentions and motives cannot be enforced through external coercion (RL 219). Kant's point is that the threat of sanctions serves to persuade individuals to obey the law for prudential reasons (RL 219; VE 34\28).

much like T. H. Green's belief that while "in enforcing its commands by threats, the law is presenting a motive, and thus . . . affecting action on its inner side, it does this solely for the sake of the external act."[12]

Second, juridical laws are concerned with inner states insofar as some such states, notably intentions, are constitutive of human actions. Kant recognizes as much when he asserts that every action contains an "end," for an end is simply a state of affairs an agent intends to bring about through his actions.[13] Because intentions are part of the fabric of human action, they must be taken into consideration by jurisprudence. For criminal law, especially, they are of great interest. Very often, for instance in cases of murder, burglary, robbery, fraud, larceny, and criminal conspiracy, intentions figure conspicuously in the definitions of criminal offenses.[14] Kant is aware of this. In the *Rechtslehre*, he characterizes a crime as an "intentional transgression" of the law.[15] Committing a murder, Kant insists,

[12] Green 1980, 19.

[13] TL 381, 385.

[14] Some crimes, especially serious ones, are defined at least partially in relation to specific intentions. Murder statutes in Western countries, for instance, often require an intention to kill, or to commit serious bodily harm. The same applies to offenses such as larceny and forgery, which typically require an intent to defraud (Edwards 1955, 166). There are, it is true, occasional examples in some legal systems of strict liability under criminal statutes, e.g., contempt of court under English law (Smith 1965, chap. 6). But strict liability for criminal offenses is rare, in the West at least. On the general topic of the role of intentions and *mens rea* in the criminal law see Denning 1961; Stephen 1890, chap. 5; Edwards 1955; Smith 1965, chap. 4; Beattie 1986, 77–81, 84, 87, 91.

[15] RL 224. There is a problem here for Kant, an obvious one he ought to have noticed. Kant appears to hold two incompatible views. The first is that it is possible to identify and ascribe intentions in criminal cases. The second is that acts of volition—and along with them motives and intentions—are hidden in an inaccessible noumenal realm (G 407–8, 457). The second belief commits Kant to the idea that in principle it is impossible to verify the existence of intentions, even one's own (REL 20\16). I am not certain that Kant has any way out of this quandary. Suffice it to say that he

involves more than killing a human being; it requires in addition the intention to do so under particular circumstances.[16]

Third, inner states are relevant to jurisprudence because they affect ascriptions of legal responsibility. Kant argues that imputations of responsibility must take into consideration "the state of mind of the subject, namely, whether he committed the deed with emotion or in cool deliberation."[17] No formula is provided by Kant for determining how to factor different kinds of mental states into assessments of legal responsibility, but the direction of his thinking is clear from his examples. In the case of a starving man who steals food to survive, Kant holds that the "degree of his responsibility is diminished by the fact that it would have required a great deal of self-restraint for him not to do it."[18] Or again, if one man kills another in a "fit of jealous temper," he should not be held as responsible as the person who "in cold blood" plans the death of another.[19] As these examples demonstrate, Kant believes that punishments and legal responsibility should be apportioned with due attention to motives, intentions, and other mental states. We should therefore not accept the suggestion that Kant regards justice and law as purely external in the sense that intentions, motives, and other inner states are of no consequence for jurisprudence. Such a view is far from Kant's.

Equally distorted is the converse supposition, (Hart's) that Kantian ethics is entirely internal, *merely* a matter of having a good will or the right intentions. This view misconstrues the real difference between ethics and justice. Kant claims that one may be obligated to perform the same duty (the same action) by

assumes, as a practical matter, that intentions can be identified and ascribed solely on the basis of the observable character of actions (REL 20, 39n, 70, 77\16, 34n, 64n, 71).

[16] VE 69–70\57–58.
[17] RL 228.
[18] VE 75–76\63.
[19] VE 75–76\63.

different types of laws.[20] In other words, if I have a duty not to steal, that prohibition may derive both from laws of justice and from ethical laws. If it derives from juridical laws, it ought to be enforced through external coercion. If it derives from ethical laws, the agent is required to make it her end not to steal, and she must to do so voluntarily, for she cannot be compelled to adopt particular ends.[21]

So, pace Hart, it is not Kant's view that there are two disjoint sets of duties—one internal and ethical, the other external and juridical. All juridical duties are external insofar as they require (or prohibit) only external actions without also demanding any special motives or ends.[22] Some ethical duties are also purely internal (for example, the duty to perform duties out of respect for the moral law). But there are "external duties" in ethics, too.[23] Not all external duties belong exclusively to the theory of justice—in fact, *none* do. All external/juridical duties, Kant says, are "indirectly" ethical duties "just because they are duties."[24] Put differently, all duties, including ones requiring external actions, are ethical duties because, whenever there is a genuine duty of any kind, there is also an ethical duty to make it one's end to perform the duty in question. In this way, all external/juridical duties become indirect ethical duties, without ceasing to be juridical duties. Juridical and ethical duties are therefore not mutually exclusive. Far from it: juridical duties are a proper subset of ethical duties.

The difference between ethics and the theory of justice is not, then, that one contains only internal and the other only external duties. The difference is that they are imposed by different types of laws and enforced by different means. Juridical duties are imposed by juridical laws, which use external coercion to

[20] RL 223.
[21] TL 381.
[22] *Reflexion* 7271, Ak XIX, 299.
[23] RL 219–21.
[24] RL 221.

ensure compliance. Ethical duties are products of ethical legislation and must be adopted voluntarily by the agent.

There is, nevertheless, a limited sense in which ethical duties are internal and juridical duties external. Ethical duties are internal in that they never, strictly speaking, require more than the adoption of an end. So long as the agent makes a genuine effort to achieve a moral end she satisfies the demands of ethical legislation, even if she fails to perform the relevant external actions. If, for example, there is an ethical duty to pay one's taxes, one does all that ethics strictly requires if one does everything in one's power to pay the taxes. Success is not necessary; all that counts from the standpoint of ethics is sincere effort. Laws of justice, however, are enforceable through external coercion, and are capable of requiring the actual performance of specific external actions, such as the payment of taxes.

It does not follow that laws of justice *must* invariably require specific external actions. On the contrary, it is always possible for juridical laws to stop short at requiring a "reasonable" or "good faith" effort.[25] Continuing with the previous example, for instance, a law of justice might require no more than a good faith effort to pay one's taxes. Even in this case, though, a law of justice is always distinguishable from an ethical law. The pertinent distinction here, as in all other cases, is that laws of justice, as opposed to ethical laws, are always *capable* of requiring the performance of specific actions through external coercion.

Justice and Enforceability

Juridical laws must be enforceable by means of external coercion and so must be restricted to the domain of external ac-

---

[25] The "reasonable man" test in tort law (now the "reasonable person" test) is a prime example.

tions. The enforceability constraint has a number of other consequences, some obvious, some less so. One of the obvious consequences is that juridical laws should not attempt to regulate beliefs, opinions, or ideas. These are internal phenomena that cannot be enforced directly through coercion, for it is always possible to dissemble and mislead others about one's views. Ideas, opinions, and beliefs therefore lie outside the sphere of juridical laws. Laws such as the archaic rule of English common law that it is treasonable to "imagine" the death of the monarch could never, therefore, have any place in a Kantian system of jurisprudence.[26] Nor can there be obligatory religious or political beliefs. Official tolerance of differing religious and political views is mandated by the fact that juridical laws are restricted to the sphere of external actions.

No doubt these restrictions are formally compatible with various kinds of state-sponsored efforts to control religious and political beliefs. They do not, for example, prohibit laws that make party membership, church attendance, or the recitation of particular creeds mandatory. Although laws of this sort are logically consistent with the enforceability constraint, their *purpose* is almost always inconsistent with it, for they are almost invariably intended as means of enforcing officially sanctioned beliefs. So if the spirit as well as the letter of Kant's enforceability constraint is adhered to, the result will be a fairly far-reaching principle of legal tolerance for conflicting beliefs of all kinds.

Another limitation on juridical laws is that although they should attempt to control *only* external actions, rather than beliefs or opinions, *not all* external actions are properly subject to juridical regulation. In particular, actions that cannot *effectively* be regulated by the threat of coercion and punishment should not, Kant holds, be prohibited or required by juridical laws. This restriction emerges especially from a passage in

[26] Salmond, *First Principle of Jurisprudence,* 204.

Theory and Practice in which Kant discusses the case of a ship-wreck victim who, to save his own life, pushes another man from a plank on which they are both adrift.[27] In a situation of this sort, Kant argues, where the first man's life would be at risk were he not to bring about the other's death, there "could be no penal law" prohibiting the actions in question: "For the authorities cannot combine a *penalty* with this prohibition, since this penalty would have to be death. But it would be a nonsensical law which threatened anyone with death if he did he did not voluntarily deliver himself up to death when in dangerous circumstances."[28] In the *Rechtslehre*, Kant expresses essentially the same thought when he says there could be no legitimate law imposing a penalty in cases of this kind, because such a law "could never have its intended effect" given that "the threat of a punishment that is still uncertain (being condemned to death by a judge) cannot outweigh the fear of an evil that is certain."[29] The general principle underlying these statements is that juridical laws should never attempt to regulate forms of external conduct that, in view of the contingent facts of human psychology, cannot effectively be controlled through the coercive apparatus available to legal systems. Any positive law that ignores this constraint thwarts its own purpose, for the purpose of a positive law is to regulate external conduct, and if it cannot effectively do so it is useless.

I have not yet mentioned the most important restriction Kant places on juridical laws. The essential distinction between ethical duties and duties of justice is that the latter are enforceable through external coercion. What is at stake here,

---

[27] TP 300n\81n.

[28] TP 300n\82n. Kant's point is not that death is the worst possible penalty a positive law could impose, but that it is the most severe punishment that can be morally justified. Clearly, one can imagine worse punishments—e.g., torture, the murder of one's children or parents, and so on. These, however, are morally prohibited, according to Kant.

[29] RL 235.

though, is not coercion *simpliciter.* Not every coercive positive law counts as a law of justice by Kant's standards. The essence of a juridical duty is that its enforcement through coercive laws is "morally possible"—that is, *morally justified.*[30] Because the objective of juridical laws is to enforce juridical duties, all such laws are constrained by the rule that they should impose only those duties whose enforcement by coercive means can be morally justified.

But which duties are these? Or, to put the matter differently: when is the state morally justified in using coercion to regulate external conduct? This question should not seem unfamiliar. For all intents and purposes it is the same question we encountered in Chapter 1 when we considered Kant's view of the proper limits of individual freedom. The answer must also be the same: legal coercion is justified only when it is required to ensure the proper operation of Kant's principles of legal equality, political freedom, and civil liberty. These principles define the legitimate limits of individual freedom; hence they also determine the proper scope of coercive laws.

Wide and Narrow Duties

By way of describing duties of justice, I have pointed out so far that they require external actions, that they can justifiably be enforced through the use of coercion, and that their limits are determined by Kant's principles of legal equality, civil liberty, and political freedom. More, however, needs to be indicated than this. Juridical duties are part of Kant's larger system of duties, and cannot be fully understood outside of this system. We have already considered some of the relations between juridical and ethical duties. Ethical duties require the adoption

[30] TL 383.

of ends; juridical duties require (or prohibit) external actions. Ethical duties cannot be enforced by the state; juridical duties can and should be so enforced. What remains to be explained, and what will occupy us in the next two sections, is how juridical duties are related to Kant's other main types of duties, namely "wide," "narrow," "perfect," and "imperfect" duties.

The difference between a "wide" and a "narrow" duty is not obscure; nor by itself does it seem to add anything to what we already know about juridical or ethical duties. A duty is narrow if it requires the performance or omission of an external action.[31] All juridicial duties are thus narrow duties.[32] A duty is wide, on the other hand, if it requires the adoption of an end.[33] All ethical duties are thus wide duties, for ethics is the "system of the *ends* of pure practical reason."[34] Initially, there appears to be nothing new or problematic in this. To speak of "wide duties" seems to be simply another way of referring to ethical duties, while to speak of "narrow" duties seems to be simply another way of referring to duties of justice.

Complications soon arise, however. Onora (nee Nell) O'Neill points out that Kant classifies lying, mockery, and other similar moral offenses as violations of ethical duties.[35] But, as she observes, duties of this sort seem to require the performance or

---

[31] TL 388–89.

[32] TL 411.

[33] TL 395. Kant sometimes says that wide duties are duties to adopt "maxims" rather than duties to adopt ends (TL 393). This distinction is of no consequence. A maxim is a policy or rule one follows for the purpose of achieving an end. To be required to adopt a maxim is, therefore, essentially the same as being required to adopt an end.

[34] TL 381. In the *Tugendlehre*, Kant claims that there is one ethical duty that is not a duty to adopt an end—viz., the general duty to act from the motive of duty (TL 383). Perhaps this should be accepted as an exception to the rule that ethical duties are duties to adopt ends. I am inclined, though, to think that Kant is simply mistaken on this score, and that, contrary to his own contention, the duty to act from the motive of duty is just a duty to make it one's end to perform all duties from the motive of duty.

[35] O'Neill 1975, 46.

omission of specific actions instead of the adoption of ends, which would seem to indicate that Kant should have classified them as juridical rather than ethical duties. Accordingly, if O'Neill is correct, there is an inconsistency in Kant's classification of ethical and juridical duties. Even more problematic is the further consequence that if not lying and not mocking others ought to be juridical duties, Kant seems to be stuck with the implausible view that all such actions should be legally prohibited; for all juridical duties, in Kant's view, should be legally enforced.

Fortunately, this difficulty is more apparent than real and its solution is simple. The very fact that Kant classifies all ethical duties as wide duties to adopt ends means that when he lists not lying and not mocking others as ethical duties he *intends* them to be understood as wide duties to adopt the ends of not lying and not engaging in mockery. Because they are classified in this way, they are *not* to be understood as narrow and enforceable duties to desist from particular actions. One's duty, Kant believes, is to adopt not lying and not mocking others as personal rules of conduct. Since they are not listed as juridical duties, Kant evidently feels that rules of this kind should not be enforced by the state.

Although this is a satisfactory response to the difficulty raised by O'Neill,[36] it leaves another problem in its wake, namely *why* Kant classifies these duties as ethical instead of as juridical duties. After all, even if Kant does not wish them to be construed as narrow and enforceable duties to perform or omit certain actions, they *could* nonetheless be treated that way. Governments could in principle enforce laws against lying and

---

[36] I should note that O'Neill proposes her own solution. I have not discussed it because I can find no explicit textual justification in Kant's writings for the distinction she draws between duties of "narrow requirement" and those of "wide requirement" (O'Neill 1975, 47). This distinction is supposed to help resolve Kant's problem, but the solution I propose here is both simpler and more textually defensible.

mockery, albeit with only limited chances of success. Why, then, should lying and mockery be ethical offenses, not juridical ones? We need not look far for the answer; we have in fact already come across it in our discussion of the kinds of laws whose enforcement through coercion is morally justified. If an action does not infringe anyone else's legitimate freedom or rights, as defined by the principles of civil liberty, legal equality, and political freedom, it does not contravene any duties of justice, and should therefore not, on Kant's view, be legally prohibited. As long as actions stay within these boundaries, they do not qualify as offenses against justice. Wrong and immoral they may be, but not unjust. Apparently, that is how Kant regards ordinary cases of lying, mockery, and similar offenses. There are moral duties not to lie or mock others, but these can only be ethical duties.

Perfect and Imperfect Duties

With the division between "perfect" and "imperfect" duties we arrive at the least clear distinction in Kant's moral theory, as well as the one whose relation to ethical and juridical duties is the most difficult to determine. Kant frequently uses but never adequately explains this distinction. He gives his readers only two definite pieces of information, both in a footnote in the *Groundwork*. We are told first that a perfect duty is one that "permits no exceptions in the interest of inclination"—so it appears that imperfect duties do permit these exceptions—and second that "this runs contrary to the usage adopted by the schools."[37] Nothing further is said in the *Groundwork* on the subject of perfect and imperfect duties. They are referred to

[37] G 421n.

once in the *Critique of Practical Reason*, where no further explanation is given, and are mentioned on several occasions in the *Tugendlehre* as well as in the *Reflexionen*, but again Kant says nothing to dispel the darkness.[38] If Kant's brief remarks in the *Groundwork* were unambiguous, the absence of further explanations would not be disturbing. The trouble, though, is that Kant never indicates in the *Groundwork* exactly *what* the "exceptions in the interests of inclination," which are the hallmark of imperfect duties, are exceptions *to*.

The reason Kant's distinction between perfect and imperfect duties is of concern to us at the moment is that, depending on how it is interpreted, it may or may not influence our understanding of the more important distinction between duties of justice and ethical duties. Consider, for instance, the following interpretations. H. J. Paton claims, without benefit of supporting evidence, that perfect duties are just narrow ones and that imperfect duties are just wide ones.[39] If so, the perfect/imperfect distinction is redundant, merely another way of talking about the narrow/wide distinction, in which case it tells us nothing about either juridical or ethical duties, for we already know that all of the former are narrow and that all of the latter are wide.

A different interpretation of the perfect/imperfect distinction is proposed by Mary Gregor.[40] According to Gregor, Kant employs two different versions of this distinction.[41] The *Groundwork*, she argues, contains a nonrigoristic view that treats imperfect duties as permitting an "arbitrary and subjective choice not to act toward" a morally obligatory "end."[42] Contrasting with this is the rigoristic view of the *Metaphysik*

---

[38] KPV 66; TL 390, 409; *Reflexionen* 7264 and 7410, Ak XIX, 297, 308–9.
[39] Paton 1949, 148–49.
[40] Gregor 1963, chaps. 7 and 8.
[41] Gregor 1963, 96.
[42] Gregor 1963, 111.

der Sitten, which allows no such arbitrary and subjective decisions to abandon morally obligatory ends, but instead permits individuals only "to limit one maxim of duty by another."[43]

If Gregor is right, if Kant does sometimes employ this nonrigoristic version of the perfect/imperfect distinction, our understanding of juridical and ethical duties will be duly colored by that fact. Like Paton, Gregor assumes that the perfect/imperfect distinction coincides with the narrow/wide distinction.[44] All imperfect duties are thus wide and all perfect duties are narrow. We have already seen, however, that all juridical duties are narrow and all ethical duties wide. Hence it follows that all juridical duties should be perfect and all ethical duties imperfect. Gregor's nonrigoristic interpretation accordingly leads to the conclusion that ethical duties—in the *Groundwork* at least—permit arbitrary and subjective exceptions to morally obligatory ends, whereas juridical duties permit no such exceptions. If this interpretation is sound, it tells us something new about ethical and juridical duties. Indeed, it provides a new way of understanding the difference between them. Because differing interpretations of the perfect/imperfect distinction thus affect the contrast between juridical and ethical duties, it is worth considering this distinction in more detail. I will begin by explaining why, in my view, Paton's and Gregor's interpretations should be rejected.

The main reason for being suspicious of Paton's interpretation is that it contradicts Kant's claim that he intends to depart from the usage of "the schools," or scholastic philosophers. The schools had traditionally equated perfect duties with enforceable (juridical) duties and imperfect ones with unenforceable (ethical) duties.[45] Kant, however, holds that narrow duties are duties to perform or omit external actions and are therefore

---

[43] Gregor 1963, 96.
[44] Gregor 1963, 97, 100.
[45] See Beck 1961, 151n; Krieger 1965, 87, 100; Morris 1981, 86.

enforceable, whereas wide duties are duties to adopt ends and are therefore unenforceable.[46] If, therefore, as I noted earlier, all narrow, enforceable duties are juridical and all wide, unenforceable duties are ethical, it is a consequence of Paton's interpretation that Kant does not, despite his own assertion to the contrary, differ from the schools in his view of perfect and imperfect duties. On Paton's interpretation, Kant agrees with the schools that all perfect duties are narrow/juridical ones and that all imperfect duties are wide/ethical ones.

Paton's is not a desirable interpretation. Perhaps Kant's view is as Paton describes it, but before we ascribe to Kant a position that contradicts his own explicit claims, especially without evidence, we should explore other available options. There is, in any event, another reason for being wary of Paton's interpretation. On his view, Kant should classify all narrow/juridical duties as perfect and all wide/ethical ones as imperfect. But that is not what Kant does. It is true that he lists all juridical duties as perfect and some ethical duties as imperfect, but he also classifies some ethical duties as perfect.[47] This classification is inexplicable on Paton's interpretation, except by way of simple error, yet it is not surprising in light of Kant's claim that his usage of the perfect/imperfect duties differs from that of the schools.

Gregor's interpretation is problematic for other reasons, principally that it is difficult to imagine Kant ever having subscribed to her nonrigoristic version of the perfect/imperfect distinction, for it runs contrary to his entire view of moral duty. The moral law, Kant insists in the *Critique of Practical Reason*, "holds for all irrespective of their inclinations."[48] In the *Groundwork*, Kant likewise says that an "act of duty

---

[46] TL 381, 383, 390–91.
[47] TL 421.
[48] KPV 67.

wholly excludes the influence of inclination."[49] Similarly, Kant asserts in his unpublished notes that moral duties allow no "exceptions" for human weakness.[50] Given these rather clear statements that duty and the moral law make no allowance for inclinations or human weakness, it is hard to believe that Kant ever intended to admit a class of duties that permits a person arbitrarily, as his inclinations dictate, to abandon efforts to achieve morally obligatory ends. Such a conception of duty is altogether foreign to Kant.

Insofar as Paton's and Gregor's interpretations seem dubious at best, we should consider available alternatives. I should now like to outline a more promising approach. As I have already indicated, Kant's explicit statements about the perfect/imperfect distinction underdetermine any specific interpretation, leaving room for conflicting views. The evidence on which a viable interpretation must be based can therefore only be indirect. Nonetheless, three constraints should govern any interpretation of this distinction.

1. It should, if at all possible, be consistent with Kant's general view of moral duty.
2. It ought to fit Kant's explicit statements, as well as his use of the perfect/imperfect distinction.
3. It should attempt to explain why Kant classifies all juridical duties as perfect, yet lists some ethical duties as perfect and others as imperfect.

To start with, let us consider what Kant *could* plausibly mean when he characterizes imperfect duties as duties that allow exceptions in the interest or for the benefit of inclination. The interest of inclination cannot, in this context at least, be the whims of transient desire. All duties, for Kant, are products

[49] G 400.
[50] *Reflexion* 6715, Ak XIX, 139.

of pure practical reason; hence all exceptions having to do with the concept of duty must be based on principles of pure practical reason. In the *Critique of Practical Reason*, Kant suggests that inasmuch as "Man is a being of needs" and "belongs to the world of sense" his "reason certainly has an inescapable responsibility from the side of his sensuous nature to attend to its interest."[51] Reason is thus obligated to take account of the claims of humankind's sensible nature; but this obligation must of course be a rational one as it is imposed by reason on itself. The claims of humanity's sensible nature, for which reason bears a responsibility, must likewise be the *rational claims* of humanity's sensible nature. Imperfect duties must, consequently, in some fashion or other, be duties permitting individuals to make *reasoned exceptions* in light of their own personal needs.

We still do not know, however, what these exceptions are exceptions to. The following line of reasoning leads, I think, in the right direction. The fact that Kant classifies some ethical duties as perfect, other ethical duties as imperfect, while never listing any juridical duties as imperfect, implies that he intends imperfect duties to be a subset of ethical duties. Moreover, all ethical duties are wide, so imperfect duties should also be a subset of wide duties. Notice next that since all wide/ethical duties are duties to adopt ends, it follows that imperfect duties should be a subset of duties to adopt ends. Finally, if this train of thought is sound, it would be natural to conclude that imperfect duties are duties that permit us to make reasoned exceptions, on behalf of our sensible needs, to those ends whose adoption is required by wide/ethical duties, and conversely that perfect duties are duties that permit no such exceptions.

The plausibility of this interpretation depends in large part on whether it can be reconciled with Kant's belief that duty completely excludes the influence of inclination. If anything is

[51] KPV 61.

certain about Kant's view of morality, it is that he never meant to allow a class of duties that permit individuals to ignore the demands of morality for the sake of satisfying their own inclinations. Although the interpretation I have proposed may seem to violate this requirement, it does not in fact do so. Kant believes that there is a wide/ethical duty to ensure one's own essential needs: "To provide oneself with such comforts as are necessary merely to enjoy life . . . is a duty to oneself."[52] This belief reflects Kant's general view that morality should not be taken to "monkish" or "fanatical" extremes.[53] We are not called upon to ignore our own basic needs in order to fulfill all of our other duties. At least *some* other duties are limited by the condition that they cannot require us to ignore our duty to attend to our own needs. I suggest that imperfect duties are concerned with the *interplay* between one's duty to provide for one's own needs and all other wide/ethical duties to adopt ends. If an imperfect duty is one that permits an individual to make reasoned exceptions for the sake of his own needs to the ends whose adoption is required by other wide/ethical duties, then it is reasonable to suppose that imperfect duties are just duties that allow an individual some leeway (Kant's word is *Spielraum*)[54] to *balance* his duty to satisfy his own needs against his other wide/ethical duties.

Here there is no question of making exceptions, either arbitrary or carefully reasoned, to what morality *requires* us to do in pursuit of morally obligatory ends. Rather, it is a question of taking into account one's duty to ensure one's own needs when one calculates *what* morality requires one to do in pursuit of morally obligatory ends.[55] In other words, once a person has determined what duty demands of her, she is not permitted to take her own needs or desires into account; but in the course of

[52] TL 452.
[53] VE 198\158.
[54] TL 411.
[55] TL 390.

deciding what duty in fact demands of her, she is permitted, in the case of at least certain wide/ethical duties, to factor her own needs into her assessment of *how* she ought to pursue morally obligatory ends.[56]

Let us consider how this interpretation fits the three constraints I mentioned earlier. It is, first of all, plausible in the sense that it is the *sort* of view one might reasonably expect Kant to hold inasmuch as it dovetails comfortably with his general understanding of moral duty. It also provides a way of understanding what he could be referring to in the *Groundwork* when he speaks of imperfect duties allowing exceptions in the interests of inclination. The exceptions in question do not permit "arbitrary choices" to abandon the pursuit of morally obligatory ends, as Gregor would have it. They are instead *counterfactual* exceptions to what an individual *would* be required to do in pursuit of morally obligatory ends *if* she had no countervailing duty to attend to her own needs.

This interpretation further allows us to make sense of Kant's classification of all juridical duties as perfect, while he lists some ethical duties as perfect and others as imperfect. Kant believes in an absolute prohibition against, for example, suicide and lying. These are listed as perfect ethical duties, because Kant wishes to insist that our individual needs can have no say when it comes to deciding what morality requires of us with respect to obligatory ends of this sort.[57] Similarly, all juridical duties are listed as perfect.[58] These are duties to perform external actions and ought to be enforced by law. They allow no leeway for individuals to take their own needs into account. When an action itself is morally required, not merely the adoption of an end, there can be no room for personal discretion. Ethical duties such as benevolence, on the other hand, are classified as

[56] TL 393–94.
[57] TL 421–22, 428–29.
[58] RL 240.

imperfect, and if my interpretation is correct, that is because, even though Kant believes we must make it our end to aid others, he does not think that duties of this kind should be pursued without regard to the agent's own personal needs.[59] Unlike perfect/juridical and perfect/ethical duties, they permit us to factor our own needs into our assessment of the demands of morality.

Wide and Narrow Rights

We know already that duties of justice are narrow and enforceable duties to perform external actions and that ethical duties are wide and unenforceable duties to adopt ends. We can expect that whatever rights may correspond to duties of justice should be narrow, enforceable rights and that whatever rights may correspond to ethical duties should be wide, unenforceable rights. Consistently with such an expectation, Kant writes in the *Tugendlehre:* "To every duty there corresponds *one* right in the sense of a *moral title (facultas moralis generatim)*; but only a particular kind of duty, *juridical duty,* implies corresponding *rights* of other people to exercise compulsion *(facultas iuridica)*."[60] Juridical duties, Kant asserts, correspond to narrow and enforceable rights, whereas ethical duties correspond to wide and unenforceable rights.[61] This view is the natural one for Kant to take. His position shifts suddenly and oddly, however, in the *Rechtslehre.* He still holds that all ethical rights are wide and unenforceable. Juridical rights, though, are no longer always narrow and enforceable. Instead, Kant now

---

[59] TL 393.

[60] TL 383.

[61] George Flechter claims that Kant recognizes only juridical ("legal") rights, never ethical ("moral") ones (Flechter 1987, 544–55). The quoted passage from the *Tugendlehre* indicates Flechter is wrong.

insists there are two kinds of juridical rights: "All justice and every right in the narrower sense (*jus strictum*) are united with the authorization to use coercion. But one can also think of justice or rights in a wider sense (*jus latum*), where the authorization to use coercion cannot be stipulated by any law."[62]

Here, the wide/narrow contrast appears in a new light. Rather than distinguishing between enforceable, juridical duties to perform actions and unenforceable, ethical duties to adopt ends, the contrast differentiates enforceable from unenforceable juridical rights. Besides being somewhat surprising, this raises a difficulty. Narrow juridical rights are not the problem: they are simply the enforceable rights that correspond, as one would anticipate, to narrow and enforceable juridical duties. The problem lies with wide, juridical rights. Because they are wide and unenforceable, it is unclear how they are supposed to differ from ethical rights, which have the same characteristics.

Kant discusses two "true or alleged" wide rights of justice: equitable rights and the right of necessity.[63] The right of necessity is described in the *Rechtslehre* as a "pretended" right that purports "to give me permission to take the life of another person when my own life is in danger."[64] As an example of the circumstances under which this right applies, Kant refers to the shipwreck case discussed earlier. For reasons already noted, Kant argues that although the man is "not inculpable" when he pushes the other fellow from the floating log, and despite the fact that his act is "unjust in itself," it is still not juridically "punishable," since no law "could have the intended effect" of preventing it.[65] Kant does not, therefore, think that acts of this

---

[62] RL 233–34.

[63] RL 234.

[64] RL 235.

[65] RL 235–36. Courts have not always come to the same conclusion as Kant on this matter. The most famous criminal case on the right of necessity is *R. v. Dudley and Stephens* (1884), 14 Q.B.D. 273 (C.C.R.), an English

sort should be prohibited by law, but neither does he believe they can be justified by a real right of necessity. Indeed, he denies in his unpublished notes that there is any genuine right of necessity.[66] Necessity cannot be a narrow and enforceable juridical right, that is, a right that should be recognized in courts of law, because "it is monstrous to suppose that we can have a right to do wrong in the direst (physical) distress."[67] Neither is Kant willing to recognize necessity as a wide juridical right. He calls it a pretended right that seeks to admit "coercion without any right."[68] Insofar as necessity can be neither a wide nor a narrow juridical right it cannot be a juridical right at all.

Unlike the spurious right of necessity, Kant accepts equitable rights as genuine, albeit wide and unenforceable, rights of justice. The history of equitable rights is long and ancient, tracing back at least to early Roman law.[69] One of the earliest and most characteristic conceptions of equity is contained in Aristotle's remark in the *Rhetoric* that it is "equitable to pardon human weaknesses and to look not to the law but to the legislator, not to the letter of the law but to the intention of the legislator, not to the acts but to the moral purpose."[70] Aristotle here articulates what has come to be the traditional jurisprudential view that equity seeks a "higher" justice than is to be found in positive law. Its aim is to mitigate the severity of overly rigid or badly framed laws, whose strict application may result in substantial injustice.[71]

---

case dealing with three men and a boy who found themselves adrift in a lifeboat when their ship sank. After several days without food, the men killed and ate the boy. At trial they raised the defense of necessity, but it was rejected and they were sentenced to death, although the sentence was later commuted to six months imprisonment.

[66] *Reflexion* 7473, Ak XIX, 397.
[67] TP 300\81.
[68] RL 234.
[69] Main 1939, chap. 3.
[70] Aristotle 1984, 1:13:13.
[71] Vico, *New Science*, 4:7; Sidgwick 1981, 485–86; Cairns 1949, 319.

Kant's discussion of equity in the *Rechtslehre* generally harmonizes with this traditional view, and to the extent that it does it is uncontroversial. But Kant additionally holds, as the traditional doctrine of equity did not, that rights of equity must be unenforceable. Kant's argument is as follows. In a typical equity case for example, one in which a domestic employee contracts to work for a specified period at a particular rate of pay in a particular currency, if the currency depreciates before payment is to be made in accordance with the terms of the contract, the employee cannot seek redress in the courts: "He can only appeal to equity (a silent goddess who cannot be heard), because nothing was stipulated about this in the contract, and a judge cannot pronounce in accordance with unstipulated conditions."[72] Kant goes on to say that a "court of equity" would contain a "self-contradiction." The reason is not explicitly stated, but Kant's point is tolerably clear. Kant believes that the proper function of a court of justice is to enforce legally recognized rights, which in turn are those protected by statutory law. Equitable rights are by hypothesis not statutory rights. A court of equity would therefore be a court that enforced nonexistent legal rights, and as such would contradict the very idea of a court of justice.

Kant's rejection of equity courts and legally enforceable rights of equity has generated criticism. Morris Cohen's objection is typical: "When Kant urges that it is impossible to have courts of equity . . . he ignores the actual existence of . . . the English court of chancery in its original form. The principle of contradiction cannot prove existing institutions to be impossible."[73] Cohen's argument is specious. When Kant asserts that courts of equity are impossible he is making a normative claim, not an empirical one. His contention is not that there cannot in fact be courts that render verdicts in equity

[72] RL 234.
[73] Cohen 1950, 125.

cases, but rather that such courts misuse judicial powers. To understand exactly why Kant takes this position, consider once again his view of the state. Kant believes the only fully legitimate state is a republican one with a separation of powers between a sovereign legislature, a judicial branch, and an executive authority.[74] Any state lacking this structure is normatively deficient: it fails to correspond to the "idea" of a political state.[75] The proper function of the sovereign legislative authority is to produce positive laws—these being for Kant always "statutory" laws.[76] The proper function of the executive authority is to enforce statutory laws, and the purpose of the judiciary is to determine when and how these laws should be applied to particular cases. Kant likens this arrangement of legal powers to the "three propositions in a practical syllogism": "The law of the sovereign will is like the major premise; the command to act is like the minor premise . . . and the adjudication (the sentence) that establishes what the actual law of the land is in the case under consideration is like the conclusion."[77]

The point that needs to be stressed if we are to understand Kant's rejection of equity courts is that in his syllogistic model of law there is no room for *judge-made* law. All positive law, Kant believes, should be statute law, enacted by legislatures, applied by courts, and enforced by the executive authorities.[78] The task of judges is to apply pre-existing legislative statutes to the case at hand.[79] Judges should not themselves make law. Consequently, they should not apply extrastatutory rules or principles to the cases with which they deal. To this extent,

[74] *Reflexion* 7781, Ak XIX, 515.
[75] RL 313.
[76] RL 313–14, 316.
[77] RL 313.
[78] This view has been standard among continental jurists, though also much criticized. See, e.g., Gray 1972, 93–125; Pound 1954, chap. 3.
[79] *Reflexion* 7653, Ak XIX; RL 316.

there is no place for "judicial discretion" in the Kantian picture of law.[80]

From Kant's perspective, the difficulty with the traditional system of equity in common law countries is that it relies on extrastatutory rules and principles that he believes judges should not be permitted to use.[81] J. H. Merryman's description is succinct: "In its general sense, equity refers to the power of a judge to mitigate the harshness of strict application of a statute . . . Equity is, in other words, a limited grant of power to the court to apply principles of fairness in resolving a dispute being tried before it."[82] Kant's syllogistic model of law prohibits any such grant of discretionary powers to the judiciary, for it does not allow judges the liberty of supplementing laws with extrastatutory principles of fairness. This restriction is why Kant rejects courts of equity, notwithstanding their actual existence at different times. From the normative point of view, they are impossible because they contradict what Kant regards as the proper function of a court.

Rights of equity cannot, therefore, be narrow, legally enforceable rights in a Kantian theory of law.[83] Yet it is easy to see why

[80] I am not suggesting that Kant's model of law is unable to accommodate *any* sort of judicial discretion. Obviously such a position would be untenable. Kant seems never to have given the matter much thought, but there is no reason to suppose that his understanding of law cannot permit judicial discretion in the interpretation of statute law. What his model of law does not permit is the judicial employment of principles that plainly are *not* contained in legislative statutes.

This whole subject is extremely thorny, especially in light of theories of law such as Dworkin's, which seek to incorporate into the proper interpretation of positive laws whatever principles may best be used to justify them. If a theory like Dworkin's is correct, that would spell serious trouble for Kant's view of positive law. See Dworkin 1978, 81–130; Dworkin 1986.

[81] For a discussion of the rules used in modern equity cases see Stafford, 14–42, 440–44.

[82] Merryman 1985, 49.

[83] Kant's rejection of enforceable rights of equity was by no means an aberration in the history of German legal thought. On the contrary, it has

Kant wished to accord them *some* recognition as rights of justice. Equity has always been thought of as a branch of justice—not of strict or narrow justice, to be sure, but of "justice" taken in a broader sense. The problem for Kant was how to reconcile this traditional view that equity belongs to the sphere of justice with his own system of rights and duties. The solution he developed in the *Rechtslehre* was to distinguish wide from narrow justice and to place rights of equity in the former category, thereby allowing unenforceable juridical rights. Most likely, this solution was suggested to him by earlier writers. The distinction between wide and narrow justice (*jus strictum* and *jus latum*) was familiar in Kant's time, having been used by many other writers.[84] Leibniz, among others, had previously contrasted equity with narrow or strict justice, so Kant's description of equitable rights as wide rights of justice was hardly a departure from established usage.[85]

Even if this classification was sanctioned by tradition, it did not fit into Kant's larger system of rights and duties. Kant claims that every duty corresponds to a right, and conversely that every right corresponds to a duty.[86] There is no difficulty deciding what kind of duties correspond to narrow, enforce-

---

been the mainstream position of German legal theorists. Thus, Cohn, e.g., notes that "German law—like the other continental laws—knows no parallel to the two distinctions which are of paramount importance in English law, i.e. the distinctions between common law and equity law and between case law and statute law. German law has always been one unified system of law in which there was and is neither need nor room for a separate system of equity" (Cohn 1968, 3).

[84] Tuck 1978, 67.

[85] Riley 1972, 56, 60, 172.

[86] TL 383; RL 239. David Lyons describes the belief that every right corresponds to a duty as the "correlativity doctrine" (Lyons 1970, 45–55). Using counterexamples, Lyons argues that it is implausible, and that there are indeed rights without duties. R. M. Hare also uses counterexamples to make the same point (Hare 1981, 149). Counterexamples, however, do not affect Kant's position directly. Kant *defines* a right as a "capacity" or "moral title" to "obligate others to a duty" (RL 239). Kant thus stipulates

able, judicial rights: they must be narrow, enforceable juridical duties. But what kind of duties might correspond to wide, unenforceable juridical rights? Kant does not say. Any answer, though would encounter obstacles. What "essentially" distinguishes a duty of justice from an ethical duty is that the former are enforceable but the latter are not. Assuming that enforceable duties must correspond to enforceable rights, and that unenforceable duties must likewise correspond to unenforceable rights, then all juridical rights should be enforceable, and hence narrow, whereas all ethical rights should be unenforceable, and hence wide.

This conclusion is unavoidable. But it makes wide, unenforceable juridical rights impossible. Indeed, when Kant says, in a passage from the *Tugendlehre* which I quoted earlier, that a *juridical duty* implies corresponding *rights* of other people to exercise compulsion," he effectively excludes the possibility of wide rights of justice, although this did not prevent him from asserting their existence in the *Rechtslehre*.[87] Just as Kant ought to have classified all juridical rights as narrow, enforceable rights, he should also have listed all wide, unenforceable rights as ethical rights. No other scheme of classification is consistent with his claim that the essential difference between duties of justice and ethical duties is that the former but not the latter are enforceable through coercion. Two decades or so before he wrote the *Rechtslehre*, Kant treated equitable rights in exactly this way. In his early lectures on ethics he said that "*Jus aequitis* . . . belongs only to ethics."[88] Rights of equity are the only wide rights Kant ever attempted to include among

---

that there are no rights without corresponding duties. Perhaps this is a nonstandard conception of a right, and perhaps it is open to criticism on that ground, but it cannot be knocked down by counterexamples.

[87] TL 383.

[88] VE 42–43\35.

rights of justice, but he would have avoided significant problems had he maintained this classification of equity rights instead of attempting to incorporate them into his theory of justice.

Natural and Positive Laws

Kant recognizes two kinds of external laws: natural laws and positive laws. Natural laws are external laws to which "an obligation can be recognized a priori without external legislation."[89] Positive laws are external laws that would "neither obligate nor be laws without external legislation."[90] Natural laws are laws of justice; they provide the "immutable principles for all positive legislation."[91] Positive laws therefore "must not be incompatible with . . . natural laws," and the former "cannot be abrogated" by the latter.[92]

Within the natural law tradition these are familiar ideas. They also raise familiar questions connected with the relation between natural and positive laws—questions about the conditions under which natural and positive laws may conflict, as well as about the status of unjust positive laws. Hobbes argued, notoriously, that because the social contract confers absolute power on rulers, the people thereby consent to whatever laws it pleases the head of state to create. Consequently, positive laws can never be unjust or inconsistent with natural laws, for any law approved by the ruler has already been consented to by the people, which is sufficient in Hobbes's view to eliminate the

[89] RL 224.
[90] RL 224.
[91] RL 229.
[92] RL 256, 315.

possibility of injustice.[93] Kant finds this conclusion "terrifying."[94] Against Hobbes, he argues that individuals have natural rights that cannot be overridden by positive laws— most notably those corresponding to his three a priori principles of justice. Any positive law that violates these rights is unjust, regardless of whether a people might in fact consent to it.[95]

In this way Kant subordinates positive law to natural law. Despite his strong affiliations with the natural law tradition, however, he stops short of accepting its most controversial thesis: that unjust positive laws are in some sense not really "laws" at all. Aquinas and Augustine are the best-known exponents of this view. Commenting on Augustine's contention that an unjust law "seems to be no law at all," Aquinas adds approvingly that these so-called "laws" are merely "acts of violence rather than laws."[96] Somewhat later, Althusius arrived at a similar view, claiming that if a civil law conflicts with natural or divine law "it is not to be called a law (*lex*)."[97]

Kant appears never to have subscribed to this belief. He argues that one should not obey positive laws that conflict with natural laws, but he does not deny that unjust laws are real laws.[98] Legal positivists insist that even if a law is immoral, it can still be technically valid in the limited sense that it may satisfy the empirically identifiable "rules of recognition"

---

[93] Hobbes, *Leviathan*, 1:13; 2:17; 2:20; 2:30. Thomas Pogge has pointed out to me that this assertion is unfair to Hobbes unless it is qualified by the observation that even though a Hobbesian sovereign cannot commit injustices against his subjects, he can fail to act on his (legally unenforceable) duty to make "Good Lawes" and to act for the "Good of the People." (Hobbes, *Leviathan*, 1:30). A Hobbesian sovereign can thus fail to promote the good, but he cannot commit an injustice.

[94] TP 303–4\84.

[95] REL 99n\90n; IAG 39–40\57; TP 290–91\74.

[96] *Summa Theologica* Q. 45, A. 2, 4. Quoted in Golding 1966, 24.

[97] Althusius, *Politics*, 67.

[98] VE 166\133.

(Hart) that determine matters of legal and constitutional validity within a particular legal system. Kant's conception of law is
able to accommodate this particular tenet of positivism. In line
with the positivist doctrine of the separation of law and morality, Kant admits that a "purely empirical theory of . . . law is
possible."[99] A theory of this kind, he writes, would "tell us
what the actual law of the land is (*quid sit juris*), that is, what
the laws say or have said at a certain time and in a certain
place."[100] Even though Kant goes on to say that a purely empirical theory of this sort would be "beautiful" but entirely
without a "brain," like the "wooden head in Phaedrus' fable,"
he does not conclude that it would not be legitimate solely as
an account of a system of positive laws. Nor does he suggest
that any criteria of moral adequacy must be satisfied in order
for these laws to qualify as positive laws.

Nevertheless, if Kant does not disagree with legal positivists
on this subject, he does part company with them on another
closely related issue. Positivists typically suppose that there is
a distinct type of legal obligation that differs from moral obligation. This obligation is usually thought to rest on the capacity of a legal system to enforce its laws through brute power.
John Austin was of course the most famous advocate of this
idea. As he put it, I am "*bound* or *obligated* by your command"
so long as I am "liable to evil from you if I comply not with a
wish which you signify."[101] Critics were quick to point out that
this view leads to preposterous results, not least that there is
obligation to obey the thief who demands one's possessions at
gunpoint.[102] Due to its implausible consequences, Austin's
theory has been universally rejected, but only in its crudest
forms. In more disguised language the same view is still widely

[99] RL 230.
[100] RL 229–30.
[101] Austin, *Lectures on Jurisprudence*, 89.
[102] Lyons 1984, 42–45.

accepted, a prime example being Hare's functional characterization of "legal obligations" as whatever obligations "the
legislature has determined and the courts will enforce."[103]
For practical purposes Hare's view differs not in the slightest
from Austin's.

Kant's position is different. For Kant there is only one kind of
obligation: moral obligation. An obligation is a moral constraint, that is, a constraint of pure practical reason.[104] In
Kant's moral theory there is no distinct form of legal obligation
resting only on force. "Compulsion," Kant asserts without
qualification, "does not make an obligation."[105] Surely this is
the only defensible conclusion. There is no credibility whatsoever to the idea that brute force, be it employed by a government or a lone gunman, is capable of producing any kind of
obligation; and it follows from this that there can be no sui ge-
neris category of legal obligation.

[103] Hare 1981, 151.
[104] KPV 32; RL 222; VE 19, 41\15, 33.
[105] VE 39\32.

CHAPTER FOUR

Political Legitimacy,
Obedience, and Revolution

I HAVE FOCUSED MAINLY ON KANT'S BASIC PRINCIPLES OF JUS-
tice, their origins in his larger moral theory, and how he distinguishes justice from ethics, as well as the different kinds of
rights, duties, and laws in his theory of justice. These issues are
fundamental, but they are also preparatory. Justice is preemi-
nently a political virtue, a virtue of properly exercised political
authority, and the topics we have covered in the preceding
chapters, although they provide the framework for understanding Kant's conception of political justice, are nonetheless intro-
ductory to that task. Having addressed these preliminary
topics, therefore, I now turn to the problem of the legitimate
state.

We have already seen the rough outlines of Kant's conception
of the legitimate state and its role as a guarantor of justice. A
fully just state must be republican in structure, which, for
Kant, means that it must have a popularly elected legislature
along with separate executive and judicial branches. It must
also protect individual rights, primarily civil liberty, legal
equality, and political freedom. These are the essentials of the

just Kantian state. If they exhausted Kant's views on the subject, there would be little need for further discussion; nor would further interest be warranted. Kant's view of political legitimacy, however, is far more complex. Included in the general problem of the legitimate state are many subsidiary questions, such as how political authority can be justified; how far the powers of the state should properly extend; who should exercise political authority; whether citizens are obligated to obey laws; and whether they are entitled to rebel against oppressive and unjust governments. To understand Kant's conception of political legitimacy we shall need to consider his responses to all of these questions. The responses are diverse and not always predictable. What gives them a curious kind of unity, as will soon become evident, is a pervasive dualism running through every aspect of Kant's approach to political authority, but which is most apparent in the alternating strands of liberalism and conservatism in his view of the state.[1]

Kant's emphasis on individual rights, legal equality, personal freedom, and popular sovereignty establish his credentials as a liberal. For a time, his support of the ideals, though never the practices, of the French Revolution even earned him a reputation for Jacobinism.[2] Indeed, many of his beliefs appeared to set him in opposition to established authority. In contrast with Hobbes, for instance, he refused to identify justice with the arbitrary commands of kings and princes, insisting instead that all individuals have "inalienable" natural rights that rulers are morally required to respect in all circumstances.[3] Nor was Kant's opinion of most rulers very flattering. The idea of jus-

---

[1] The theme of dualism in Kant's political philosophy is explored well in Williams 1983, especially 52–67, 128.

[2] See Lewis White Beck's Introduction to *Kant on History* (Indianapolis: Bobbs-Merrill, 1984). A more broad-ranging discussion of Kant's relation to the French Revolution can be found in Burg 1974.

[3] Hobbes, *Leviathan*, 2:30; TP 304\84.

tice, he complained in his lectures on ethics, has "no authority with princes," who care for nothing except "despotic power" and have contributed "not one iota" to the "worth of mankind."[4] Harsh words, certainly, yet characteristic of Kant's contempt for the political morality of rulers.[5] On other occasions he remarks, with the same severity, that rulers "look upon their subjects merely as tools for their own purposes," that what passes for "statecraft" is nothing other than disguised "trickery," and that the rebelliousness of citizens is to be explained, not by a natural truculence, but by the "unjust coercion" and "treacherous designs" of governments.[6]

Views of this sort leave the impression that Kant is a defender of oppressed citizens against unjust governments. But there is another equally prominent though quite different side to Kant's approach to political authority. If the rights of citizens are important to Kant, so are the prerogatives of rulers. All existing governments possess an indisputable right to rule, no matter how unjustly they may exercise that right: "The authority that is now here and under which you live . . . possesses the right of legislation."[7] It is a "crime," Kant alleges in a moment of hyperbolic overstatement, even to "doubt" this right.[8] Citizens are instead required "to obey the legislative authority that now exists regardless of its origins."[9] Not even under the worst provocation or tyranny are they permitted to rebel, for rebellion is always the "greatest and most punishable crime in a commonwealth."[10] Far from having a right to overthrow governments they deem oppressive, citizens are obligated "to en-

[4] VE 318–19\52–53.
[5] Frederick II, about whom Kant has admiring things to say, appears to have been an exception (WIA 40–41\58–59).
[6] PAD 448\15; APH 332–33n\250–51n; SF 80, 89\178, 185.
[7] RL 372.
[8] RL 318.
[9] RL 319.
[10] TP 298–300\80–81.

dure even the most intolerable abuse of supreme authority."[11] Injustices must certainly be rectified and reforms, when necessary, must be carried out; but these goals should be pursued only by peaceful means.[12] Progress toward greater justice must always be "gradual" and "evolutionary," must rely on initiatives from "the top downwards," and above all must occur through legally permissible channels.[13]

No serious conflict exists between Kant's liberal principles and his policy of gradualism. It is perfectly feasible to condemn unjust rulers while holding, on moral or pragmatic grounds, that increased justice can and should be achieved only by means of slow, peaceful, incremental reforms. But Kant's insistence on the legitimacy of existing authority, whatever its composition or disposition, goes far beyond the demands of this sort of moral or pragmatic gradualism. Kant does not merely prohibit violent opposition to ruling authorities, he also goes to considerable lengths to strengthen the claims to power of regimes whose methods of governing contrast sharply with his own ideals of justice. It seems appropriate, therefore, to speak of a "dualism" in Kant's approach to political authority, and it is this dualism, more than any other aspect of Kant's view of political legitimacy, that stands in need of explanation.

Justifying Political Society

I propose to begin with Kant's reasons for believing that political society, in any shape or form, is morally necessary. In Chapter 1 I briefly discussed Kant's most general justification of the state. Now we can examine more closely and more crit-

---

[11] RL 320.
[12] RL 319.
[13] ZEF 373–74\118; SF 87, 91–93\184, 187–89.

ically that argument. Kant claims in the *Rechtslehre* that civil
society is necessary because the state of nature is inherently devoid of justice. It is devoid of justice because justice requires an
impartial means of arbitrating disputes between individuals
about their respective rights, and no such mechanism is available in the state of nature.[14] Political society provides—or can
provide—this mechanism through a system of public legal justice. The political state is consequently morally necessary as a
condition of the possibility of justice, and therefore "all men
ought to enter" a "civil society" or "juridical state of affairs."[15]

This argument is open to a harmless as well as a not-
so-harmless interpretation. The harmless (and platitudinous)
interpretation is that one has a duty to leave the state of nature
if it is possible to join a just political society. Such a conclusion
would be uncontroversial, but it is not the one Kant intends.
The fact that Kant employs the term "civil society" (*bürger-
liche Gesellschaft*), which in his usage is morally neutral between just and unjust political societies, indicates his belief
that there is a duty to be a member of political society, regardless of whether it is just or unjust, as long as it provides an alternative to the lawless state of nature.[16] It is equally clear that
this is a highly controversial notion.

Besides being controversial, this conclusion derives little if
any support from Kant's argument. We may grant that there is
a duty to quit the state of nature in favor of joining a political
society that protects individual rights and enforces laws of justice. By no means does it follow that there is a duty to leave the
state of nature in order to enter a civil society that is not just
and fails to protect individual rights. Kant's argument manages
to show that *some* form of political society is a necessary con-

[14] RL 256, 312.
[15] RL 306.
[16] RL 256, 305–6; ZEF 371\117. For an extended analysis of Kant's concept of civil society and its origins in Aristotelian political philosophy, see
Reidel 1976.

dition of justice, but what he wishes to establish, without having succeeded in doing so, is that *any* political society in which an individual may find herself is a necessary condition of justice and is thus morally preferable to the state of nature. Kant's argument is not adequate to support this latter claim. He does nevertheless have other reasons for believing it, and I will return to these after examining another of his arguments.

In a sequel to the argument we have just considered, Kant claims in the *Rechtslehre* that alongside the duty to enter civil society there is a right to force others to do so as well. If men "deliberately and intentionally resolve to remain" in the state of nature, he argues, "they cannot wrong each other by fighting among themselves; for whatever goes for one of them goes equally for the other as though they had made an agreement to that effect."[17] Every person in the state of nature therefore is "authorized" or has a "right" to use "violent means" to compel others to enter civil society.[18] We may rephrase Kant's argument: choosing to remain in the state of nature is equivalent to abrogating all rules of justice, in which case no one can commit an injustice against anyone else, and then no rights can be violated if someone is compelled to join civil society. The situation Kant has in mind is comparable to a game in which all the players agree among themselves to suspend the normal rules. In that event, any move is as acceptable as any other, and no player is entitled to complain about another player's moves.

Kant's reasoning is inventive but far from compelling. The principal difficulty becomes apparent as soon as we look more closely at the notion of a *right* to compel others to enter civil society. We sometimes assert that a person has a *right* to do something as long as it is not morally wrong. A right of this kind is simply a moral permission or liberty. It is the kind of right at stake when we say, for instance, that a professional

[17] RL 307.
[18] RL 312; cf. 257, 307.

boxer has a *right* to strike his opponent or that a prisoner of war has a *right* to escape.[19] In locutions of this sort we mean only that the actions in question are not wrong—for instance, to continue with the same examples, that a prisoner of war does nothing wrong by attempting to escape or that, subject to certain limitations specified by the rules of boxing, it is permissible for boxers to hit each other. When we speak of rights in this way we definitely do *not* intend to imply that, in addition to the prisoner's moral liberty to escape or the boxer's rightful freedom to strike his opponent, there is also a duty on the part of the opposing boxer to allow himself to be struck or on the part of guards in prisoner of war camps not to hinder the escape of prisoners.

Rights of this kind are appropriately called *weak* rights, because they entail no corresponding duties on the part of others not to violate them.[20] If we are concerned to find a philosophical lineage for these rights we need only recall Hobbes's claim in *Leviathan* that every person possesses an indefeasible right of self-preservation.[21] When Hobbes insists that no one can ever lose this right of self-preservation he means that everyone retains under all circumstances a moral liberty to defend themselves. He does not further assume that there is always a corresponding duty not to take or threaten the lives of others when they attempt to exercise their rights of self-preservation. Hobbes's right of self-preservation is thus a weak right.

If Kant had meant to use the notion of a right in the weak sense in which it entails no more than a moral permission or liberty to act in a certain way, with no assumption of a corresponding duty on the part of others not to violate it, his claim

[19] The prisoner of war example comes from Dworkin's essay "Taking Rights Seriously," as does the distinction between strong and weak rights which I discuss in the next few pages (Dworkin 1978, 184–205).

[20] Within a legal context, these weak rights correspond to what Weslay N. Hohfeld calls "privileges" (Hohfeld, 1964, 38–39).

[21] Hobbes, *Leviathan*, 2:28.

that everyone has a right in the state of nature to compel others to enter into civil society might be unobjectionable. Kant would have then implied only that it is not wrong in the state of nature to force others to enter civil society—a claim that could have been supported by his argument that refusing voluntarily to enter civil society is tantamount to abrogating all rules of justice, so that those who do so cannot be wronged if they are forced to join civil society. Kant does not use the notion of a right in this weak sense. A right, as Kant defines it, is a "moral title" or "capacity to obligate others to a duty," and every right therefore entails a corresponding obligation on the part of others to respect it.[22] Understood in terms of this *stronger* conception of a right, Kant's argument is manifestly unsatisfactory.

In Kant's moral theory all enforceable, coercive rights are rights of justice, as I noted in Chapter 3. All such rights, by the preceding definition of a right, entail corresponding duties on the part of others not to violate them. Whenever there is a right to exercise coercion it must therefore be a right of justice and must entail a corresponding duty not to interfere with or violate it. Clearly Kant's argument fails to substantiate a right in the state of nature to force others into civil society. Because it would be coercive, this right would be a right of justice, and in keeping with Kant's conception of a right it would also imply a corresponding duty of justice to respect it. The trouble is that if Kant's argument is sound, there can be no duty of this kind in the state of nature. When individuals in the state of nature refuse to enter civil society voluntarily, that is tantamount to abrogating all laws of justice, from which if follows that no one can any longer do an injustice to anyone else. If, however, no one can do an injustice to anyone else, because all laws of justice have been abrogated, it follows *not only* that no injustice can result from forcing others into civil society *but also* that

---

[22] TL 383; RL 237, 239.

none can be caused by resisting such a use of force. There can be no right, therefore, in the state of nature to force others into civil society. Given Kant's view that every right entails a corresponding duty and that all coercive rights are rights of justice, the right to force others into civil society would have to correspond to a duty of justice to comply with this coercive right, and there can be no such duty inasmuch as the failure to comply with it could not violate any principles of justice.

Kant has failed to notice that his argument cuts two ways. In an attempt to establish a right in the state of nature to compel others to enter civil society Kant contends that refusing to enter civil society voluntarily is equivalent to abrogating all rules of justice. If all rules of justice have been dispensed with, however, then no action can be either right or wrong, just or unjust. A condition of this sort is one in which there can be neither rights nor duties of justice in Kant's sense, because all distinctions between justice and injustice have by hypothesis been obliterated. If one person compels others to enter civil society by force, he perhaps does nothing wrong; but that is not because there is a right to use force in this way. It is rather because all rights and duties of justice have been erased. Kant's error, to make use of the game metaphor once again, is not seeing that dispensing with the rules of a game means acknowledging both that there are no *wrong* moves and that there are no *right* ones.

Kant's argument falls short of its goal, but it is not entirely a failure. Assuming that Kant is correct in alleging that the refusal to leave the state of nature voluntarily is equivalent to abrogating all rules of justice, he is entitled to maintain at least that if individuals in the state of nature refuse to enter civil society of their own accord, it is not unjust or wrong to force them to do so. In a suitably weak, Hobbesian sense of the term- "right" there may still be a right to compel others to enter civil society, but Kant's own moral theory does not allow him to speak of rights in this limited sense.

The preceding discussion has shown that neither of the arguments Kant uses in the *Rechtslehre* to legitimize civil society are full-fledged successes. The first suffices merely to establish a duty to belong to a just civil society; the second shows no more than that it is not wrong to found civil society on conquest. The more interesting question, however, aside from whether either of these arguments is effective, is *why* Kant bothers with them at all. What, we may ask, is Kant's underlying agenda? What does he hope to gain by defending a right of conquest in the state of nature or a general duty to submit to civil authority? The initial answer, correct though superficial, is that Kant wishes to provide an across-the-board legitimization of political power, especially of governments whose authority is most open to doubt. But this is not a very satisfying response; it only moves the problem back a few paces, for we can now ask why Kant wishes to provide a general legitimization of political society.

The answer to this second and more difficult question is connected with the *project* that underlies Kant's theory of justice. Here, as in other areas, Kant follows the lead of Rousseau. Rousseau claims in his introduction to the *Social Contract* that he intends to take "men as they are and laws as they can be made" and within this context to "reconcile what right permits with what interest prescribes."[23] Kant's goal is similarly to develop a conception of justice that avoids utopianism or "empty ideality."[24] Like Rousseau, his objective is to show that "politics" can be "reconciled" with "morality."[25] But the politics Kant wants to reconcile with morality is not a narrow or parochial politics. In the *Groundwork*, Kant claims that whoever "wills" an end must, insofar as he is rational, also will the

---

[23] Notwithstanding anti-utopian statements of this sort, Rousseau is regularly presented as a utopian. See, e.g., Shklar 1969, chap. 1.
[24] TP 276\63.
[25] ZEF 385–86\130.

requisite "means" to its attainment.[26] This entails, among other things, that nothing can be a genuine moral end—an object of moral volitions—unless it can be achieved in the practical world, against the backdrop of human history and human nature. Relating this to the reconciliation of politics with morality, we should understand Kant to be saying, in part, that a theory of justice must operate within the confines of what is historically and humanly possible.

If we interpret Kant's project in this way, it becomes easier to appreciate why he wishes to provide a general legitimization of political authority. Kant believes that only a republican state is "absolutely just."[27] No other state attains more than "provisional" justice. From the point of view of morality, a nonrepublican state is never better than a pale copy of a just state. A fully just republican state cannot, however, simply spring into existence at the beginning of political history. It can only be the end product of a "laborious" and lengthy "process" of evolution.[28] Political history cannot begin with a completely just state because political society must initially be founded on "force" and "power" rather than on popular consent and natural rights.[29] Kant claims that we can know this from the "very nature of uncivilized men."[30] Although Kant does not elaborate, what he has in mind should be apparent from our previous discussion of his philosophy of history in Chapter 2. The early stages of human history are marked by the dominance of "animal inclinations" over reason. To the extent that human beings are at first slaves of their passions and desires, they are prone to "abuse" their natural freedom. As much as they would like others to respect their rights and liberties, they tend to "exempt" them-

---

[26] G 417.
[27] RL 341.
[28] SF 91\187.
[29] ZEF 371\117.
[30] RL 339.

selves from the same requirements.[31] "Man" is therefore "an animal who needs a master."[32] Hence the need for civil society.

Forcing human beings to respect each other's rights is the main purpose of civil society. At its inception, however, civil society must leave a great deal to be desired. The "master" who unites others under his own authority will be no different from the rest—he too will abuse his freedom to the detriment of others. Consequently "this master will also be an animal who needs a master," only in his case none will be available since there will be no one capable of forcing him to respect the rights of others.[33] Such is the problem of the unjust ruler. As I noted before, and for reasons I will discuss in detail later, Kant holds that violent opposition to political authority is always morally prohibited. Reforms must therefore always come from the top downwards. Yet Kant also recognizes that "power corrupts" those who possess it.[34] Rulers exercise control over their subjects and must be relied on to enforce laws of justice, but they themselves stand in need of external constraints, for they are no more inclined to act justly than those they govern. The result is a dilemma for Kant: he must depend on rulers for progress toward greater justice, while believing that they care little, if at all, about justice for its own sake. Because the problem of the unjust ruler appears so intractable, Kant describes it as the "most difficult and the last to be solved by the human race."[35] A "perfect solution," he admits, is "impossible."

Kant nonetheless offers a partial solution in the form of rulers' self-interest. A perfectly just state is one that provides "the greatest possible freedom" for its citizens, and Kant believes that considerations of self-interest must eventually compel rulers to allow ever increasing amounts of personal freedom for

[31] IAG 23\46.
[32] IAG 23\46.
[33] IAG 23\46.
[34] ZEF 369\115.
[35] IAG 23\46.

their subjects. Whenever individuals are prevented from pursuing their own goals as they see fit, "commerce" suffers, the "vitality of business" is eroded, and ultimately the "state's power in its external relations" declines.[36] Rulers, accordingly, need only consult their own interests to see that they will "profit" from permitting greater "civil freedom," and therefore greater justice.[37]

We may or may not be convinced by this argument, but what is clear is that it cannot take Kant far enough. Suppose we grant that increased civil freedom is, by and large, conducive to the growth of commerce, of benefit to nations generally, and (to that degree) in the interests of rulers. Even so, justice requires more than civil freedom: it requires, as well, in Kant's scheme of things, political freedom and a republican form of government. This, however, is the sticking point, for on the whole it does not appear to be in the self-interest of nonrepublican rulers to relinquish power in order to institute a republican form of government. Kant cannot therefore rely entirely on rulers' self-interest to bring about complete political justice. Of this he is well aware, so he eventually falls back on the vague hope that "education" will ultimately provide the solution: only when rulers receive the right moral education will there be sustained progress toward justice.[38] Education is thus Kant's final answer to the problem of the unjust ruler. On the vital question of how it may be possible to ensure that rulers receive the proper education Kant unfortunately has little to say, and this means he is unable to specify with any confidence how progress can be made toward a fully just republican state.

Whatever may be the shortcomings of Kant's attempt to find a mechanism within history capable of guaranteeing progress toward complete justice, reviewing this issue has at least put us

---

[36] IAG 27–28\50–51.

[37] IAG 27–28\50–51; WIA 41–42\59–60.

[38] PAD 448–49\15–17; SF 92–93\189; VE 318–19\253; APH 325\242.

in a better position to understand why he wishes to provide a general legitimization of political authority. Without political society, Kant believes, justice is impossible, and so the political state is a necessary condition of justice. Because of the problem of the unjust ruler, however, political history must start with less than optimal justice—indeed, probably with a significant amount of injustice. As a result, imperfectly just states are historically necessary presuppositions of progress toward full justice, even if there is no certainty of such progress. Reconciling the demands of justice with the realities of history and human nature therefore requires accepting the paradox that less than fully just states are unavoidable precursors of fully just states. From this acceptance it is a small step to the further conclusion that all such states must be recognized as legitimate; otherwise we would be demanding justice without being prepared to pay the unavoidable price of attaining it.

In Kantian terms: if we will an end, we must also, insofar as we are rational, will whatever conditions are necessary to its attainment.[39] To fail to will the necessary means to an end is to fail to will the end at all. As long as we are not prepared to accept the necessary means to an end, we may wish, hope, or desire it, but we cannot be said to will it. Therefore, if we will the development of fully just states, we must will—and accept the moral necessity of—whatever unjust states are historically necessary precursors of fully just states. This conclusion by itself should explain why Kant was eager to legitimize political authority. If we also take into account two of Kant's other beliefs, first that rebellion is never morally permissible, and second that progress toward greater justice should come always from the top downwards, it becomes even more apparent why he was anxious to provide a general legitimization of political authority.

---

[39] G 417.

Standards of Legitimacy and the Social Contract

Kant holds that the moral legitimacy of governments can be measured in degrees and that some governments are therefore more (or less) legitimate than others. This idea is reflected in his use of different standards for assessing the moral status of governments. Unqualified legitimacy belongs only to republican governments that rule in accordance with laws of justice. At the other end of the spectrum any existing government is legitimate in the restricted sense that it must be regarded as a historically necessary precursor of a fully just state. Between these two poles or standards of legitimacy, however, there is a third. Kant believes that nonrepublican rulers may govern in a republican "spirit" even when their states are formally non-republican, for instance, monarchical or oligarchic.[40] To govern in a republican spirit is to rule "by analogy" with the "laws which a people would give itself in conformity with universal principles of right"—by analogy, that is, with a republican constitution guaranteeing civil liberty, legal equality, and political freedom.[41] When nonrepublican rulers govern in this way, they acquire increased legitimacy because their mode of governing approximates to the principles that underlie a republican form of government.

At this point Kant's social contract theory comes into view, for governing in a republican spirit means framing laws by reference to the *idea* of the social contract. An idea (*Idee*), for Kant, is a "concept of a perfection that has not yet been experienced."[42] The idea of the social contract is consequently the concept of a perfect or ideal social contract that has never existed in the historical world. Since Kant's social contract is ideal rather than historical, he diverges from Locke, who be-

[40] ZEF 372\118; SF 91\187.
[41] SF 88\184.
[42] PAD 444\8.

lieved that at least some political societies were founded on a
historically determinate "original" contract.[43] Like Hume, and
for substantially the same reasons, Kant rejects the notion of a
historical contract. Hume had argued that civil society could
not have had a contractual foundation because the concept of a
social contract was "far beyond the comprehension" of the
"savages" who were supposed to have been party to it.[44] Kant
echoes this objection when he claims that the "original contract" could not have occurred "in reality" since "savages do
not draw up documents when they submit themselves to the
law."[45] On Kant's view, as we saw earlier, civil society must
rather have been founded originally on force and conquest.[46]

Kant's critique of the social contract tradition is hardly decisive. Hume understood that contract theorists like Locke rely
more on the notion of a "tacit" agreement than on anything so
improbable as an oral or written contract.[47] Many of Hume's
arguments were geared accordingly.[48] Kant, on the other hand,
seems to have had an overly literal understanding of previous
social contract theories. When he criticizes the concept of a
historical contract he speaks exclusively of "documents" and
demands an "authentic record . . . orally or in writing" of the
putative transaction.[49] Contract theorists such as Locke would
not have considered themselves threatened by this demand, for
they never imagined that it could be satisfied.[50]

---

[43] Locke, Two Treatises, 2:8:95–110.
[44] Hume, "Contract," 468.
[45] TP 297, 301–2\79, 83.
[46] RL 339.
[47] Plamenatz's discussion of the tacit character of Locke's contract theory is useful on this point (Plamenatz 1965, 220–41).
[48] Hume, "Contract," 475.
[49] TP 297\79.
[50] I do not mean to suggest that Kant's objections to a historical contract
are entirely irrelevant. He might have developed convincing objections to
Locke's contract theory had he bothered to develop his somewhat crude demand for documentation of an explicit contract into a more realistic demand for evidence of tacit consent.

In any event, whether for good reasons or bad, Kant rejected the notion of a historical contract. This was due not only to an implausibly literal understanding of the social contract tradition but also to his awareness that contract theories had commonly been used to undermine the authority of governments, a result Kant was anxious to avoid.[51] Locke, for instance, though hardly a radical, absolves citizens of their duties of obedience as soon as rulers betray the terms of the social contract.[52] Kant did not intend his social contract to have such subversive implications. The idea of the social contract, as Kant conceives it, is a "rational principle for judging any lawful public constitution."[53] It obligates "every legislator to frame his laws in such a way that they could have been produced by the united will of an entire people"[54] If a "whole people could not *possibly* agree" to a law, or if it would be "self-contradictory" for them to consent to it, then the law is unjust.[55] So long as it is possible for an entire people to agree to a law, however, even if they "would probably refuse" to consent to it, it must be considered just.[56] Kant avoids the delegitimizing consequences of other contract theories by stipulating that the people are not entitled to use the social contract principle as an excuse for rebelling against governments. Only rulers are permitted to judge whether a law qualifies as just or unjust by the standards of the social contract principle.[57]

The concept of an ideal social contract is familiar nowadays, thanks largely to John Rawls's *A Theory of Justice*. Rawls bor-

---

[51] TP 301–2\83; RL 318\84.
[52] Locke, *Two Treatises*, 2:18:199–208.
[53] TP 302\83.
[54] TP 297\79. Kant's "united will of the entire people" (*vereinigten Willen eines ganzen Volks*) or "general will" (*allgemeine Wille*) is an a priori rational will, like Rousseau's (ZEF 378\123). I discuss it further in the next chapter.
[55] TP 297–300\79–81.
[56] TP 297\79.
[57] TP 297\79.

rows the concept of an ideal contract from Kant, but develops it in far greater detail and in a quite different direction. His objective is to determine the fundamental principles that "free and rational" individuals, conducting their deliberations in a situation of "equality," would chose to regulate the basic institutions of political society.[58] Rawls begins with what he calls the "original position," an abstract, ahistorical analogue of the state of nature, whose function is to provide a set of hypothetical circumstances in which free, equal, and rational individuals may arrive at a fair agreement about the principles of justice that are to govern their society. To ensure that none of the parties to the contract are inequitably advantaged or disadvantaged by knowledge unavailable to others, Rawls imposes a "veil of ignorance" in the original position: no one is to be aware of his own social or economic position, or of his own talents, aptitudes, temperament, or psychological disposition. Without this constraint, the parties to the contract, who are assumed to be self-interested as well as rational, would attempt to tailor principles of justice to benefit themselves at the expense of others.[59]

Another limitation on deliberations in the original position is that they are not concerned with every aspect of the basic institutions of political society, but only with the distribution of "primary goods." Primary goods, as Rawls describes them, are those goods such as rights, liberties, health, opportunities, income, and wealth that every rational individual requires as ingredients or means to the attainment of his or her particular wishes, goals, and desires.[60] The principles of justice that emerge out of the original position are designed to regulate the distribution of these goods by the basic institutions of society. Rawls argues that the parties in the original position will agree

[58] Rawls 1971, 11.
[59] Rawls 1971, 18.
[60] Rawls 1971, 62.

to two principles governing the distribution of primary goods. The first is that everyone is to be guaranteed the most extensive liberty compatible with a similar liberty for all others. The second is that social and economic inequalities are to be arranged so that they benefit all members of society and are attached to positions open to everyone.[61] These principles, Rawls goes on to argue, must be "lexically" ordered with the first taking absolute priority over the second in the sense that it can only come into play as a rule governing the distribution of primary goods so long as it does not violate the first principle.[62]

Even this very brief outline of Rawls's theory is enough to indicate that it has points of contact with Kant's conception of justice. For one thing it relies on the notion of rational consent, which, as I suggested in Chapter 1, is also true of Kant's view of justice. For another there is a family resemblance between Rawls's first principle of justice and Kant's belief, reiterated in a variety of texts, that a just political state must guarantee each citizen the greatest possible freedom consistent with a like freedom for all other citizens.[63] Kant and Rawls are thus united in regarding maximum equal liberty as one of the foremost requirements of justice.

There are, then, obvious similarities between Rawls's and Kant's conceptions of justice.[64] In many respects Rawls's theory can be seen as a further articulation and refinement of ideas that appear only germinally in Kant's remarks on the social contract. Nevertheless, for present purposes there is little to be gained from extended comparisons of Kant's views with those of Rawls. Rawls develops the concept of an ideal contract in ways that never occurred to Kant. One looks in vain, for instance, for anything corresponding to Rawls's original position or veil of ignorance in Kant's discussion of the social contract.

[61] Rawls 1971, 60.
[62] Rawls 1971, 42–43.
[63] See Chapter 1; also KRV A316\B373.
[64] I suggest some further similarities in the next chapter.

Nor does Kant provide an explicit or fine-grained characterization of the parties to his social contract. Moreover, Rawls does not find the Kantian roots of his theory of justice in Kant's social contract principle or larger political philosophy, but rather in his ethical theory, particularly in the categorical imperative, the principle of autonomy, and the concept of a realm of noumenal beings divorced from the ordinary conditions of sensibility, which Rawls sees as a model for his veil of ignorance in the original position.[65]

It seems unlikely therefore that much insight into Kant's social contract principle can be derived from a closer examination of Rawls's ideal social contract. We may thus leave Rawls aside for the moment, concentrating instead on Kant's own statements concerning the social contract principle for clues about how it should be interpreted and applied. Unfortunately Kant's direct comments are few and meager, far too few and meager to provide sufficient illumination on their own. Besides indicating that he intends the social contract principle to serve as a test of unjust laws, Kant tells us only that an unjust law is one which an entire people could not agree to without self-contradiction. As with the categorical imperative in the *Groundwork*, Kant seems to think that his social contract principle is intuitively clear and easy to apply. Plainly it is not, and on the crucial issue of what it means to say that an entire people could not agree to a law without contradicting itself Kant provides no direct guidance.

Some clues are nonetheless available. When Kant refers to a contradiction involved in consenting to unjust laws, he seems to allude to the contradiction in conception and contradiction in the will tests found in the *Groundwork*. The contradiction in conception test is meant to identify maxims that cannot be made into coherent laws of nature. The contradiction in the will test is intended to identify maxims that, although capable

[65] Rawls 1971, 11n, 139–41, 251–57; Rawls 1980.

of being made into coherent laws of nature, would be "impossible to will" as universal laws because they would "contradict" the will of any rational being.[66] For a number of reasons, it is natural to look to the contradiction in conception test for an interpretation of Kant's social contract principle. In the first place, the social contract principle is a principle of justice and Kant believes that justice is purely formal in the sense that it is not concerned with the "matter" or "ends" of any particular will, but only with the "form" of the relation between individual wills.[67] Ethics, on the other hand, is concerned with the content of volitions because it is a doctrine of the "*ends* of pure practical reason."[68] A contradiction in the will, however, arises only when one end conflicts with another, so the contradiction in the will test ought to be associated with ethics. By default, the contradiction in conception test should be associated with the theory of justice.

This is the obvious conclusion to draw, one supported by Kant's claim in the *Groundwork* that the contradiction in conception test determines "narrower (imprescriptible)" duties, while the contradiction in the will test determines "broader (meritorious)" duties.[69] We have already seen that narrow duties are duties of justice and that wide duties are ethical duties.[70] It follows that the contradiction in the will test must be associated with ethics and the contradiction in conception test with the theory of justice.

If we accept this reasoning, we seem to be halfway to an understanding of Kant's social contract principle. If all duties of justice are determined by the contradiction in conception test,

---

[66] G 424. A detailed discussion of the contradiction in conception and contradiction in the will tests would involve too lengthy a digression here. By far the best analysis is in O'Neill 1975, chap. 5.
[67] RL 230.
[68] TL 381.
[69] G 424.
[70] TL 387–91.

then this test ought to provide a means of understanding the social contract principle, as that principle is a rule of justice. Assuming the correctness of this reasoning, all that would remain to be done in order to arrive at an understanding of the social contract principle would be to develop an interpretation of the contradiction in conception test. Even though it appears this solution should work, it does not. The main difficulty is that it does not fit any of Kant's specific applications of the social contract principle. Kant applies the social contract principle on three different occasions. Each time he argues that an entire people could not possibly agree to a particular law, and each time his argument turns on the tacit premise that all rational beings have certain ends that are inconsistent with the law in question.

The first example is in *Theory and Practice*, where Kant claims that a "whole people could never agree to" a law that inequitably imposed a tax on some members of an economic group while allowing arbitrary exemptions for other members of the same group.[71] Kant does not suggest that there is any conceptual impossibility involved in agreeing to such a law, so the contradiction in conception test should not apply. But his claim makes sense if we take him to mean that no rational individual would voluntarily consent to being arbitrarily disadvantaged by a law, and that consequently an "entire people" could not consent to it because it would contradict the rational will of those who would thereby be disadvantaged.

The second example is similar. This time, in the *Rechtslehre*, Kant criticizes laws permitting a hereditary nobility. "Inasmuch as it can be assumed that no man would throw away his freedom," Kant says, "it is impossible that the general will of the people would consent to such a groundless prerogative."[72] Kant is relying on the assumption that every ra-

[71] TP 297–98n\79n.
[72] RL 329.

tional being seeks to maximize her own freedom—or, what is the same, to minimize restrictions on her liberty. In relation to an entire people, this means that maximum equal liberty is one of rational ends of the general will, or of a people considered as a whole. For if each individual seeks to maximize her own freedom, rational agreement can only be reached if each consents to as much freedom as is consistent with a like amount of freedom for all others. A hereditary nobility, whose members enjoy special rights and privileges denied to members of other classes, must then be considered unjust insofar as an equal distribution of freedom, which is a universally shared rational end, is inconsistent with allowing unearned rights and privileges for members of a particular social class.

The third and final example is in *What Is Enlightenment?* In this essay Kant argues that neither ecclesiastical nor civil authorities should attempt to establish an "unalterable" canon of religious doctrines.[73] Kant's concern is not primarily with legal attempts to enforce religious beliefs, but with efforts by clerics or civil legislators to establish a perpetual and unchangeable standard of orthodoxy. To do so, Kant says, would be to attempt to prevent "all further enlightenment from the human race."[74] This would be a "crime," Kant goes on to suggest, and no people could "be permitted" to "impose such a law upon itself," since it would conflict with the "destiny" of humanity which lies in steadily increasing enlightenment.[75]

Kant doubtless exaggerates the truth when he claims that establishing an unalterable canon of religious orthodoxy would amount to an attempt to prevent *all* further enlightenment. It would be possible to suppress religious inquiry while encouraging, say, artistic, scientific, or philosophical investigations. Kant's main point, however, is unaffected by this piece of hy-

---

[73] WIA 38–39\57.
[74] WIA 39\57.
[75] WIA 39\57; cf. TP 305\85.

perbole. His main point is that all attempts to prevent the development of new ideas and the spread of knowledge, of which the establishment of a perpetual canon of religious orthodoxy would be a prime example, conflict with one of humanity's rational ends: the intellectual freedom required for progress toward complete enlightenment. Because all attempts to stifle intellectual inquiry conflict with this rational end, none could rationally be agreed to by an entire people.

As the preceding examples suggest, Kant's social contract principle relies implicitly on the idea of rational ends. When a law conflicts with those ends, it cannot rationally be willed by an entire people, and for that reason cannot be considered just. The self-contradiction involved in unjust laws is one that emerges when a people is asked to consent to a law that conflicts with its rational ends. Judging from the above examples of Kant's application of the social contract principle, we can conclude that the most important rational end he ascribes to every individual is freedom—as much freedom as possible subject to the constraint that it must be distributed equally among all citizens.

This should not come as a surprise. Kant's social contract principle is not an independent rule of justice. Its purpose is to enable nonrepublican rulers to govern in the spirit of a republican state. The central principle of republicanism in turn is freedom; for Kant believes that a republican form of government is morally optimal solely because it offers the greatest possible amount of liberty for all citizens.[76] A republican state thus fulfills the objective of the social contract principle, which is why Kant says that the idea of the social contract is "realized" in a perfect republican state.[77] We should accordingly interpret Kant's social contract principle as requiring nonrepublican rulers to maximize their citizens' freedom. In

[76] ZEF 349–52\99–100; KRV A316\B373.
[77] TP 311\91; PAD 444\8.

Kant's view, this cannot be achieved outside of a republican state. Nonrepublican rulers are therefore required to move gradually toward a republican form of government and in the interim to approximate to that ideal.

Sovereignty and Constitutionalism

By tradition a sovereign is thought to be the "final and absolute political authority" in a nation or state.[78] As this suggests, the idea of sovereignty is closely tied to the idea of political legitimacy. The idea of sovereignty has also traditionally been laden with ideological assumptions. "Its function in the history of politics," F. H. Hinsley observes, "has been either to strengthen the claims of power or to strengthen the ways in which political power may be called to account."[79]

The delegitimizing potential of the idea of sovereignty is evident in the works of many political philosophers, Rousseau being a case in point. According to Rousseau, sovereignty belongs exclusively and inalienably to the general will. The defining characteristic of sovereignty is the power of legislation, and so the general will alone possesses the right to make laws. Since the general will can express itself only in an assembly of the whole people, the sovereign power of legislation can be exercised only when the whole people gather together as a single body to ratify laws.[80] Nothing else counts as a law for Rousseau. Nor does he hesitate to draw the obvious conclusion that in light of these stringent requirements "very few nations would, upon careful examination, be found to have laws."[81]

[78] Hinsley 1986, 17.
[79] Hinsley 1986, 25.
[80] Rousseau, *Social Contract*, 2:6; 3:15.
[81] Rousseau, *Social Contract*, 3:15.

Bold as it is, however, this remark understates the real effect of Rousseau's view: by his standards no state in modern times has contained any laws. All have instead been lawless, with the obvious corollary that their legitimacy is highly dubious. This result is a direct consequence of Rousseau's belief that sovereignty belongs only to the general will and that the general will can express itself legislatively only in a citizens' assembly.

In several respects Kant's theory of sovereignty is similar to Rousseau's. Kant, though, is anxious to avoid the delegitimizing implications of Rousseau's doctrine. He retains Rousseau's identification of sovereignty with the highest legislative authority; but whereas Rousseau locates this sovereign in an ideal and incorporeal general will, Kant holds that "sovereign authority resides in the person of the legislator."[82] By this, Kant does not mean that sovereignty is located in whomever ought to possess legislative authority; he means that it belongs to the current holder of legislative power—that is, to the legislative authority "that is now here and under which you live."[83]

Kant asserts this in passing, apparently unaware that it is in need of any defence. Yet it is certainly a controversial claim inasmuch as it immediately confers a measure of legitimacy on those who possess legislative power, no matter how they may use it. More than anything else, this claim distinguishes Kant's view of sovereignty from Rousseau's. On Rousseau's theory, sovereignty always belongs to an abstract general will; it is never located in a historical person. Rulers, princes, monarchs, and others who possess the legal power to legislate are never more than "officers" of the sovereign general will.[84] If their commands conflict with the general will (which is to say, if they rule unjustly) the "body politic" is immediately "dissolved" and along with it all obligations on the part of citizens

[82] RL 313.
[83] RL 372.
[84] Rousseau, *Social Contract*, 3:1.

to obey governments.[85] Kant's decision to locate sovereignty in the current possessor of legislative power has quite different consequences: it confers a mantle of respectability and legitimacy on all governments.

As the discussion above indicates, Rousseau and Kant put the concept of sovereignty to different uses, but not entirely different. Although Kant locates actual sovereignty in the existing legislator, he also holds that the power of legislation—and therefore of sovereignty too—belongs by right to "the people" or the "general will."[86] Even if the people do not at any given moment in fact possess sovereign legislative authority, they ought to, and in a republican state they do possess it and exercise it through their elected representatives. In effect, though without directly saying so, Kant makes the people into the *de jure* or ultimately rightful sovereign and the current possessor of legislative power into the *de facto* sovereign.[87] This fact might seem to cast doubt on the legitimacy of governments that are neither popularly elected nor republican, since they are not the ultimately rightful possessors of sovereignty. Kant forestalls such an inference by claiming that if the people do not at any particular time possess actual sovereignty, they are entitled to reclaim it "only on condition that the means employed to do so are compatible with morality."[88] The *de jure* sovereignty of the people is limited, in other words, by the principle that their right to *de facto* sovereignty is conditional upon the use of morally acceptable (that is, peaceful and nonseditious) methods of acquiring it. Kant's acknowledgment that sovereignty ought to belong to the people does not therefore seriously jeopardize the authority of nonrepublican governments.

The evidence suggests that Kant's tacit division of sovereignty into *de facto* and *de jure* components is an attempt to

[85] Rousseau, *Social Contract*, 3:1.
[86] RL 313, 319.
[87] RL 313, 319, 341, 371; WIA 40\58.
[88] SF 87–88n\184n.

balance his desire to legitimize existing governments against his belief that justice requires giving citizens the right to live by laws of their own making. Had Kant followed Rousseau in locating sovereignty exclusively in the general will, he would have risked undermining the authority of governments that in his own view are historically necessary precursors of a fully just republican state. Had he, on the other hand, located both *de facto* and *de jure* sovereignty in the existing holder of legislative power, he would have betrayed one of his own most basic principles of justice: popular sovereignty. In the event, he settled for a compromise between these two dangers. Only *de jure* sovereignty confers full legitimacy, but the legitimacy that flows from *de facto* sovereignty is nonetheless adequate to maintain the everyday authority of governments. For insofar as Kant holds that revolution is never morally permissible, even a *de facto* sovereign possesses the right to remain in power without having his authority challenged by rebellious subjects through extralegal means.

While the compromise effected through this bifurcation of sovereignty may seem strained, is not obviously untenable. The same, however, cannot be said of all aspects of Kant's theory of sovereignty. Some in fact contain contradictory elements, most notably Kant's doctrine of sovereign illimitability. In addition to being the "highest" and "supreme" authority in the state, Kant's sovereign possesses "absolute power."[89] Absolute power is illimitable, and Kant takes seriously the notion that the legislative authority of the sovereign cannot be restricted in any way. Kant's sovereign is not subject to any laws of the state; neither is he bound by any legal duties.[90] He is, in a word, legally omnipotent, making laws at his own pleasure without being subject to any legal restraints, for the simple reason that all laws are products of his own will which he is free to

[89] RL 372.
[90] RL 317; TP 291\75.

change as he sees fit. According to Kant, it is conceptually impossible to limit the powers of the sovereign: "To permit any opposition to this absolute power (any opposition which might limit that supreme authority) would be to contradict oneself, inasmuch as in that case the power (which may be opposed) would not be the lawful supreme authority."[91] The point is explicit: there can be no limitations on sovereign power, none at all. The concept of sovereignty is inconsistent with legal constraints. Any such restrictions would imply the existence of a superior power in the state capable of limiting the authority of the sovereign.[92] That, however, would involve a contradiction, for the sovereign is, *ex hypothesi*, the highest authority in the state. The sovereign must therefore possess absolute and legally illimitable power.

There are many difficulties with this doctrine, but the one most damaging to Kant is that it is incompatible with his own constitutionalist tendencies. Kant repeatedly insists on the overriding importance of constitutional government, more particularly on the necessity of a republican constitution.[93] Constitutionalism of any kind, however, does not go well with the idea of absolute or illimitable government. The idea of constitutional government has always been synonymous with the idea of limited government.[94] A constitution that placed no restrictions whatsoever on governmental powers would be a historical anomaly. It would also be pointless, because the purpose of national constitutions has always been to limit the power of government in order to prevent tyranny and protect individual rights. There is consequently a historical incompatibility between constitutionalism and the idea of absolute sovereignty, for constitutionalism has always been conceived as a solution to the problem of absolute sovereignty.

[91] RL 372.
[92] *Reflexion* 7953, Ak XIX, 563.
[93] RL 340.
[94] See, e.g., Wheare 1962, chap. 1.

The difficulty for Kant, though, runs deeper than this historical inconsistency between constitutionalism and absolute sovereignty. Kant is both a constitutionalist and a republican. The essential characteristic of a republican constitution, as he understands it, is that it provides for a separation of powers between executive, legislative, and judicial branches of government. Kant's sovereign is the highest legislative authority, but within a separation of powers system his powers are exclusively legislative.[95] The sovereign legislator is specifically not permitted to perform executive or judicial functions; otherwise the constitutional separation of powers is breached and the sovereign becomes a "despot."[96] Yet this presents an insuperable problem for Kant insofar as restricting the authority of the sovereign to legislative matters entails limiting his powers. A truly illimitable sovereign power would have the legislative authority to take over the functions of the executive and judicial branches. A truly illimitable sovereign power would thus be inconsistent with a constitutionally guaranteed separation of powers. Kant failed to see this, and therefore failed to realize that he could not consistently maintain a doctrine of absolute sovereignty alongside his theory of a constitutional separation of powers.

The question we should now consider is why Kant attached himself so firmly to the idea of absolute sovereignty when it was manifestly at odds with his republican and constitutionalist principles. The answer seems to be disturbingly simple: it was part of the political geography of his time and he inherited it from previous political theorists without inspecting it critically, a lapse that caused him to overlook its incompatibility with many of his own principles of justice. Prior to Kant's time,

[95] RL 316–17.
[96] ZEF 352\101; RL 317; *Reflexionen* 7781, 7783, 7952, 7953, 7971, Ak XIX, 515–16, 563, 567.

absolutism had gained wide though not universal acceptance in Europe through the writings of Bodin, Grotius, Hobbes, and Rousseau, among others,[97] all of whose theories of sovereignty, though differing on many points, shared the assumption that the power of the sovereign must be legally illimitable.[98] Kant rarely mentions Grotius and Bodin by name, so their influence on him was likely to have been only indirect; but Hobbes and Rousseau turn up frequently in Kant's political writings, and even when he disagrees with them he shares many of their assumptions. Rousseau's sovereign, for instance, possesses "absolute power" just as does Kant's, and like Kant's is above the law insofar as he cannot be subject to any legal restrictions.[99] Hobbes's conception of sovereignty was likewise similar to Kant's. He, too, regarded the sovereign as legally omnipotent, incapable of being constrained by any positive laws.[100] In Hobbes's covenant of submission the people confer "all their power and strength on one Man," the sovereign, and his power is either "absolute . . . or else there is no sovereign,"[101]

[97] See, e.g., Tuck 1978, 77–79; Friedrich 1958, 66; Hinsley 1986, 120–21; Bodin 1955, 25–30; Franklin 1973, chap. 7; Cassirer 1979, 256–57.

[98] There were some exceptions. Puffendorf, for example, preferred absolutist regimes but recognized that unlimited sovereignty was neither a logical nor a legal necessity (Gierke 1957, 142–47; Krieger 1965, 145–47). Closer to Kant's own time, the American Constitution of 1787 as well as the French Constitution of 1791 restricted the powers of their respective central governments, and thus in effect rejected absolute sovereignty (Thompson 1985, 81–90, 171–88). Kant was certainly aware of these constitutions. There is no evidence, however, that he understood their unsettling implications for the doctrine of absolute sovereignty.

[99] Those sympathetic to Rousseau may object to the suggestion that he was an absolutist. It is true that his absolutism was different from most other varieties. He did not, as was common, grant absolute power to existing rulers. Nevertheless, he was certainly an absolutist insofar as he refused to permit legal or constitutional restrictions on the powers of the sovereign. See Rousseau 1970, 1:4; Cassirer 1967, 52.

[100] Hobbes, *Leviathan*, 2:26.

[101] Hobbes, *Leviathan*, 2:17; 2:20.

Kant seems not to have appreciated that as an advocate of constitutional republicanism this conception of sovereignty was not available to him. Neither Hobbes nor Rousseau were committed to a constitutionally entrenched separation of powers.[102] They were consequently able to adhere consistently to a doctrine of absolute sovereignty. Not so with Kant: his constitutionalist principles precluded admitting an absolute sovereign, and he should not have done so. Other possibilities were open to him. In this century, a number of writers have proposed abandoning the concept of sovereignty altogether, principally on account of its historical ties with absolutism.[103] Kant might have done the same. There was also a less drastic alternative: retaining the concept of sovereignty while stripping away its absolutist assumptions. The only kind of sovereign consistent with Kant's constitutionalism is a limited sovereign whose authority derives from and is restricted by the terms of a national constitution. A limited sovereign of this sort can be subject to law inasmuch as its legislative acts may be treated as legally void if they conflict with the constitution.[104] Such a

[102] Not all scholars accept the notion that Kant was committed to such a separation of powers doctrine. Thomas Pogge, in particular, holds the contrary view that Kant intended no legally binding separation of powers, only one binding on the sovereign's conscience. On Pogge's view, Kant meant to impose no constitutional restrictions on the powers of the sovereign legislator, merely an ethical obligation not to usurp the functions of the executive and judicial branches or government (Pogge, 1988, 419–27). I find this interpretation difficult to accept for several reasons. The main problem, though not the only one, is that Kant describes his republican separation of powers doctrine as a "political principle" (*Staatsprinzip*) rather than an ethical principle, indicating that he intended it to be a legal and constitutional principle, not just an ethical one (ZEF 352\101).

[103] See Laski 1951, 271; Maritain, 61–64; Gray 1972, 79.

[104] There is nothing novel about this idea. In many countries—e.g., Italy, Spain, Australia, India, West Germany, Canada, and the United States—the constitution is regarded as legally binding on all branches and all levels of government, including the highest legislative body. See Setalvad 1967, 84; Wynes 1970, 29; Rossiter 1964, 540; Strong 1963, 169–70; Dworkin 1986, 356; Cohn 1968, 5; Merryman 1985, 139–40; Merkl 1963, 213.

sovereign may still be the "highest" and "supreme" law-making authority in the land, but only within constitutionally determined boundaries. Contrary to Kant's assumption, legislative sovereignty need not be identified with legislative omnipotence.[105]

Complex issues surround the question of *how* exactly a sovereign legislator can effectively be made subject to constitutional restrictions. The chief difficulty lies in determining who should be empowered to render legally binding decisions concerning the constitutionality of legislation. Kant was aware of this problem. It seems in fact to have been one of the main obstacles that prevented him from developing a theory of limited sovereignty. Kant believed that no one other than the sovereign (*Beherrscher*) or head of state (*Staatsoberhaupt*) can have "a right to judge how the constitution should be administered."[106] Only the sovereign therefore is entitled to decide whether his own laws are constitutionally valid. On this issue Kant's reasoning runs parallel to Hobbes's. Hobbes argued that if another authority in the state were permitted to judge the sovereign, this other authority would ipso facto be the "new Sovereign" because his power to judge the original sovereign would show him to be the real possessor of supreme authority.[107] Kant similarly claimed that allowing another authority to judge the constitutionality of legislation produced by the head of state would

---

[105] Some of Kant's contemporaries in Germany understood this clearly enough. Writing at roughly the same time as Kant, Fichte developed a theory of limited sovereignty which called for the creation of an "Ephorate" to oversee the constitutionality of all governmental operations. Fichte's Ephor was to be responsible for ensuring that governments act only within the limits of their constitutional authority. If they overstepped these limits the Ephor would be empowered, *inter alia*, to "suspend the administration of the law and the government in all its branches" (Fichte, *Science of Rights*, 253–77).

[106] TP 300\81; cf. RL 318.

[107] Hobbes, *Leviathan*, 2:29.

involve setting up "another head [of state] above the head of state . . . which is self-contradictory".[108]

Kant's reasoning is defective. Hobbes had no separation of powers doctrine. His sovereign, unlike Kant's, controls all legislative, executive, and judicial authority, though he may delegate as much of it as he wishes. Hobbes is thus able to claim that allowing another authority to judge the sovereign is equivalent to placing a second sovereign over the first. Kant's sovereign, on the other hand, is only the highest legislative authority. He possesses no executive or judicial powers. Permitting another authority to judge the constitutionality of the sovereign's legislative acts would not compromise his position as the highest lawmaking authority under the constitution, nor therefore would it undermine his sovereignty. The task of deciding the constitutionality of legislation is most easily conceived as a judicial function, analogous to determining whether a particular action counts as a breach of civil or criminal law. Responsibility for deciding the constitutionality of legislation may accordingly be placed in the hands of the judiciary, or some part thereof, without threatening the prerogatives of the legislative branch.[109] Kant could (and should) have adopted this solution to the problem of subjecting sovereigns to constitutional restraints. Had he done so, he might have been able to avoid the difficulties connected with his ill-advised attempt to combine absolute sovereignty with constitutionalism and a separation of powers theory of government.

---

[108] TP 300\81; cf. *Reflexion* 7953, Ak XIX, 563.

[109] This approach is common in liberal democracies and is a cornerstone of the theory of judicial review that developed out of Justice Marshall's ruling in *Marbury* v. *Madison* 5 U.S. (1 Cranch) 137, 163 (1803). (See Tribe 1985, 111–12; Cox 1976, chaps. 1 and 2; Cox 1987, chap. 2; Miller 1978.) A similar but not identical theory developed somewhat later in the civil law countries of Europe (Merryman 1985, chap. 18).

Political Obligation and Passive Disobedience

At the beginning of this chapter, I quoted some of Kant's more conservative remarks about political legitimacy and political obligation, for instance, that it is a "crime" to question the authority of governments and that citizens must "obey the legislative authority that now exists regardless of its origins."[110] In view of Kant's belief that the powers of the sovereign are legally illimitable, and more particularly his decision to locate this exalted authority in the hands of the current legislator, these statements are not surprising. They merely reflect Kant's desire to legitimize all existing authority. They have nevertheless earned him a good deal of opprobrium, one of the milder accusations being that, together with his rejection of revolution, they show him to have markedly "authoritarian" tendencies.[111]

To some degree, the charge of authoritarianism is certainly warranted. By no stretch of the imagination can Kant's view of political obligation be said to pose any threat to ruling authorities. It is also true, however, that Kant's authoritarianism has often been overstated. Thomas Grey claims, for instance, that according to Kant "the citizen has no right to disobey or resist substantively unjust positive law."[112] In the same vein, Joseph Grcic ascribes to Kant the belief that the "moral obligation" of citizens "to obey the law is not *prima facie*, but absolute and overriding in all circumstances."[113] Needless to say, if Kant in fact held these views his position would be utterly indefensible. As it happens, though, Kant's position is not what Grcic and Grey suggest. Kant does believe that "active resistance" to political authority is always morally prohibited, and he is firmly

---

[110] RL 318–19.
[111] Friedrich 1958, 129.
[112] Grey 1987, 581n.
[113] Grcic 1986, 450.

opposed to all rebellion. It is equally clear, though, *pace* Grcic and Grey, and despite Kant's own occasionally sweeping statements to the contrary, that he does not believe citizens are always morally required to obey laws. To put the matter briefly: although Kant rejects all violent opposition to ruling authorities, he accepts the moral permissibility in some circumstances, and the moral necessity in others, of passive disobedience to unjust laws.

Evidence of this position comes from several sources. Toward the end of the *Rechtslehre*, Kant claims that a "categorical imperative" requires us to "obey the suzerain . . . in everything that does not conflict with inner morality (*nicht dem inneren Moralischen widerstreitet*)."[114] Kant makes no effort to explain what might qualify as a "conflict" with "inner morality," but the *Critique of Practical Reason* provides an example of the sort of situation he probably had in mind. In the concluding chapter, "The Methodology of Pure Practical Reason," Kant discusses a number of hypothetical, mythological, and historical instances of honest men being induced to acts of slander by unscrupulous rulers. One case involves a prince who threatens the honest man "with loss of freedom and even of life itself" if he refuses to join in groundless calumnies.[115] Kant leaves no doubt as to the correct course of action: the upright man should remain "true to his resolution to be honest."[116] If he is made to suffer for his honesty, he should take comfort in the thought that "virtue is here worth so much more . . . because it costs so much."[117]

Generalizing from this example, one might interpret Kant's view as being that an individual is allowed, even morally required, to disobey a law or command if complying with it

[114] RL 371.
[115] KPV 155–56.
[116] KPV 156.
[117] KPV 156. Kant discusses a similar case and draws a similar conclusion in his lectures on ethics (VE 192\153).

would make him a participant in acts of injustice. Peter Nicholson reads Kant in this way. Largely on the basis of this example, Nicholson concludes that according to Kant disobedience is "only permissible when obedience means acting unjustly, and not simply whenever the law is unjust."[118] Interpreting Kant in this way has definite advantages, not least that it makes his view seem familiar and easily recognizable by bringing it within striking distance of the traditional Lutheran and Calvinist belief in divinely mandated submission to temporal authorities, except when obeying the laws of men necessitates violating the laws of God—or of justice, these being the same; at which point passive disobedience becomes a religious duty.[119] With Kant's pietistic background, it is not hard to picture him falling within the general orbit of this doctrine. Moreover, many of his own statements on the subject of disobedience seem to be consistent with this model, as when, for instance, he says in the *Religion* that although obedience to rulers is a "divine command," we "dare not and ought not, obey them" when they "command anything which is in itself evil (directly opposed to the law of morality) (*dem Sittengesetz unmittelbar zuwider*)."[120]

Despite its initial plausibility, however, Nicholson's interpretation does not stand up to scrutiny, either as an account of Kant's views or as a viable moral position. When he interprets Kant as holding that one should obey unjust laws unless they require one to act unjustly, Nicholson commits Kant to what is best described as a *clean-hands* policy. A clean-hands policy of this kind is highly problematic. If the idea of "acting unjustly" is interpreted broadly, then merely obeying a law that inflicts injustice on others qualifies as acting unjustly, for compliance

---

[118] Nicholson 1975, 219.

[119] On the traditional Lutheran and Calvinist views of political obligation see Skinner 1980, 16–18, 192–95.

[120] REL 99n\9on.

easily blends into complicity and obedience to a law that causes injustice may plausibly be construed as indirect participation in injustice. But if we interpret "acting unjustly" in this broad way, it may be impossible ever to obey an unjust law *without* acting unjustly, which is surely not the result Nicholson envisages, since he wants in at least some instances to *contrast* "acting unjustly" with simply "obeying an unjust law."

Presumably, therefore, Nicholson intends to interpret the idea of acting unjustly more narrowly, so that it includes only direct, as opposed to indirect, participation in injustice. This distinction is inherently vague, yet reasonably serviceable. In practice, if not in theory, we are able to tell the difference between direct and indirect injustice, for this is the familiar distinction between actively committing an injustice and passively allowing it to occur without taking steps to prevent it. I commit a direct injustice, for instance, if I physically abuse a child, whereas I commit a indirect injustice if, knowing that someone else is engaged in child abuse, I take no measures to prevent it. Limiting the idea of acting unjustly to cases of direct injustice is more in keeping with the spirit of Nicholson's clean-hands interpretation. The resulting policy, however, is much more dubious. The narrower interpretation entails not only that one should submit quietly to official injustices against oneself, no matter how grievous, but also that one should obey laws which inflict injustices on others, for instance, racially discriminatory laws of all kinds up to and including policies of genocide, as long as they can be obeyed without directly contributing to the injustice they cause.

A policy of this sort is difficult, indeed impossible, to defend. It endorses a see-no-evil, hear-no-evil attitude under cover of which official injustices thrive and multiply. Tyrants depend on such policies, and without them they cannot accomplish their goals. Thankfully, there is no reason to suppose that this policy represents the best interpretation of Kant's claim in the *Rechtslehre* that one should not obey positive laws that "conflict" with "internal morality," or of his statement in the *Religion* that one should not obey laws that are "opposed" to the "law of morality."[121] Positive laws may conflict with moral laws other than by requiring private citizens to participate directly (or even indirectly) in official wrongdoing. Simply *being* unjust is enough to bring a positive law into conflict with moral laws. A positive law that violates the principles of legal equality or civil liberty, for instance, conflicts with the demands of morality because these principles are laws of justice and all laws of justice are moral laws.

For this reason, Nicholson's clean-hands policy does not adequately convey the meaning of Kant's principle that one should not obey positive laws that conflict with the moral law. How then should we understand Kant's position? Before attempting a complete answer, a few preliminary points should be canvassed. In the first place, Kant's repeated admonitions to obey existing authority indicate that he believes disobedience to rulers must be held firmly in check and permitted only on rare, perhaps very rare, occasions. A well-known incident from Kant's personal life bolsters this impression. As a result of his rationalistic approach to theology in the *Religion*, Kant ran afoul of the Prussian censors, eventually receiving a letter in October, 1794, from Frederick William II warning him to desist from further "distortion and debasing" of Christian doctrine on pain of unpleasant consequences.[122] Kant's response was one of quiet submission to what he clearly regarded as an injustice. In his reply to Frederick William II, he assured the monarch that he remained a "loyal subject" and promised not to publish any further writings on the topic of religion.[123]

---

[121] RL 319.

[122] See Vörlander 1977, bk. 4, chaps. 2 and 3, as well as Cassirer 1981, chap. 7, for discussions of this incident and the background leading up to it.

[123] Kant's letter to Frederick William is reprinted in the preface to *The Conflict of the Faculties* (Ak VII, 7–11).

Two factors seem to have convinced Kant of the wisdom of acquiescence. First, he wrote in a note during this period that although "retraction and betrayal of one's inward conviction is base . . . keeping silent in a case like the present one is a duty of the subject."[124] Second, he had a healthy reluctance to court personal disaster by flouting the wishes of a sovereign who was capable of considerable ruthlessness. Showing a sensible aversion to unnecessary personal risks, Kant wrote in a letter over a year before this incident that when "the strong men of the world" are in a "state of intoxication" it is advisable for a "pygmy who is fond of his skin" not to get in their way.[125] About six months after Frederick William's warning, Kant expressed a similar sentiment in a letter to Schiller, writing that because "discussions of political and religious topics are currently subject to certain restrictions," the wisest policy is to "conform prudently to the times."[126]

As these remarks suggest, Kant's response, when personally subjected to what he regarded as an unjust interference with his freedom as a thinker, was to submit quietly to the dictates of those in authority, partly as a matter of principle, partly as a matter of prudence. Although it is doubtless true that Kant's personal attitude toward civil disobedience was conservative, it would be a mistake to make too much of his submissive response to Frederick William II on this occasion. Foolishness is never a virtue, not even in the service of justice, and Kant's actions in this incident reflect elementary common sense in dealing with a situation where defiance would have been unlikely to produce desirable results.

Remember, too, that Kant's response might have differed had the victim of injustice been someone else. Our duties to our-

[124] AK XII, 406.
[125] Letter to Spener, March 22, 1793 (Ak XI, 402–4).
[126] Letter to Friedrich Schiller, March 30, 1795 (Ak XII, 10–12).

selves are different from our duties to others. We have a right to relinquish some of our own rights, though not all, but we have no right unilaterally to relinquish anyone else's rights. We have, therefore, moral latitude in allowing encroachments on our own rights that we do not have in relation to the rights of others. I can, for instance, decide not to enforce my property rights against a trespasser; I have no right, however, to allow a trespasser to walk on my neighbor's property. Kant may consequently have been willing to tolerate injustices against himself that he would not have tolerated toward others. Considerations of this sort therefore make it difficult to generalize about Kant's attitude to civil disobedience based solely on the censorship incident.

We have still not resolved the question of how to interpret Kant's principle against obeying positive laws that conflict with the moral law. This question can be dealt with more easily by dividing it into two narrower questions. (1) Under what circumstances is it morally *necessary* to disobey unjust laws? (2) Under what circumstances is it morally *permissible* to disobey unjust laws? Judging from his remarks in the *Critique of Practical Reason* about the honest man who refuses to join in groundless calumnies, Kant evidently believes that disobedience to unjust laws is sometimes a moral duty. Yet there is no evidence to indicate that Kant believes there is a duty to disobey all unjust laws. Nor, indeed, is this view plausible. Consider, for instance, an immigration law prohibiting members of one race from being admitted to legal citizenship, or a housing law prohibiting members of a particular religious group from living in a particular area. Laws of this sort would no doubt be unjust, though not everyone could disobey them. The first is incapable of being disobeyed, except possibly by a renegade immigration official; and the second can be disobeyed directly only by members of the religious group in question. As these examples show, there cannot be a general duty to disobey all unjust laws. Kant's recommendation to disobey positive laws that conflict with the moral law therefore cannot entail such a duty.

Can Kant's principle be interpreted as implying a general right to disobey unjust laws? Kant would certainly have said no; for he believed that citizens should never "actively resist" unjust laws,[127] and many unjust laws can only be disobeyed by actively opposing them, for instance, laws prohibiting public demonstrations or flag burning.[128] Kant would therefore not have interpreted his principle against obeying positive laws that conflict with the moral law as implying more than a right passively to refuse to comply with such laws. Does this mean that it should be interpreted as implying such a right? The answer is yes; but to see why this is correct it is necessary to look at the relevant issues in more detail.

If there is a right to disobey immoral and unjust laws, as Kant's remarks in the *Rechtslehre* and *Religion* suggest, it must be either a right of justice or an ethical right. It cannot be a right of justice because, according to Kant, rights of justice must be legally enforceable, in principle at least, and it makes no sense to suppose that a right to disobey laws could be enforced by law.[129] Insofar as a right to disobey unjust laws could not be a legal right, neither could it entail immunity from prosecution, a factor that would have to be considered by those wishing to exercise it. Since it could not be a legal right or right of justice, it would have to be an ethical right, for there is no third alternative in Kant's moral theory. As I noted before, ethics is a "system of the ends of pure practical reason"; hence

---

[127] RL 319.

[128] I owe this point to Thomas Pogge, whose comments on an earlier draft of this section were helpful.

[129] TL 383. This is not to say that there could not be a legal right to be *exempt* from legal duties. An absolute sovereign possesses exactly this sort of right, but it is not the same as a right to *disobey* positive laws. One can disobey a positive law only if one is *not* legally exempt from the obligations it imposes.

ethical rights and duties are concerned with the adoption of ends.[130] Rights and duties of this kind therefore pertain directly only to the inner determining grounds of the will, not to external actions. They guide an agent's choice of morally acceptable ends. Only indirectly, through an agent's choice of ends, do they affect external actions. It follows that if there is a right to disobey unjust laws, it must be an ethical right and must consist in the moral freedom to adopt a policy, or make it one's end, (passively) to disobey unjust laws.

This conclusion dovetails nicely with Kant's principle in the *Religion* against obeying positive laws directly opposed to the moral law. Positive laws cannot directly conflict with ethical rights or duties, for the simple reason that all ethical rights and duties involve the adoption of ends and no one can be directly compelled by positive laws, or by any other means, to adopt an end that she does not wish to adopt. As Kant says in the *Tugendlehre:* "Another person can indeed compel me to perform actions which are means to his end, but he cannot compel me to have an end; only I myself can make something my end."[131] Consequently, if positive laws conflict directly with the moral law, the conflict must be with rights or duties of justice. A positive law that conflicts with rights or duties of justice is an unjust law. So Kant's rule against obeying positive laws that directly conflict with the moral law is a rule against obeying unjust positive laws. But the right entailed by Kant's rule against obeying positive laws that conflict with the moral law must, for reasons indicated a moment ago, be an ethical right to adopt a policy of noncompliance with unjust laws. Accordingly, Kant's principle in the *Religion* against obeying positive laws that conflict with the moral law implies an ethical right to adopt a policy of not complying with unjust laws.

[130] TL 381.
[131] TL 381.

I anticipate two objections. One is that even if this is a reasonable interpretation of Kant's principle in the *Religion*, it goes farther than Kant *intended* in allowing citizens to disobey governments. The other is that even if the suggested interpretation is exegetically defensible, it is morally and politically unsound. There is some merit in the first objection, though none in the second. Several times I have noted that Kant's personal attitude toward political authority is conservative. Nevertheless, it is in keeping with own Kant's view of interpretation to suggest that he may not always have been the best interpreter of his own principles. In the *Critique of Pure Reason*, Kant said precisely the same about Plato, insisting that he (Kant) understood Plato "better than [Plato] . . . understood himself," and that the proper interpretation of Plato's theory of Ideas is "in opposition to his own intention."[132] My present suggestion is similar, that Kant's conservative predilections may have prevented him from recognizing some of the implications of his own belief that one should not obey positive laws that conflict with the moral law.

The other objection is more troublesome. The voluminous literature on political obligation and civil disobedience contains a myriad of arguments against a right to disobey unjust laws, which I have not the leisure to address at the moment. Without responding to all of the relevant arguments,[133] however, it may be worthwhile to consider the most common one, briefly at any rate. This is the anarchy argument, so-called because it relies on the contention that if individuals were allowed to disobey laws they regard as unjust, the result would be

---

[132] KRV A314\B370

[133] Two of the more significant arguments that I will not discuss here derive from Socrates and Rawls. The interested reader is referred to Plato's *Crito* (50a–53e\Plato 1981, 52–56) and Rawls's essay "The Justification of Civil Disobedience" (Bedau 1985, 240–55), as well as Rawls 1971, 342–77. A useful analysis and reply to these argument can be found in Pateman 1985, 98–100, 103–29.

a breakdown of order, mass confusion, the disintegration of authority, and eventual chaos.[134]

There are a number of ways of responding to this argument. The first is to note that although the anarchy argument is based on an empirical assumption about human behaviour, namely, that widespread acceptance of a right to disobey unjust laws would inevitably lead to chaos, its adherents never bother to provide empirical support for such a speculative premise. One might also wonder whether this assumption does not betray a deep distrust of the human capacity for self-government. The principle of popular self-government, in most of its forms, is based on the notion that citizens are generally capable of distinguishing what is just from what is unjust, and moreover that they will usually choose the former over the latter. If so, then it is hard to see why, in a passably just state, there should be great danger of anarchy from citizens acting on their sense of justice. Only if a political system is substantially unjust is principled—as opposed to criminally motivated—disobedience to laws likely to be widespread enough to produce anarchy. Then one might reasonably wonder, however, whether anarchy would not be a better alternative than continued injustice under the guise of law.

The last suggestion is one Kant would have rejected out of hand inasmuch as he believed that any functioning legal system is preferable to the state of nature. Even if we share Kant's horror at the prospect of anarchy, though, there are important reasons rooted in Kant's own moral theory, beyond those already cited, for accepting a right to disobey unjust laws. In the framework of Kantian morality, a right to disobey unjust laws must, as I indicated earlier, be an ethical right to adopt a policy of noncompliance with unjust laws. Another way of characterizing this right is to say that it is a right to exercise *freedom of conscience* in deciding whether to disobey unjust laws.

[134] See, e.g., Waldman in Bedau 1985, 109–10.

Kant describes conscience in the *Tugendlehre* as an "inner court" before which a person examines his conduct as a judge would the actions of an accused criminal.[135] Kant also characterizes conscience as "practical reason holding a man's duty before him."[136] Conscience, in other words, is the inner voice of the moral law. Kant believes that anyone who sincerely acts on the basis of conscience is morally irreproachable: "If someone is aware that he has acted with the approval of his conscience, then so far as guilt or innocence is concerned nothing more can be required of him."[137] Not that human beings are incapable of moral error. Kant is not saying that someone who acts in conformity with her conscience cannot mistake the actual requirements of justice or ethics. He means only that as long as a person acts from sincere moral conviction, then even if her actions are morally wrong, she as an agent is morally blameless.[138] Naturally, this applies as much to principled acts of civil disobedience as to any other type of action grounded in the promptings of conscience.

The concept of conscience is closely linked with the idea of autonomy in Kant's moral theory. To act on the basis of conscience is simply to express one's moral autonomy. Autonomy, for reasons indicated in an earlier chapter, is one of the most fundamental values in Kant's moral theory, manifesting itself not only in the ethical principle of autonomy but also in the principle of civil freedom, which seeks to ensure a maximum of external freedom for each individual, and in the principle of political freedom, which serves to translate the idea of autonomy into a rule of political self-determination by means of participation in representative elections. If we take the idea of indi-

---

[135] TL 438; VE 164–68\132–35.

[136] TL 400.

[137] TL 401. This is similar to the *Groundwork's* doctrine that a good will is an absolute and unqualified good regardless of its effects in the phenomenal world (G 393–94).

[138] TL 400–401.

vidual autonomy seriously, as one of the controlling principles of ethical, political, and personal life, we must be wary in the extreme of allowing any encroachments on the liberty of each individual to follow his own conscience. There must be, as the old cliche affirms, a "balance between freedom and authority," but the balance is not properly struck when individuals are asked to relinquish their liberty to follow their own consciences in a matter so close to the core of moral autonomy as whether or not to act on the honestly held conviction that a law is unjust and should be disobeyed. To relinquish this liberty is tantamount to transferring control over one's conscience to the government of the day. This is not a balance between liberty and authority. It is an abdication of moral autonomy, and therefore of moral responsibility. Indeed no moral autonomy or responsibility remains when an individual trades away custodial rights over her conscience.

Rebellion and Revolution

Passive disobedience to unjust laws marks the outermost threshold, in Kant's eyes, of legitimate opposition to political authority. As soon as opposition becomes violent, Kant's limited sympathy for challenges to governmental power disappears completely. Kant is unwilling to tolerate any form of active resistance to governments. In *Theory and Practice,* he leaves little room for doubt: "All resistance against the supreme legislative power, all incitement of the subjects to violent expressions of discontent, all defiance which breaks out into rebellion, is the greatest and most punishable crime in a commonwealth. . . . This prohibition is *absolute.*"[139] In the *Rechtslehre* he is equally emphatic: "There can . . . be no legit-

[139] TP 299\81.

imate resistance of the people to the legislative chief of state. . . . There is no right of sedition (*seditio*), much less a right of revolution."[140] The slightest tendency in this direction, Kant adds, is "high treason," warranting no less a punishment than death. Rather than take up arms against their rulers, citizens must put up with the worst abuses of authority.[141] If they perceive themselves to be victims of injustice, they may petition for redress, but only peaceful means of affecting change are permitted.[142] When reforms arrive they must, as I said before, come from the top downwards.[143] Until governments choose to reform themselves, the people must wait patiently, if not contentedly, for the desired changes, including the morally necessary transition to a republican form of government.[144] In the meantime, rebellion is strictly prohibited.

On the whole, this is an accurate restatement of Kant's attitude toward rebellion. Nevertheless, on two occasions his position seems to shift, or at least to develop hitherto unsuspected ambiguities. The most noticeable deviation is in the *Reflexionen zur Rechtsphilosophie,* where in a much-quoted remark Kant seems to license rebellion in special circumstances: "[The private employment of] [f]orce, which does not presuppose a judgement having the validity of law, is against the law; consequently [the people] cannot rebel except in cases which cannot at all come forward in a civil union, e.g., the enforcement of a religion, compulsion to unnatural sins, assassination, etc., etc."[145] Kant appears to argue that if governments cross certain elementary boundaries of justice—such as enforcing observance of a religion or compelling citizens to commit grave moral offenses—then rebellion may be justi-

---

[140] RL 320.
[141] RL 320.
[142] SF 87–88n\184n; RL 319.
[143] SF 92\188.
[144] RL 322.
[145] *Reflexion* 8051, Ak XIX, 594.

fied.[146] On the face of it, this passage represents a significant departure from his otherwise unqualified rejection of rebellion. We may even be glad of Kant's apparent change of heart, thinking perhaps that it represents a more humane approach to the issue of rebellion, but we should nonetheless be wary of this text. One of the reasons for caution is that it is an isolated passage, apparently at odds with the position Kant persistently asserts. Another is that it occurs in unpublished notes. Kant never saw fit to commit the same ideas to print, and this suggests that they do not represent his considered opinion, particularly since his published views are vastly different.

The other deviation is in a footnote in the *Rechtslehre*, where Kant says that when citizens suffer under an oppressive monarch, they may by "appealing to a right of necessity" have "at least have some excuse" for "forcibly" causing the monarch to "relinquish his authority."[147] On no account, however, should this result be achieved by "laying hands" on the ruler himself.[148] Superficial appearances to the contrary, Kant is not expressing approval of rebellion, not even in the most dire circumstances. When he says that rebellion may sometimes be excusable, he does not mean that it is ever justified.[149] Excuses are appropriate only when an action is wrong; otherwise no excuse is required. An effective excuse, furthermore, does not usually diminish the wickedness of an action. Typically its function is to point to mitigating circumstances, thus establishing that although the *action* is wrong, the *agent* should not be held fully accountable. So Kant is not claiming that rebellion is ever morally permissible; only that, in rare instances, it may be pardonable. Nor is Kant's reference to a "right of neces-

[146] There is a useful discussion of this *Reflexion* and related issues in Henrich 1976, especially 362–63.

[147] RL 321n.

[148] RL 321n.

[149] Nicholson makes this point in commenting on the same *Rechtslehre* passages (Nicholson 1975, 228).

sity" meant to indicate acceptance of a genuine right of this kind. I argued earlier that Kant does not recognize necessity as a real right, and no exception is intended here. If one could appeal to a genuine right of necessity in the circumstances Kant describes, that presumably would *justify* rebellion, not merely *excuse* it; for a right is an entitlement rather than simply a ground of plausible excuses.

To sum up, Kant's view of rebellion is fairly straightforward: leaving aside the single recalcitrant passage in his unpublished notes, and granting that he regards rebellion as occasionally excusable, he nonetheless believes that it is never morally justifiable. Some commentators have found this distressing. Kant, it is felt, betrays his moral principles—especially his emphasis on the importance of individual rights—and gives the upper hand to tyrants, when he condemns what frequently seems to be the only practical means of regaining lost rights and liberties, namely, revolutionary violence. Howard Williams, for instance, seems to take this view when he construes Kant's apparent faintheartedness as a disappointing sign that his conservative inclinations triumphed in the end over his liberal convictions.[150]

Whether or not this reaction is justified, it is at least understandable. In some cases, though, objections to Kant's view of rebellion have not the slightest merit, among them Joseph Grcic's argument that Kant's rejection of revolution is "inconsistent with his own moral theory."[151] Grcic begins by observing (correctly) that Kant describes the preservation of the state as an "absolute duty," which precludes admitting any right to destroy it for the purpose of attaining greater justice.[152] By means of a rhetorical question, Grcic then implies that such a duty can have no place in Kant's moral theory; for "how," Grcic

[150] Williams 1983, 198, 201–6.
[151] Grcic 1986, 447.
[152] TP 300n\81n.

asks, "can the preservation of the state be an *absolute* duty, since the only absolute imperative is the categorical imperative, which makes no mention of the state."[153] A more misguided objection would be hard to imagine. It is on all fours with the contention that there can be no absolute duty not to commit murder or rape, because none of Kant's formulations of the categorical imperative specifically refer to these crimes.

Most objections to Kant's view of rebellion deserve more attention than Grcic's. Before considering some of them in detail, we should examine Kant's arguments against rebellion, the first of which is: "Revolution under an already existing constitution means the destruction of all relationships governed by civil right and thus of right altogether. And this is not a change but a dissolution of the civil constitution."[154] The questionable move in this argument from the *Rechtslehre* is Kant's assertion that revolution inevitably destroys civil society. The same idea is repeated in *Theory and Practice*, where Kant insists that as soon as a revolution has occurred "the state of anarchy supervenes, with all the terrors it may bring with it."[155] T. H. Green once accused Hobbes, in a similar context, of confusing the "dissolution of government" with the "dissolution of political society."[156] Kant may appear to have made the same error. Save for the odd anarchist, revolutionaries do not usually desire a return to the state of nature, nor is that what they typically achieve. Revolutions can and often do leave intact the structural elements of the state: courts of law, legislatures, police systems, bureaucracies, and so on. When they do not, the same or similar structures are generally rebuilt immediately. In most cases, the outcome of a revolution is merely a different government, not the end of government altogether. It is the complete end of government that Kant fears, however, since that would

[153] Grcic 1986, 450.
[154] RL 339–40.
[155] TP 302n\83n; cf. RL 355.
[156] Green 1980, 51.

destroy the very possibility of justice. So Kant's argument does in fact rest on a false premise, that revolution necessarily involves the destruction of government as an institution instead of the elimination of a particular government. We should not imagine, though, that Kant is unaware of the relevant distinction or that he has overlooked it. Why else, after all, would he bother to assert that revolution entails a "dissolution" of, rather than a "change" in, the civil constitution? Nonetheless, Kant merely asserts this, and although it suggests that he has not conflated the dissolution of a government with the dissolution of the state, it gives us no reason to believe that the one must follow from the other.

Kant's next argument is different. It turns on the same logic of sovereignty that proved so problematic before. Kant says in the *Rechtslehre* that resistance to the supreme legislative authority

> can only be unlawful . . . because, in order for it to be authorized there would have to be a public law that would permit the resistance. That is, the supreme legislation would have to contain a stipulation that it is not supreme and that in one and the same judgement the people as subjects should be sovereign over him to whom they are subject.[157]

Few of Kant's arguments have received more scorn than this one. Lewis White Beck describes it as an example of Kant's "formalism . . . *in extremis.*" The only point Kant succeeds in making, according to Beck, is one of "boring obviousness, namely that there can be no *legal* right of revolution."[158] The main issue, which Beck accuses Kant of missing, is that revolution "by its very nature is a denial that established legal and constitutional claims are indefeasible. . . . To tell a revolution-

[157] RL 320.
[158] Beck 1971, 414.

ary that he should desist from his revolutionary activity because he is breaking the law would be met with derision."[159]
Beck thus implies that Kant has begged the real question:
whether there can be an extralegal or moral right of revolution.

I will return to this criticism later. First, though, we should
look more closely at Kant's argument in the quoted passage,
since Beck's breezy dismissal does not tell us what is wrong
with it, or why a legal right of revolution is so obviously impossible. Kant has sound reasons—similar to the ones I mentioned in connection with the impossibility of a legal right of
civil disobedience—for rejecting a legal right of revolution. I
will discuss these reasons later, but they are not the ones Kant
sets out in this argument. Kant claims in the present text that
there would be a hidden incoherence in any public law or constitution that permitted a right of rebellion, for it would
thereby tacitly declare that the supreme legislative authority is
not supreme.[160] This reasoning is comparable to Kant's assertion that the sovereign cannot be subject to legal constraints
because that would be tantamount to admitting a sovereign
over the sovereign. It is also just as wrongheaded. Within any
particular jurisdiction, a supreme legislative body must, admit-
tedly, possess supreme lawmaking power; that much is probably analytic, even tautological. But, as I argued earlier, a
sovereign legislative body need not be legally omnipotent: it
can be subject to law in the sense that it may derive its authority from a constitution that may limit its authority in various
ways. For a constitution to permit a right of revolution would
not be for it to acknowledge, even tacitly, a higher *lawmaking*
authority than the sovereign legislative authority. A right of

[159] Beck 1971, 414.
[160] I am not aware of any national constitutions that allow a right of rebellion, but several state constitutions in America—specifically, Virginia,
Pennsylvania, New Hampshire, and Delaware—have at one time or another recognized a right of rebellion when governments become oppressive.
See Cairns 1949, 452; Gray 1988, 22.

revolution is not a right to legislate, but a right, among other things, to overthrow the current legislator(s). Such a right, because it is *not* a right to create laws, may, if it is contained in a constitution binding on the highest legislative body, be logically consistent with that body's claim to be the highest lawmaking authority. Once more, therefore, Kant has failed to provide compelling reasons against a legal right of revolution.

Kant's final argument, from *Theory and Practice*, is more persuasive.[161] He begins with the premise that the "head of state" (*Staatsoberhaupt*)—which here means the highest executive authority, though elsewhere[162] Kant uses the same term to refer to the highest legislative authority—is the person "through whom alone the rightful coercion of all others can be exercised."[163] It follows that the head of state cannot himself be subject to legal coercion: "For if he too could be coerced, he would not be the head of state."[164] This time the contradiction Kant believes he has uncovered is real. If we assume, as is probably analytic, that the use of coercion for the purpose of enforcing laws is exclusively an executive function, and that the highest executive authority in a state directly or indirectly controls all legal uses of coercion (for example, through his power to appoint and dismiss subordinate executive officials), then the highest executive authority cannot itself be subject to legal coercion, since no other authority could be empowered to use coercion against it. A legal right of revolution, however, would be a legal right to use coercion against the highest executive authority, and because that is legally impossible there can be no such legal right. This does not mean that the powers of the chief executive cannot be restricted in any way. Kant rightly

[161] TL 291.
[162] *Reflexion* 7971, Ak XIX, 567. The explanation for this confusing use of *Staatsoberhaupt* appears to be that Kant finds it a convenient way of referring to monarchs who possess supreme legislative and executive powers.
[163] TP 291\75.
[164] TP 291\75.

holds that the chief executive or ruler is "subject to law," just as are all private citizens.[165] Kant's point is that the chief executive cannot be subject to legal coercion, and that if he violates the laws of the state, the only legal remedy is for the sovereign legislator to "depose" him and strip him of his authority.[166]

Although Kant does not mention it, there is another, closely connected reason why a legal right of revolution would be impossible. Recall our earlier discussion of the right of passive disobedience to unjust laws. I indicated then that this could not be a legal right because it could not be legally enforced. The same is true of a legal right of revolution. The final responsibility for enforcing laws and legal rights, by physical coercion if necessary, belongs to the chief executive. If there were a legal right of revolution, the chief executive would, in the last resort, bear responsibility for its enforcement. However, to require the chief executive to enforce a right of revolution would be to require him to enforce a right against himself, and if need be, to coerce himself pursuant to his duty to ensure compliance with a legally guaranteed right. It makes no sense, though, to speak of enforcing a right against oneself, or of being required to do so. Still less does it make sense to speak of coercing oneself, or of having a legal obligation to coerce oneself. The idea of coercion does not lend itself to this kind of reflexivity, nor does the idea of an enforceable right. So there can be no legally enforceable right of revolution, and if we follow Kant in believing that all legal rights must in principle be enforceable, we must concede that the idea of a legal right of revolution is incoherent.[167]

I return now to Beck's implication that Kant begs the question whether there is a moral right of revolution. We should have no difficulty concluding that he has not. Kant's theory of

[165] RL 317.
[166] RL 317.
[167] RL 232.

justice is an ideal theory of law, a theory of the rights and duties that should form the basis of a fully just legal system.[168] This means two things: first that rights and duties of justice are coercive; second that they must be enforceable through legal channels.[169] A right of revolution, however, could not be enforced by legal coercion; so it could not be a right of justice. The only other alternative within Kant's moral theory would be for it to be an ethical right, but that is also impossible. Ethical rights correspond to ethical duties, which are voluntary and unenforceable duties to adopt ends. Ethical rights, though never explicitly defined by Kant, must therefore be rights to the performance of voluntary ethical duties. Accordingly, they cannot be coercive rights, because one cannot coercively enforce voluntary duties. It follows that there can be no ethical right of revolution.[170]

Clearly, therefore, there can be no moral right of revolution in the existing framework of Kant's moral theory. Kant's reasons for rejecting a right of revolution are neither arbitrary nor superficial, but are deeply rooted in his understanding of the nature of ethical and juridical rights. Ethical rights exclude a right of revolution because they are not coercive rights; juridical rights exclude a right of revolution because the coercion they allow must in principle be capable of being administered through a legal system. If we accept Kant's method of dividing all moral rights and duties into ethical and juridical categories, along with his conception of the nature of ethical and juridical rights, we must therefore also accept his conclusion that there cannot be a moral right of revolution.

---

[168] RL 229, 305–6, 313.

[169] RL 231–32.

[170] The impossibility of an ethical right of revolution is grounded on the same fact that makes an ethical right of passive disobedience possible. A right of revolution implies a right to use coercion. All coercive rights are rights of justice (RL 232; TL 383). Therefore a right of revolution cannot be an ethical right. But a right of passive disobedience is not a right to use coercion. So it can be an ethical right.

At this stage we have two alternatives: we may accept Kant's conclusion that there can be no moral right of revolution or we may reject the premises that force this conclusion upon him. The first alternative will have very little appeal to contemporary minds. Just as the time has passed when one could defend slavery and expect to be given a serious hearing, so too (and for many of the same reasons) has the time passed when one could expect to be taken seriously while arguing that rebellion against unjust governments is never morally defensible. If such a position ever had any plausibility, that could only have been in more naive times.

We must consequently reject one or more of the premises that forced this conclusion upon Kant. The crux of the problem is that Kant holds two beliefs that cannot consistently be maintained if we are to accept a right of revolution. He holds (1) that the "essential" distinction between justice and ethics is that juridical rights and duties are enforceable through coercion whereas ethical rights and duties must be voluntarily self-imposed.[171] Kant also believes (2) that a theory of justice is an ideal theory of law, and hence that all rights of justice should in principle be legally enforceable. These beliefs are consistent with each other, but are jointly inconsistent with the fact that force is the medium of revolution and therefore that a right of revolution must be a coercive right. (1) entails that a right of revolution must be a right of justice. (2) entails that a right of revolution cannot be a right of justice, because no right of revolution could be legally enforced. To escape this contradiction, we must abandon (1) or (2). Abandoning (1) would mean removing the central pillar of Kant's taxonomy of rights and duties. It would imperil Kant's distinction between justice and ethics, throwing much of his moral theory into confusion. It is better to abandon (2), for (2) is not as central to Kant's moral theory as (1).

[171] TL 383.

This alteration is a significant but not fatal revision of Kant's theory of justice. We can still conceive of a theory of justice *primarily*, though not exclusively, as an ideal theory of law. We can also still retain Kant's central principle that the essential difference between ethics and justice is that rights and duties of justice, in contrast with ethical rights and duties, are enforceable through coercion. All rights and duties of justice will still be enforceable through coercion, though not every right of justice will be enforceable through legal coercion. There will instead be at least one right of justice that must be enforced against legal systems rather than through them.

CHAPTER FIVE

Justice and Social Welfare

Each of the previous chapters dealt with a variety of connected issues. This chapter attempts to answer only one question: How does Kant understand the relation among justice, the state, and the satisfaction of human needs? Most Kant scholars accept what I will call the "minimalist interpretation," which holds that the proper function of the state, according to Kant, is to protect individual liberty, to enforce contracts, and to prevent fraud, but involves very little else. The minimalist interpretation further holds that Kant disapproves of social welfare legislation, except insofar as it may be instrumentally necessary to ensure the stability of the state— for instance, during times of revolutionary upheaval or economic crisis. The minimalist interpretation, in short, pictures Kant as a theorist of the night watchman state.

Defenders of the minimalist interpretation include Jeffrie Murphy, Bruce Aune, Mary Gregor, Morris Cohen, as well as Howard Williams (though Williams's reading of Kant is more nuanced and ambiguous than the rest).[1] Aune's account of the Kantian state and its relation to social welfare legislation is representative:

[1] Gregor 1963, 35–36; Aune 1979, 156–59; Cohen 1950, 105–27; Murphy

Although Kant insists that the end to be promoted by public law is not the happiness of citizens but a "juridical condition" that ensures and protects their rights (or lawful liberty), he claims that end can only be realized in a stable, enduring social order. To ensure that the state or civil society is stable, "strong enough to resist foreign enemies," and able to maintain itself as a community, the lawmaker may pass laws that do contribute to the prosperity of the people. . . . What we should call "welfare legislation" is therefore justifiable, according to Kant, when and only when it is necessary for the continued existence of civil society.[2]

This view of the Kantian state needs revision—not with respect to the idea that Kant sees the primary responsibility of the state as protecting individual rights and liberties (that is doubtless true), but rather in connection with the dogma that Kant is hostile to social welfare legislation unless it can be justified as instrumentally necessary for the preservation of the state. After we examine the issues carefully, it will be clear that Kant's final view is that, quite apart from instrumental considerations relating to its own stability, the state has a moral responsibility to ensure the well-being of its citizens. On the interpretation I recommend, therefore, Kant is no advocate of the night watchman state.

1970, 109, 144–46; Williams 1983, 196–98. Harry van der Linden's recent book, published after this chapter was written, has some points of contact with the view I develop here. Ultimately, however, van der Linden also sees Kant as a supporter of the minimal state, which is the view I argue against (van der Linden 1988, vii, 35, 38, 76–77, especially 157–63).

[2] Aune 1979, 157.

The Minimalist Interpretation

In many ways the minimalist interpretation seems textually well-grounded. It represents the commonsense interpretation of Kant's position, and I concede at the outset that the burden of proof lies with anyone who would reject it. Before I criticize it, therefore, I want to bring out its strong points so as to explain why it is so often accepted.

A number of factors make the minimalist interpretation seem not merely reasonable, but compelling. To start with, there is Kant's analysis of the concept of justice in the *Rechtslehre*, much of which will be familiar from Chapter 1. On Kant's view, justice is not concerned with any individual's "wishes or desires (or even . . . his needs)."[3] Justice is concerned exclusively with the "form of the relationship between wills insofar as they are regarded as free, and whether the action of one of them can be conjoined with the freedom of the other in accordance with a universal law."[4] Similar language recurs in some of Kant's shorter essays, especially in *Theory and Practice*, where he says that justice "has nothing to do with the end which all men have by nature (the aim of achieving happiness)," but consists rather in "the restriction of each individual's freedom so that it harmonizes with the freedom of everyone else (insofar as this is possible within the terms of a general law)."[5] Kant's point is that although justice requires individuals to restrict their freedom for the purpose of making it compatible with the freedom of all others within the terms of a law governed society, it does not require anyone to provide for the needs or desires of anyone else. This fact alone, one might reasonably conclude, is enough to show that social welfare leg-

---

[3] RL 230.
[4] RL 230.
[5] TP 289–90\73.

islation cannot, according to Kant, be grounded in principles of justice.

More support for the minimalist interpretation seems to come from Kant's hostility to paternalistic laws.[6] Paternalistic legislation directed only toward making citizens happy is severely condemned by Kant.[7] To the extent that it involves treating individuals as "immature children who cannot distinguish what is truly useful or harmful to themselves," legislation of this kind produces the "greatest conceivable despotism," for it takes away an individual's most basic right—her right to pursue her own ends so long as they do not contravene laws of justice.[8]

Further evidence in favor of the minimalist interpretation seems to come from Kant's belief that the variability and indeterminacy of the concept of happiness render it unfit to serve as a basis for legislation. No two individuals have quite the same needs or desires, and since on Kant's reckoning happiness is no more than the satisfaction of the largest consistent set of an individual's desires, there can be no universal or objective content to the concept of happiness.[9] Because the concept of happiness is infinitely variable—one person's meat being another's poison—it lacks the sort of universality Kant regards as essential for ethical or judicial legislation.[10]

The case for the minimalist view already appears quite strong. Still more, however, can be said for it. The idea that the state ought not, all things being equal, to engage in social welfare activities seems to follow naturally enough from Kant's taxonomy of duties. Kant, as we have seen, divides duties into

---

[6] Aune and Williams both understand Kant's opposition to paternalism as involving that the state ought not to make laws intended to promote the happiness of citizens, except for the instrumental reasons already discussed. See Aune 1979, 159; Williams 1983, 196–97.

[7] TP 290–91, 298\74, 80.

[8] TP 291\74.

[9] E.g., KPV 73; G 399, 405; TP 290–91\74. See also Chapter 2.

[10] TP 298\80.

two main categories: duties of justice, which require the performance or omission of external actions, and duties of virtue, which demand the adoption of specific ends of goals.[11] The state can only regulate external actions; it cannot compel anyone to adopt an end. An end, by hypothesis, is a goal that an individual freely chooses.[12] Kant, however, classifies the duty of benevolence as a duty of virtue, so it follows directly that the state cannot enforce duties of benevolence. Yet the duty of benevolence is our only duty to promote the well-being or happiness of others. It appears, therefore, that the state has no license to tax or otherwise coerce any group of citizens for the purpose of aiding members of any other group, and this would seem to rule out social welfare legislation.[13]

The final point in support of the minimalist interpretation, like the preceding one, has to do with how Kant draws the boundaries of legitimate state interference with individual freedom. Near the beginning of the *Rechtslehre*, Kant introduces the "first principle of law," the rule that coercion is justified when it is necessary to prevent interference with the legitimate liberty of others.[14] Some of Kant's interpreters believe that the first principle of law is the *only* principle he accepts in justification of governmental coercion.[15] If that were so, it would follow that Kant should hold that the state is not entitled to coerce some citizens merely for the purpose of *improving* the lives of others.

My survey of the evidence in favor of the minimalist interpretation is now complete. All sides recognize that Kant is prepared to tolerate social welfare legislation under special circumstances, such as when the security and stability of the state require it for instrumental reasons to ensure the well-

[11] TL 382, 288–89, 406–7.
[12] TL 381, 384–85.
[13] Gregor accepts roughly this line of reasoning (Gregor 1963, 35–36).
[14] RL 231; TL 396.
[15] Murphy 1970, 94–95, 109, 144.

being of its subjects. The relevant text on this question is from *Theory and Practice:* "If the supreme power makes laws which are primarily directed toward happiness (the affluence of the citizens, increased population etc.) this cannot be regarded as the end for which a civil constitution was established, but only as a means of *securing the rightful state,* especially against the external enemies of the people."[16] Only in the context of ensuring the stability of security of the state, Kant seems unequivocally to say, is social welfare legislation justifiable. Taking into account all of the previous evidence we have examined, this passage appears to make the minimalist interpretation unassailable.

The evidence indeed seems overwhelming. Justice is not concerned with the welfare of individuals. Paternalistic legislation aimed at the happiness of the people must be prohibited. The concept of happiness is too indeterminate to serve as a basis for legislation. The state is not permitted or able to enforce duties of benevolence. The first principle of law does not license the state to tax or otherwise coerce some citizens merely for the benefit of others. The state may pass social welfare legislation only when such laws are instrumentally necessary for its own stability. All of these claims can be found in Kant, and together they certainly make the minimalist interpretation, the prima facie correct understanding of Kant's view of the responsibilities of the state.

A Different Analysis

Consider some of the evidence in favor of a quite different reading of Kant's position. Two sets of remarks especially, one

---

[16] TP 298\80.

from the *Rechtslehre*, the other from *Perpetual Peace*, spell trouble for the minimalist interpretation. The *Rechtslehre* passage begins: "Indirectly, inasmuch as he takes over the duty of the people, the supreme commander possesses the right to levy taxes on them for their own preservation, in particular, for the relief of the poor, foundling hospitals, and churches; in other words, for what are generally called charitable and pious institutions."[17] Kant says that rulers take over a duty from the people. Presumably, the duty he has in mind is benevolence; no other duty fits the description.[18] Kant, we must further assume, does not mean that when a ruler takes over this duty from the people, private individuals are thereby discharged from their duties of benevolence. Kant's moral theory does not suppose that others can relieve us of duties imposed on us by categorical imperatives. Therefore, if this text is to be understood as consistent with Kant's ethical theory, we must interpret Kant as claiming that the ruler's duty of benevolence is derived from, without reducing or eliminating, private citizens' duties of benevolence.

A second point to notice about the quoted passage is that, corresponding to the ruler's duty of benevolence, there is a right to levy taxes for the preservation of the people. This right is derived "indirectly" from the people's duty of benevolence, and as the passage continues Kant attempts to explain the origin of this duty and the corresponding right:

The general Will of the people has united itself into a society in order to maintain itself continually, and for this purpose it has subjected itself to the internal authority of the state in order to support those members of society who are unable to support themselves. Therefore it follows from the nature of the

[17] RL 325–26.
[18] TL 393–94.

state that the government is authorized to require the wealthy to provide the means of substance to those who are unable to provide the most necessary needs of nature for themselves.[19]

Kant's reasoning here is not altogether transparent. As an advocate of the minimalist interpretation, Murphy suggests that although "we may applaud this rare instance of benevolence on Kant's part, it is by no means clear that this view is consistent with his general theory."[20] Williams similarly finds it difficult to reconcile this argument with Kant's general view, though he is more chary than Murphy of accusing Kant of inconsistency.[21] With considerable implausibility, Aune reads the argument as supporting his belief that Kant is willing to countenance social welfare legislation only when the continued existence of the state requires such laws.[22] With regard to Aune, however, we must note that what is in question is a duty of benevolence on the part of rulers toward the people, not a duty to ensure the existence of the state, which would be quite another matter; for, as Kant remarks on another occasion, the "well-being of the state must not be confused with the happiness or welfare of the citizens of the state."[23] Without reading the quoted remarks tendentiously, trying to squeeze them into an interpretive framework they do not fit, there is no reason to interpret them as asserting that the survival of the state requires it to accept a duty of benevolence toward its subjects.

How, then, should we understand Kant's argument? The most straightforward reading is as follows. The general Will creates civil society for a specific purpose: its own preservation. Insofar as the general Will is the united Will of an assemblage of individual wills, ensuring its own preservation

[19] RL 326.
[20] Murphy 1970, 144–45.
[21] Williams 1983, 196–98.
[22] Aune 1979, 157.
[23] RL 318.

necessitates ensuring their preservation. The nature of the state, therefore, as a society formed for the purpose of preserving the general Will, gives it the right to tax the rich for the sake of maintaining the existence of the poor. The trouble with this argument is not that it is obviously unsound, but that it is too abstract, too sketchy, and too short on details to be persuasive. Granting, for instance, that the general Will wills its own preservation as a condition of the formation of political society, why does the preservation of the general Will require the preservation of each of its components—each individual citizen? Surely the existence of the general Will would not be threatened by the death of one or two citizens; otherwise it would cease to exist each time a citizen dies, which is clearly not Kant's view.

Problems of this sort indicate that the argument must be recast if it is to be successful. Later in this chapter, I suggest how it may be fleshed out, but for the moment my main objective is to understand Kant's position rather than to claim that it is correct or even defensible. As far as understanding Kant's position is concerned, what is evident from his remarks in the *Rechtslehre* is that he believes rulers have a duty of benevolence, grounded in the *nature* of the state, though not in *its* needs, to ensure the survival of their subjects.

These remarks in the *Rechtslehre* are not the only ones of their kind. Toward the end of *Perpetual Peace* Kant introduces two versions, one negative, one positive, of what he calls the "principle of publicity." The negative principle of publicity is designed to identify maxims that are morally unfit to serve as principles of public or international law.[24] According to this principle, a maxim is inconsistent with "public right" if its publication would arouse such general opposition that its purpose would thereby be defeated. Contrasting with the negative principle of publicity, as a test of maxims that are not consis-

[24] ZEF 381\125–26.

tent with justice, is the positive principle of publicity, whose purpose is to identify maxims that are not only consistent with but also promote the interests of justice. The positive principle of publicity asserts that "All maxims which *require* publicity if they are not to fail in their purpose can be reconciled both with right and politics."[25] Lacking further details, this principle would be difficult to apply. As with many of Kant's moral rules, it errs on the side of abstractness. Fortunately, Kant provides his own gloss: maxims satisfying this rule will be those that "conform to the universal aim of the public (which is happiness)."[26] Promoting this objective, Kant goes on to say, is the "particular task of politics," and the purpose of the positive principle of publicity is to facilitate the accomplishment of this task.[27]

Advocates of the minimalist interpretation routinely ignore the positive principle of publicity. Small wonder: it amounts

----

[25] ZEF 386\130. The positive and negative principles of publicity indicate Kant's unusual interest in the notion of publicity (*Öffentlichkeit*), an idea that I discussed earlier in connection with Kant's distinction between public and private uses of reason. The explanation for Kant's interest in the idea of publicity is that he considers it to be intimately connected with the idea of rationality. Kant believes that publicity and rationality are inextricably linked because the "verdict of reason" on any particular issue is simply "the agreement of free citizens" who are allowed to discuss questions openly in the public arena without censorship or intimidation (KRV A738–52/B766–80). The voice of reason is ultimately, therefore, the voice of public opinion when it crystallizes into unanimous agreement as a result of open and informed debate. This point applies also to morally practical reason. The function of the categorical imperative in Kant's ethical theory is to determine whether private and personal maxims of action can also be made into publicly disclosed laws of conduct for all rational beings. If maxims cannot be taken out of the secret realm of private choice and brought into the public domain for all to act on, they are morally prohibited. I cannot discuss Kant's understanding of publicity in more detail here without digressing too far from our main topic. The interested reader is, however, referred to Habermas 1976 and O'Neill 1986 for probing analyses of Kant's concept of publicity.

[26] ZEF 386\130.

[27] ZEF 386\130.

to the rule that maxims are fit to serve as public laws if their adoption as laws would promote the happiness of all citizens.[28] The moral status of the positive principle of publicity, however, is still not clear. We need to know in particular whether Kant intends it as an obligatory or merely optional test of public laws. Just before Kant formulates this principle he introduces it by noting that "both aspects [of morality], philanthropy and respect for the rights of man are obligatory. And while the former is only a conditional duty, the latter is an unconditional, absolutely imperative one."[29] Kant does not usually speak of a duty of philanthropy (*Menschenliebe*), so this comes as a bit of a surprise, but he soon identifies it with "morality . . . as ethics," indicating that he has in mind the ethical duty of benevolence.[30] The upshot, then, is that in Kant's view both the duty of benevolence and respect for human rights are obligatory in politics.

When Kant says that philanthropy or benevolence is a conditional duty, while respect for human rights is an unconditional one, he implies that there is a priority of the right over the good. In the domain of politics, therefore, as in private morality, there is an obligation to promote the happiness of one's fellow citizens, but this obligation must always take a back seat to the scrupulous observance of rights.[31] Making use of Dworkin's vocabulary, the matter is best put by saying that although both obligations are genuine, the duty to respect individual rights always trumps the duty of benevolence when they come into conflict.

---

[28] ZEF 386\130.

[29] ZEF 385\129.

[30] ZEF 386\130.

[31] ZEF 385–86\129–30. There is an obvious resemblance between this view and Rawls's "lexical" ordering of the two principles of justice. The principle of equal liberty has an "absolute weight," for Rawls, whereas the difference principle, though also an obligatory rule of justice, can be applied only when it does not infringe the former rule (Rawls 1971, 42–43, 60–63, 244–45).

All of this suggests clearly enough that Kant thinks governments have a duty of benevolence toward their subjects. The
positive principle of publicity is designed to serve as a test that
rulers may use to determine which policies and laws best fulfill
their obligations to promote public happiness, thus furthering
the "particular aim of politics." Even more than the *Rechtslehre* passages, the positive principle of publicity is a square peg
for the minimalist interpretation. Both the *Rechtslehre* texts
and this principle impose duties of benevolence on rulers, but
the positive principle of publicity is more expansive than the
Rechtslehre passages insofar as it imposes a general duty to promote the happiness of citizens instead of a limited duty to see
only to their most basic needs.

After setting out the positive principle of publicity, Kant
states that he must "postpone the further elaboration and discussion of this principle until another occasion."[32] Apparently
that occasion never arrived, for Kant never again discussed it
explicitly. Yet it may not be unreasonable to see the *Rechtslehre* passages as a restricted application of the duty of benevolence for which the positive principle of publicity is intended
to serve as a test, for they do in fact specify a restricted form of
the general duty of benevolence underlying the positive principle of publicity. Far from being inconsistent, therefore, the
Rechtslehre passages and the positive principle of publicity
complement each other.

Both versions of the principle of publicity have a fairly obvious ancestry in Kant's moral theory: they are mirror images of
Kant's two versions of the principle of the end in itself, or as he
sometimes calls it, the principle of humanity. The negative
principle of humanity requires us not to treat others solely as
means to our own ends, but rather to respect individuals as
ends in themselves, which Kant interprets as meaning, to repeat what I wrote in Chapter 2, that one should not interfere

[32] ZEF 386\130.

with the rights, property, or legitimate freedom of others. Going beyond this merely negative demand, the positive principle of humanity obliges us actively to promote the permissible ends of others; in other words, to recognize a duty of benevolence.[33]

The negative principle of publicity has much the same purpose as the negative principle of humanity. Kant supposes that if a maxim cannot be publicized without arousing such "general" opposition that its purpose would thereby be defeated, the opposition provoked by the maxim must indicate that its aim involves violating the rights and legitimate liberties of others, which is why it would be unfit to serve as a public law or governmental policy.[34] Similarly, the positive principle of publicity corresponds to the positive principle of humanity. Both involve duties of benevolence. The difference between them is just that the duty of benevolence specified by the positive principle of humanity is an obligation imposed on private individ-

---

[33] G 423, 430; TL 393–94.

[34] The negative principle of publicity requires a more detailed examination than is possible here. One or two potential misunderstandings, however, should be addressed briefly. It may seem naive to suppose that a maxim or law that arouses general opposition must infringe individual rights. After all, individuals often oppose measures that run contrary to their interests even when their rights are not threatened, and majorities often oppose policies aimed at the preservation of minority rights even when justice is on the side of the minority. Has Kant failed to notice these elementary points, or has he committed the fallacy of accepting public opinion as an arbiter of right and wrong? To assume that Kant has made these errors is to misinterpret him. The "general" opposition Kant refers to is not the opposition of the many or of the majority. It is the "necessary" and "*a priori* foreseeable" opposition of "everyone" (ZEF 381\126). It is, in other words, the *rational* opposition of an entire population. How such rational opposition is to be interpreted remains problematic. I shall not pursue the matter further at the moment, other than to note that it should be understood in light of the rational ends connected with Kant's social contract principle. What seems clear, in any case, is that Kant is neither turning public opinion into a test of justice nor confusing rights with interests. He is rather suggesting, as he also does in his discussion of the social contract, that laws are unjust when they conflict with universally valid rational ends.

uals to promote the well-being of other private individuals, while the duty of benevolence with which the positive principle of publicity is concerned is an obligation on the part of governments to promote the well-being of their subjects by adopting laws and policies appropriate to that purpose.

What distinguishes these two pairs of principles is not, therefore, any divergence of purposes. They are differentiated instead by their domains of application. The positive and negative principles of humanity are intended to apply only to the sphere of private morality, whereas the positive and negative principles of publicity are meant to provide *criteria for* applying the former principles *to the domain of politics and law.* The negative principle of publicity serves as a test of maxims that infringe individual rights and liberties, thus providing a means of discriminating between just and unjust laws. The positive principle of publicity functions as a criterion by which rulers can determine whether a maxim, if made into a law, would be a suitable application of their duties of benevolence toward their subjects.

To sum up the results of this section, we have seen that there is strong evidence to suggest that Kant recognizes a duty on the part of governments to promote the happiness and well-being of their subjects. Kant does not specify the policies that must be pursued to fulfil this duty, but he does provide criteria that he believes are capable of settling such a question.

Reassessing the Minimalist Interpretation

One option at this stage would be to conclude that Kant is grossly inconsistent. On one hand, the minimalist interpretation seems textually well-grounded. On the other, there is substantial evidence that Kant believes governments have a noninstrumental duty to promote the happiness of their subjects. The result appears to be a dilemma: both interpretations cannot be right, so we must either suppose Kant has no consistent position concerning the normative responsibilities of governments, or we must choose between the two conflicting interpretations. As a matter of interpretive charity we should not accuse Kant of inconsistency unless necessary. Although we cannot entirely avoid the conclusion that there was some waffling and confusion in Kant's position as his views developed over time (about which more later), the charge of gross inconsistency can be fended off successfully. The way to do so is to see that the evidence in support of the minimalist interpretation, strong as it appears, is almost entirely illusory.

Recall that six pieces of evidence seemed to lend credibility to the minimalist interpretation.

(1) On Kant's view, it is said, the state is entitled to use coercion only when the first principle of law allows it to do so. Since the first principle of law justifies the use of coercion only to prevent one person from interfering with the lawful liberty of another, it does not permit governments to tax some citizens merely for the benefit of others.

(2) Kant is firmly opposed to paternalistic legislation, and therefore to laws aimed only at promoting the well-being of citizens, except when the security needs of the state dictate otherwise.

(3) The variability and indeterminacy of the concept of happiness, Kant believes, render it unfit to serve as a basis for public laws.

(4) Kant's division of duties rules out allowing the state to enforce duties of benevolence; hence governments are not allowed to compel individuals to contribute to the welfare of others.

(5) The concept of justice is the foundation of all morally acceptable public laws, and this concept, in Kant's view, has nothing to do with the needs or desires of individuals.

(6) In *Theory and Practice*, Kant explicitly rejects social welfare legislation unless it is instrumentally necessary as a means of ensuring the security of the state.

I will take up these claims seriatim. The first point is the weakest piece of evidence in favor of the minimalist interpretation. It is, in fact, completely without merit, for Kant *never* says that the use of coercion is justified *only* by the first principle of law. This idea is contradicted by the *Rechtslehre* passages in which Kant employs a quite different rationale to justify taxes on wealthy citizens for the benefit of the poor. Similarly, when Kant explains the juridical basis of property taxes, he appeals not to the first principle of law, but to the ruler's "supreme proprietorship" of the land, which seems to have little to do with the first principle of law.[35] More generally, Kant holds that any legislation produced by the general Will of the people in a representative legislature is ipso facto just, and there is no indication whatsoever that he intends to restrict the legislative volitions of the general Will by the constraint that they must not go beyond the first principle of law.[36] As a republican, Kant does of course believe that there must be constitutional limits on the powers of the state; nowhere, though, does he suggests that this is one of them.

The next point has considerably more initial plausibility. Certainly Kant rejects paternalistic legislation, because he sees it as a violation of the individual's right to pursue his own ends as he himself wishes. He objects in particular to laws that impose a specific conception of the good on unwilling citizens, as is shown by a passage I quoted earlier from *Theory and Practice* that serves as the basis for part of the principle of civil freedom: "No one can compel me to be happy in accordance with his conception of the welfare of others, for each may seek his hap-

[35] RL 325.
[36] Cf. RL 313–14.

piness in whatever way he sees fit, so long as he does not infringe on the freedom of others to pursue a similar end."[37] No
doubt, Kant means to repudiate paternalism, but does it follow
that all social welfare legislation is morally repugnant? Evidently, Williams thinks so. Commenting on the *Rechtslehre*
passages in which Kant says that rulers have a duty to provide
for the most elementary needs of their citizens, Williams asks
rhetorically: "Does not this reflect a strong paternalistic attitude which elsewhere he [Kant] strongly rejects?"[38] The answer
is: no. It is one thing to act paternalistically by *imposing* a
conception of his own welfare on an unwilling recipient; it is
quite another to promote someone's welfare by granting him
entitlements to benefits he may make use of *as he sees fit*.
The duty of benevolence, according to Kant, is a duty to promote the ends *of* others. As long as social welfare legislation
does not force individuals to accept dubious "benefits" they do
not want, being limited instead to providing entitlements to
goods or services, it cannot be regarded as paternalistic. It is,
therefore, a non sequitur to suppose that a prohibition against
forcing people to accept benefits they do *not* want is simultaneously a prohibition against providing them with benefits
they *do* want.

Perhaps part of the reason some interpreters have fallen into
the same trap as Williams is that Kant describes paternalism as
being based on the "principle of benevolence" (*Prinzip des
Wohlwollens*).[39] A moment's reflection, though, will establish
that this principle cannot be equated with the duty of benevolence that Kant says governments have in relation to their subjects. The former rule attempts to force a conception of the
good on an unwilling citizenry. The latter duty requires rulers
to promote the common good in a nonpaternalistic manner

[37] TP 290–91\74.
[38] Williams 1983, 197.
[39] TP 290–91\74.

that does not infringe any individual's rights. To *ensure* that
this duty of benevolence does not infringe individual rights
Kant specifies that it is the second of an ordered pair of duties,
the first of which, respect for individual rights, always has
priority.[40] Consequently, although it may be regrettable that
Kant uses the same word (*Wohlwollens*) in both contexts, the
principle of benevolence is wholly unlike, indeed very much opposed to, the duty of benevolence.

Kant's views concerning the indeterminancy and variability
of happiness can be dealt with in a similar fashion. Kant says
that "No generally valid principle of legislation can be based on
happiness. For . . . the highly fluctuating and variable *illusions*
as to what happiness is . . . make all fixed principles impossible, so that happiness *alone* can never be a suitable principle of
legislation" (emphasis added).[41] The point here is relatively
simple, and should be familiar to any student of Kant's moral
philosophy. Kant is not an objectivist about happiness. He does
not believe that there is any definite set of goods the having of
which is sufficient to guarantee happiness. Quite the opposite,
he has a decidedly subjectivistic conception of happiness, as I
indicated in Chapter 2. To be happy, for Kant, is to have the
largest consistent set of one's inclinations satisfied—allowing
possibly for some weighting function that orders desires by
their relative importance to the agent.[42] Insofar as different individuals have different sets of desires, only illusions and tyranny can result from the supposition that there is any
intersubjectively valid content to the concept of happiness.

None of this, however, entails that governments ought not to
concern themselves with the well-being or happiness of citizens; nor that they may not have a duty in that regard. All that

[40] ZEF 386\130.
[41] TP 298\80.
[42] TP 298\80; G 399. See Chapter 2.

follows from Kant's subjectivism about happiness is that due to its variability and indeterminacy the concept of happiness cannot *alone* serve as a principle of legislation; for by itself it cannot provide any information as to *how* the happiness of different individuals may effectively be promoted. This question can be answered only by the individual concerned, because only she knows her own subjective ends and preferences. Therefore, if social welfare legislation is to be based on the duty of benevolence, it must be firmly grounded on the actual wishes and goals of individuals, not on a government's conception of what those ends ought to be according to some normative view of human happiness or well-being.

So much for the closely connected problems of paternalism and the indeterminacy of happiness. Consider next the suggestion that Kant's taxonomy of duties precludes the state from having a duty of benevolence toward its citizens. Remember that the reason adduced in support of this contention was that the duty of benevolence is a duty to adopt an end, but that insofar as the adoption of ends must be a voluntary matter, incapable of being enforced by the state, such a duty cannot be a concern of governments. Again, though, this conclusion is a non sequitur. The state cannot force any individual to accept a duty of benevolence, because this duty requires the voluntary adoption of an end from the motive of duty.[43] Nevertheless, such a prohibition does not imply that the state may not have its *own* duty of benevolence, for in Kant's view the state is a moral person, and is thus as capable of having its own moral duties as any other moral agent.[44]

Furthermore, the impossibility of governmental enforcement of individual duties of benevolence establishes only that the state cannot compel private citizens to make benevolence a

[43] TL 381.
[44] RL 343.

voluntary *end*. It does not imply that the state cannot or should not force individuals to perform *actions* that may assist it in fulfilling its own duty of benevolence. Coercion of the latter kind would not count as an attempt to enforce individual duties of benevolence, because those duties require the adoption of ends rather than the performance of specific actions. So although the state cannot enforce any private duties of benevolence, it can compel individuals to contribute to the well-being of their fellow citizens. Therefore, Kant's taxonomy of duties is not incompatible with the idea that the state may have a duty of benevolence toward its subjects.

We arrive now at one of the two reasons for taking the minimalist interpretation seriously—Kant's frequently repeated claim that justice has nothing to do with human happiness.[45] At face value, this claim certainly appears to support the minimalist interpretation. Evidently, it also seems to conflict with Kant's claims in *Perpetual Peace* that benevolence (philanthropy) is obligatory in politics and that it is the "particular task" of politics to promote public happiness. It seems to square badly, too, with Kant's suggestion in the *Rechtslehre* that the general Will confers on rulers a duty of benevolence to provide for the essential needs of their subjects.

Perhaps we should conclude that this reveals a contradiction in Kant's political philosophy. That would be a mistake. Charges of inconsistency are entirely unwarranted. The assumption that there is an inconsistency between these views depends on a tacit premise: that the state has no moral license to do *more* that justice itself might *demand*. Kant never subscribed to such a view. The minimalist interpretation *assumes* that he did without any textual basis for this assumption. Along with many other eighteenth-century philosophers, Kant believed that justice in the strict sense requires no more than

---

[45] E.g., RL 230–31; TP 289\73.

noninterference with the freedom and property of others.[46] Adam Smith advocated a similar view.[47] Kant was part of the same classical, liberal tradition to which Smith belonged. Their basic conceptions of justice hardly differed. However, and this is the important point, holding such a view of justice in no way entails the further consequence that the state can have no responsibilities beyond those required by strict justice. A state unable to do more than enforce strict justice would bear little resemblance to a modern political state. It would be unable to build roads or airports, provide public sanitation or health and educational services, manage disaster relief efforts, or perform any of the myriad other functions of a modern government.[48] Adam Smith never limited the powers of state in this way.[49] Nor is there any evidence that Kant ever considered similar restrictions. On the contrary, he clearly believed that the state should provide many of these services—that it should, for instance, bear the expense of educating its subjects.[50] Since it is unlikely that he would have held this view had he also believed that the powers of the state ought not to extend beyond the enforcement of strict justice, the latter belief is not one we should ascribe to him. Moreover, if we take seriously, as surely we must, the texts in which Kant insists that rulers have a duty of benevolence to their subjects, the appropriate conclusion is

[46] RL 230–31.

[47] Smith, *Moral Sentiments*, 82.

[48] Possibly the response will be that even though strict justice does not require the state to engage in these sorts of activities, they can still be justified by instrumental considerations relating to the security needs of the state. It might be argued, e.g., that a network of roads is necessary for defense purposes, that public health must be protected to ensure a supply of manpower in case of war, and so on. Whether or not an argument along these lines could be made plausible remains to be seen, but it would inevitably depend on empirical premises, many of which are likely to be controversial.

[49] Smith, *Wealth of Nations*, 5:1:1; 5:1:3.

[50] IAG 26\51; SF 92–93\188–89.

that he rejects the idea that the state should do no more than enforce strict justice.

If we take all of this into consideration, then it appears that Kant's conception of justice is not incompatible with his view in *Perpetual Peace* that governments have an ordered set of duties: first, to protect the rights and liberties required by principles of justice; second, to promote the happiness of their subjects as long as that can be done without diminishing their legitimate rights and liberties. We have not yet, however, examined the final point in favour of the minimalist interpretation. I said earlier that it is impossible to exonerate Kant completely of the charge that there are signs of confusion in his views as they developed over time. A prime example is the passage from *Theory and Practice* in which he says that if rulers enact laws mainly "directed toward happiness (the affluence of citizens, increased population etc.), this cannot be regarded as the end for which a civil construction was established, but only as a means of *securing the rightful state*, especially against external enemies of the people."[51] This text certainly lends support to the minimalist interpretation. It also apparently conflicts with the passages from *Perpetual Peace* and the *Rechtslehre* in which Kant claims that governments have a noninstrumental duty to provide for the well-being of their subjects.

Notice, however, that *Theory and Practice* was written in 1793, two years before *Perpetual Peace*, and four years before the *Rechtslehre*. It would not be surprising if Kant's views changed during this period; neither would it be peculiar if he abandoned in these later works a view he had held earlier. So if, as seems reasonable, we take Kant's considered position to be the one set out in these later works, it would hardly count much in favor of the minimalist interpretation that he had once accepted, only to reject later, the view it ascribes to him.

---

[51] TP 298\80.

The situation, though, is not quite this simple. It is important to see that the *Theory and Practice* passage, which is the only text lending any real credibility to the minimalist interpretation, is the product of conflicting tendencies in Kant's thought. In Part Two of *Theory and Practice,* which contains his remark that the state can enact social welfare legislation only when its own security interests require it to do so, Kant is trying to reconcile three different beliefs, without seeing how they can all be held at the same time. He wants to say, first, that the concept of happiness is too variable to provide a basis for juridical laws; second, that governments must not be paternalistic toward their subjects; and, third, that the "doctrine that *salus publica suprema civitatis lex est* [public welfare is the supreme law of the state] retains its value and authority undiminished."[52] Although Kant wishes to retain all of these beliefs, he ends up repudiating the third. When he accepts the doctrine that the public welfare is the supreme law of the state, we expect a generous treatment of the common good. What Kant goes on to do is very different. He claims that the "public welfare that demands *first* consideration lies precisely in that legal constitution which guarantees everyone his freedom within the law, so that each remains free to seek his own happiness in whatever way he thinks best."[53] To this we can have no objection: it represents the core idea of Kant's political philosophy. We expect Kant, however, to discuss next the public good that merits *second* consideration. Instead, he tells us that legislation directed toward the happiness of the public—presumably the object of the second, missing consideration—can *only* be justified by the instrumental needs of the state, which is all but to say that the happiness of the public deserves *no* consideration *in its own right.*

[52] TP 290–91, 298\74, 80.
[53] TP 290\80.

The question is why Kant here backs away from the conclusion toward which he was obviously moving, and which he later accepted in *Perpetual Peace*, that rulers have an ordered set of duties: first to protect individual rights, then to promote the happiness of their subjects? The answer, I think, is connected with a problem we noticed earlier: Kant's unfortunate use of the expression "principle of benevolence" (*Prinzip des Wohlwollens*) to designate the rule, based on objectivist illusions about happiness, that underlies the paternalistic legislation he so vigorously opposed.[54] Nothing could be further from paternalism than a Kantian duty of benevolence. Still, Kant uses the same word in both contexts, and the reason for this, I suggest, is that in *Theory and Practice* Kant does not yet see how he can balance a belief that rulers ought to promote the happiness of the public against both his opposition to paternalism and his view that the concept of happiness cannot provide valid principles of legislation.

These commitments are not inconsistent, as the preceding discussion has shown. Nonetheless it is not hard to see why Kant might have doubted their compatibility, which may go a long way toward explaining his ambivalence in *Theory and Practice* with respect to public welfare legislation, as well as his conclusion that the happiness of citizens can only be an instrumental concern of the state. In *Perpetual Peace* Kant arrived at a solution to this quandary in the shape of the positive principle of publicity. This rule is intended to screen out laws that do not *both* promote the happiness of the public *and* protect individuals against infringements of their legitimate liberties, among which paternalism ranks very high. In *Theory and Practice*, however, Kant had not yet seen his way clear to this solution.

---

[54] TP 290\74.

Provisional Summary

Our reexamination of the minimalist interpretation in the last section has shown that its textual support is very largely a mirage. Only one passage in *Theory and Practice* lends it serious support, and I have argued that this is a transitional text reflecting Kant's unclarity concerning how legislation designed to promote social welfare might be reconciled with his other moral beliefs. If this argument is not fully convincing, however, we may just as easily conclude that Kant's position shifted between *Theory and Practice*, on the one hand, and *Perpetual Peace* and the *Rechtslehre* on the other. In either case, we are left with the conclusion that Kant's considered view, contrary to the minimalist interpretation, includes the belief that governments have an obligation, albeit a conditional one, to promote the well-being and happiness of their subjects.

Why, if this is indeed Kant's position, did he not articulate it more clearly? Part of the answer may well be that here, as elsewhere, Kant is his own worst interpreter. The more specific reply, though, ought to be, as I have already suggested, that it was difficult for Kant to see how, given his opposition to paternalism, in addition to his views concerning the indeterminacy of happiness and its unsuitability as a principle of legislation, he could accept human happiness as a proper goal of politics. Even in the *Rechtslehre* and *Perpetual Peace*, where Kant commits himself to the notion that governments have a duty of benevolence toward their subjects, he never *calls* it by that name. Instead, he writes of the ruler's duty of "philanthropy" or of the ruler taking "over the duty of the people," notwithstanding the fact that he is plainly referring in both cases to a duty of benevolence."[55] This indicates that although his final position committed him to insisting that governments are obligated to

[55] RL 325–26; ZEF 385–86/129–30.

promote the happiness of their citizens, Kant had lingering, if quite unjustified, doubts about whether such a duty was consistent with the rest of his moral-political philosophy. On this point Kant seems to have made exactly the same mistake as advocates of the minimalist interpretation, and for some of the same reasons.

Reconstructing Kant's Argument

Now that Kant's settled position is tolerably clear we can return to the question of *why* he believes that governments have a duty of benevolence toward their subjects, an issue that was left hanging earlier when it became apparent that the *Rechtslehre* argument, in which Kant claims that rulers must provide for the needs of the poor, was problematic. The argument, remember, seemed to be this. Because the general Will wills its own preservation as a condition of the formation of civil society, and because its own preservation requires the preservation of each of its constituent parts, the state has a duty to provide for the basic needs of all its subjects. Hence, the nature of the state, as a society formed for the purpose of ensuring the continued existence of the general Will, gives it a right to tax the wealthy for the benefit of the poor. Recall, also, the problem with this line of thought: it is by no means obvious that the preservation of the general Will requires the preservation of all citizens.

As it stands, therefore, this argument does not seem very satisfactory. Appeals to Kant's claim in *Perpetual Peace* that philanthropy or benevolence is obligatory in politics are also not of much use, for that idea is asserted without benefit of accompanying argument. The difficulty, then, is how a plausible argument in support of the idea that governments have a duty of benevolence toward their subjects can be reconstructed from

Kantian sources. Fortunately, we need not look very far for a solution. The duty under consideration is a duty of benevolence, and just as Kant's principles of publicity have a visible ancestry in the principle of humanity in the *Groundwork*, so too, though in a less obvious way, can the *Rechtslehre* argument be seen as an attempt on Kant's part to adapt his argument for a duty of benevolence in the *Groundwork* to the domain of politics and public policy. In the *Groundwork*, Kant argues that although a maxim of never helping those in need could hold as a universal law of nature,

> it is nevertheless impossible to will that such a principle should hold everywhere as a universal law of nature. For a will that resolved this would conflict with itself, since instances can often arise in which he would need the love and sympathy of others, and in which he would have robbed himself, by such a law of nature springing from his own will of all hope of the aid he desires.[56]

The main idea here is fairly simple. Kant is constructing a reductio ad absurdum of the hypothesis that a rational being might will the universalization of the maxim of never helping others. Kant's argument is roughly as follows. As a rational being, every person necessarily wills that all his present and future needs should be satisfied.[57] No one can be certain that the satisfaction of his future needs will not require the help of others; for even the wealthiest person can never be sure that future reversals of fortune may not bring him to such a pass that his needs can only be met through the aid of others. Hence, insofar as he is rational and self-interested, every person wills that the help of others should be available to him in the event that he

[56] G 423.
[57] Cf. KPV 61.

should need it. But if the maxim of never helping others were universalized, it would be a law of nature that no one would ever help anyone else. Such a law, however, would conflict with the will of every rational being, since every such being wills that aid should be available to him if he should ever need it. Consequently, there would be a contradiction in the will of any rational being who attempted to will the universalization of the maxim of never helping others. The final conclusion is accordingly that because this maxim cannot be universalized, the adoption of its negation, the maxim of sometimes helping those in need, is a moral duty.[58]

The striking point about this argument is how easily it can be adapted to Kant's political philosophy in general and to his social contract theory in particular. Recall from our discussion of the social contract principle in Chapter 4 that Kant believes a law is just whenever an "entire people" can will it without contradicting one of their rationally necessary ends. I noted then that Kant regards freedom as one of the primary rational ends of a human will, but freedom is not the only rational end Kant recognizes. As this argument from the *Groundwork* indicates, Kant also holds that providing for one's own needs is a rationally necessary end.[59]

The connection between the argument in the *Groundwork* for a duty of benevolence and Kant's social contract principle becomes clear as soon as we ask whether an entire people could rationally agree to a positive law that stipulated that the state should do nothing to provide for the needs of citizens or even ensure their survival if they were unable to do so themselves. The argument in the *Groundwork* suggests that the answer is no. Kant claims that insofar as an individual is rational he wills the conditions necessary for the satisfaction of his present and

[58] My interpretation of this argument is similar to O'Neill's account in O'Neill 1975, 87.
[59] KPV 61.

future needs. On the basis of this premise, along with the assumption that no one can ever be certain of being able to supply his own future needs through his own resources, Kant infers that one cannot will the maxim of never helping others as a universal law of nature. If no one can rationally will the maxim of never helping others *as a law of nature,* however, then neither can an entire people rationally will *as a law of political society* that the state should allow them to perish rather than supply their basic needs. The *same* reason that makes it impossible rationally to will the maxim of never helping others as a law of nature also makes it impossible rationally to consent to a law of political society that would permit the state to ignore the basic needs of its citizens. In both cases, the reason is that the law in question would conflict with every individual's rational end of ensuring the conditions necessary for the satisfaction of his present and future needs.

This is the context within which to understand Kant's argument in the *Rechtslehre* that the general Will wills its own preservation as a condition of the formation of civil society. Kant's general Will (*allgemeine Wille*) is the collective rational will of an entire people. Its rational ends are the common rational ends of all citizens. Accordingly, if every citizen rationally wills the conditions necessary for the satisfaction of his present and future needs, that is also what the general Will wills. If the general Will wills its own preservation as a condition of the formation of civil society, that means no more and no less than that every citizen rationally wills his own preservation as a condition of the formation of civil society. Interpreting the *Rechtslehre* argument in this way removes the objection we considered earlier. The argument should not be thought of as involving the dubious claim that the existence of the general Will would be threatened by the loss of a few citizens, but instead that, insofar as the general will is the collective rational will of an entire people, it wills that each of its component parts should be preserved, because that is what each of the individual components of the general Will wills to the extent that each is rational.

When they are understood along the preceding lines, the *Rechtslehre* argument, the *Groundwork* argument for a duty of benevolence, and Kant's social contract principle jointly provide a justification for a duty on the part of governments to do more than merely ensure the survival of their subjects. They also serve to justify the broader duty of benevolence underlying Kant's positive principle of publicity. The *Groundwork* argument suggests that every individual rationally wills the conditions necessary for the satisfaction of her present and future needs. Kant's social contract principle indicates that, since this is a necessary rational end, no just and rational system of positive laws could fail to impose on the state a duty to provide for the needs of its citizens inasmuch as any system of laws that failed to do so would conflict with the rational ends of all citizens. The same point can also be restated by saying that since the rational ends of the general Will are the common rational ends of all citizens, and since the general Will determines the conditions of the formation of civil society, it includes among those conditions the proviso that the state must provide for the needs of its subjects. These needs will of course include the elementary necessities of survival, but they need not be limited to the most basic of human needs. If the state has a general duty to provide for the needs of its subjects, this duty may extend considerably beyond ensuring their continued existence; it may extend also to ensuring their general well-being.

Objections Considered

Various objections might be raised against the interpretation I have been recommending in this chapter. While I cannot now deal with all potential criticisms, one or two deserve immediate attention. In the course of explaining the principle of civil freedom in Chapter 1, I indicated that Kant believes individuals have a right to pursue their own ends without external interference. Earlier in this chapter I also noted that in *Perpetual Peace* Kant commits himself to the view that the state has an ordered pair of duties: first, to protect individual rights and liberties; second, and conditionally upon not violating this first duty, to promote the well-being and happiness of its subjects. The objection to this second duty, and more generally to my claim that Kant recognizes an obligation on the part of governments to provide for the needs of their subjects, is liable to be that such a duty would *inevitably* conflict with the principle of civil freedom and with the first of the duties just mentioned. For, it may be argued, if the state has a duty to provide for the needs of its subjects, it can only fulfil this duty by taxing some citizens for the benefit of others, and this amounts to interfering coercively with the freedom of some individuals to pursue their own ends as they see fit. Consequently, the state cannot perform its duty to provide for the needs of its subjects *except* by infringing the principle of civil freedom and hence also its duty to protect the rights of citizens. The final conclusion would then be that, contrary to what I have been arguing throughout this chapter, there is in fact an inconsistency between Kant's belief that individuals have a right to noninterference with their freedom on condition that they do not interfere with the freedom of others and his belief that the state has a noninstrumental duty to provide for the needs of its subjects.[60]

There are a number of ways of responding to this objection. One is to point out that government revenues need not be derived exclusively from coercive taxation. In principle, as well as in practice, other sources of revenue are available to govern-

---

[60] The objection outlined in this paragraph was suggested separately by Terence Irwin and Richard Moran.

ments,[61] some of which may be used to fund programs directed toward the well-being of citizens. This is a partial answer, and although it is not entirely unpersuasive, it nevertheless fails to confront the objection head on.

A more direct way of dealing with the objection is to question the assumption that taxation in support of welfare programs must inevitably infringe or violate the right of citizens to pursue their own ends. I have interpreted Kant as holding that the state's duty to promote the well-being of its subjects is conditional upon its not interfering with their right to pursue their own ends. The core of the objection to my interpretation is that this condition cannot be met. It can, however, and if we grant Kant one or two assumptions, it can be met quite easily. In a Kantian republic, governments are popularly elected and the policies they adopt, including those concerned with social welfare and taxation, are not, if honestly presented at election time, coercively imposed on an unwilling citizenry. Popularly elected republican governments rule with the consent of the people, according to Kant, even if they are elected only by a simple majority. Their governing by popular consent means that their policies bear the imprint of the popular will. Therefore, if taxation policies in support of programs directed toward the welfare of the public emerge from an electoral process of this sort, they are not, given Kant's assumptions, coercively imposed on an unwilling population. On the contrary, they can be represented, within the context of the liberal conception of electoral consent, as voluntary restrictions imposed by a people on its own freedom. So in the framework of a Kantian republic, governments can fulfill their duty to promote the public welfare without violating the rights of legitimate liberties of their subjects.

---

[61] A short list would include surplus funds from public corporations (e.g., national airlines), the sale of state property (e.g., land, oil leases), and of various kinds of rights (e.g., patent rights), as well as the proceeds from government operated lotteries.

This answer to the initial objection, however, may invite a second one. If a popularly elected legislature is entitled to limit the right of individuals to pursue their own ends by taxing them in order to provide benefits to others, then why, it may be asked, should elected legislatures not also be entitled to pass laws imposing various other more serious and direct restrictions on the right to pursue one's own ends, for instance, a law imposing compulsory servitude on unpopular minorities?[62] Clearly this is not acceptable. But why is it permissible to allow one restriction on civil freedom and not the other? How do we finesse this slippery slope?

Consider the following points. Kant regards the right to pursue one's own ends as a basic constitutional right, along with the rights to legal equality and political freedom. Like all constitutional rights (and all rights in general) it must have boundaries and limits. There cannot be a completely unrestricted right to pursue one's own ends, otherwise civil society would be impossible. Virtually every law imposes some restrictions on individual freedom. That, after all, is what laws are for. Only in the state of nature are there no restrictions on personal liberty, and then there is no effective or secure right to pursue one's own ends because the freedom of every individual is constantly threatened by the freedom of all others. The right to pursue one's own ends within civil society must accordingly have certain limitations. The most obvious ones are those that are necessary to maintain civil society itself, including laws restricting criminal activity, requiring the payment of taxes to support essential governmental services such as courts and police, and so on. These laws inevitably limit the right of individuals to pursue their own ends, but they do not qualify as *violations* of this right, for without them there could *be no* effective or enforceable right to pursue one's ends in civil society. They are consequently not external constraints on, or viola-

---

[62] This objection was suggested by Thomas Pogge.

tions of, the right to pursue one's own ends, but rather *internal* restrictions on it. They demarcate its boundaries so that it is possible to determine which *further* restrictions on personal liberty may count as violations of this right.

My suggestion is that taxation in support of welfare legislation provides an internal limitation on the right to pursue one's own ends, but that unjust policies such as subjecting minorities to servitude are violations of this right. Rights, for Kant, are creations of pure practical reason. All rights must therefore be subject to whatever restrictions are required by practical reason. If reason demands a restriction on a right, that is not a "violation" of the right in question. If it were, we would have to conclude that rights are irrationally demarcated, hardly an appealing or plausible idea, given that one can only demonstrate the existence or boundaries of a right by means of rational argumentation. Rationally required limitations on rights are instead internal limitations: they tell us how far a given right extends, and where it ends.

I have been arguing that if we understand Kant's social contract theory properly, we are led to the conclusion that no people could rationally agree to a constitution that failed to contain a provision guaranteeing (at least) the basic needs of all citizens. Constitutionally guaranteed rights to a minimal level of well-being are thus, on Kantian principles, part of the structure of any just and rational civil society.[63]

This is a perfectly defensible notion. One of the primary purposes of political society must be to ensure the continued survival of its members. As H. L. A. Hart observes in the course of discussing the fundamental principles of political society: "We are committed to" the goal of survival

---

[63] For the sake of brevity I will restrict the present discussion to the question whether there is a right to a rudimentary level of well-being, though as I suggested a moment ago, I do not think the state's duty of benevolence is this limited.

as something presupposed by the very terms of the discussion; for our concern is with social arrangements for continued existence, not with those for a suicide club.... To raise ... any ... question concerning *how* men should live together, we must assume that their aim, generally speaking, is to live.[64]

Because survival is a primary purpose of political society—indeed, as Hart implies, one presupposed by all *other* objectives—it is natural to suppose that rational participants in a social contract would give recognition to the this fact by incorporating into the constitution of their state a duty on the part of governments to provide for their basic needs. No rational goal of political society is more fundamental than survival; so no rational social contract would permit other constitutional provisions to take precedence over it. Not even individual liberty can be a more fundamental value; for liberty is of value neither to a corpse, nor to those who lack the basic necessities of life. Rights to a minimal level of well-being must therefore be recognized as central to any fully rational constitution. Such rights are demanded by reason as a sine qua non of the formation of political society, and must therefore be regarded as setting internal limitations on all other rights in political society, including the right to pursue one's own ends. From this it follows that being required to pay taxes in support of welfare legislation should not be regarded as a violation of the right of each individual to pursue her own ends, but as one of the boundary conditions imposed by practical reason on this right.

The same cannot be said about many other restrictions on personal freedom, including our previous example of a law imposing servitude on unpopular minorities. Freedom, Kant holds, is a primary rational end of humankind. It would accordingly be irrational for members of any group to accept a law imposing servitude on them. Consequently no rational social

[64] Hart 1984, 188.

contract could contain such a law. A law of this sort would be antithetical to reason, for it could not represent an internal limitation on the right to pursue one's own ends. As Kant says in connection with other morally arbitrary limitations on personal liberty, this would be a restriction that no people could "be permitted" to impose on itself.[65] Instead of being an internal limitation on the right to pursue one's own ends in civil society, such a law—along with all other morally arbitrary restrictions on the freedom of particular groups—would be a violation of this right, not to mention of the right to legal equality.

[65] TP 305\85.

The Continuing Significance of
Kant's Political Philosophy

I HAVE ATTEMPTED TO EXPLAIN AND, WHERE NECESSARY, RECON-
struct the main elements of Kant's political philosophy. It is
now time to take stock of the overall result and to ask what
our general assessment of Kant's political philosophy should
be. Does it have any claim on our attention today? Is there anything we can still learn from it? Or is it only an object of an-
tiquarian value, something Kant scholars may quibble over but
which is of concern to few others?

My own response will come as no surprise: I am persuaded
that there is a good deal of value in Kant's political philosophy.
I also believe, however, that if we are to arrive at a correct es-
timate of its merits, we must avoid the temptation to make
grandiose or exaggerated claims on its behalf. To start with, we
must acknowledge that some of Kant's views are manifestly indefensible to present-day sensibilities, particularly his property
qualification for the electoral franchise, his absolutist conception of sovereignty, and his unwillingness to admit any right
of revolution. These ideas are among the least appealing in
Kant's political writings; nothing is lost by admitting their
deficiencies.

In addition we must acknowledge that Kant's political philosophy occupies a rather modest position in the Kantian corpus. Kant's contribution to political philosophy is less significant than his contribution to ethics in the *Groundwork* and the *Critique of Practical Reason*, or to epistemology and metaphysics in the *Critique of Pure Reason*. Kant's influence on the development of epistemology and metaphysics has been massive, equaled only by a handful of other figures in the history of philosophy. The same is true in ethics. Hardly anyone nowadays accepts Kant's ethical theory without alteration or revision, yet it is nonetheless impossible to work seriously in the field of ethics without encountering Kant's shadow at every turn. Some philosophers are sympathetic to Kantian ethics, others are hostile, but few have managed to develop their own views without encountering and grappling, superficially at least, with Kant's ethical writings. We cannot credibly make the same claims for Kant's political writings. Compared with his ethical, epistemological, and metaphysical works, his political essays have had relatively little influence, doubtless in part because they are less original than the writings of other political philosophers—Marx, Hobbes, Rousseau, and Machiavelli come quickly to mind.

Given these caveats about Kant's political philosophy, what can we say about its merits or continuing importance? Let me begin to answer this question by recalling something I noted in Chapter 1 and have stressed several times since, namely that the principal value in Kant's political philosophy is freedom. Of Kant's commitment to the idea of freedom we have had ample evidence, including his repeated characterizations of a just constitution as one that assures each individual the greatest possible freedom within the context of a law-governed society. In practice, this freedom turns out to have two dimensions in Kant's theory of justice—one civil, the other political. Civil freedom—what we sometimes describe loosely as "personal liberty"—is the freedom to pursue one's own ends as one sees fit under the protection of the law. Political freedom is the liberty to participate along with others in determining the laws by which one is governed, and by which one's civil freedom is defined. Both types of liberty are morally necessary, according to Kant.

The lasting importance of Kant's political philosophy is closely connected with the central role Kant assigns to freedom in both of these senses. Kant was a liberal and like most classical liberals, including Mill, Locke, and von Humboldt, he was concerned primarily with the preservation and enhancement of civil freedom. Reflecting the laissez-faire ideology then emerging in Europe, Kant was anxious to assure the individual's freedom of action to compete in the economic marketplace. But he was also, like many other liberals, committed to the moral necessity of political freedom in the form of a popularly elected representative legislature. These are the two components of the Kantian ideal of external freedom.

Kant was not, of course, the first political philosopher to champion civil and political freedom. Among classical liberals who had already defended such liberties, we have no trouble identifying Locke in England and Condorcet in France, to whose names a host of others could easily be added. Nor can we plausibly present Kant as the most eloquent defender of liberty, for that honor ought surely to go to Mill, whose prose style, even on a bad day, far surpassed Kant's. On Kant's behalf, however, we can say two things: first, that he was one of the most clearheaded of early liberals in his understanding of the relation between civil and political freedom; second, that he was able to provide a sounder justificatory basis for these freedoms than could many other liberals, then or now.

As to the relation between civil and political freedom, Kant had a finely-tuned sense of the dangers of popular self-government. Long before Mill warned in *On Liberty* of the

threat to personal liberty originating from democratic government, and nearly half a century before Tocqueville in *Democracy in America* introduced the idea of the tyranny of the
majority, Kant saw the need in *Theory and Practice* and *Perpetual Peace* to protect individuals against the encroachments
of popularly elected governments by constitutionally entrench-
ing civil freedom alongside political freedom as an a priori right
belonging to each person in virtue of her humanity. So although Kant was not the first to appreciate the risks popular
government can pose to personal liberty, he nonetheless understood them clearly, and for this insight, as well as his resulting
effort to balance civil against political freedom, he deserves to
be ranked as one of the foremost early liberal defenders of personal liberty.

Turning to the question of justification, we discover Kant's
position to be even stronger, as can be seen by contrasting his
defense of civil liberty with those of some other well-known
liberals. Consider Mill, for instance. Mill asserts in a famous—
and famously overstated—remark in *On Liberty* that the "only
freedom which deserves the name is that of pursuing our own
good in our own way, so long as we do not attempt to deprive
others of theirs or impede their efforts to obtain it."[1] When it
comes to defending this freedom, though, Mill suffers the well-
known embarrassment of having to rest his case entirely on the
principle of utility,[2] which, as many critics have pointed out, is
ill-equipped to bear the burden. For no matter how generously
we interpret the idea of utility, or how carefully we define the
proper scope of personal liberty, it will always remain a contingent, empirical, and therefore precarious matter whether the
general utility is or is not best served by protecting individual
liberty. Surely if personal liberty is as valuable as Mill insists,
we should at least *attempt* to find a more permanent founda-

[1] Mill, *On Liberty*, 72.
[2] Mill, *On Liberty*, 69–70.

tion for it than the eminently disputable proposition that it contributes optimally to the general happiness. No individual's freedom is likely to be secure as long as its sole justification is that it promotes the general happiness.[3]

Mill is not the only liberal whose defense of civil freedom runs into trouble as soon as its normative underpinnings are questioned. Consider two more recent liberal theorists: Isaiah Berlin and Friedrich A. Hayek. Both are impassioned defenders of individual liberty. Both believe that nothing is of more importance in human affairs than that each person should have a well-defined area of personal liberty within which she may act on her own wishes and follow her own choices without hindrance from others. If we ask, however, what the justificatory basis is for placing such a premium on individual liberty, the answers provided by Berlin and Hayek are disconcerting. Hayek stakes his defense of personal liberty on skepticism about moral rationality, while Berlin resorts to a kindred species of moral relativism. In direct contradiction to Kant, Hayek claims that "reason" is powerless to determine "ends" and hence cannot "tell us what we ought [morally] to do."[4] Hayek regards it as a fatal "overestimation of the powers of reason" to suppose that reason can by itself settle questions of value, especially

---

[3] A historical aside: it is curious that although Mill was perfectly willing in *On Liberty* (1854) to base personal freedom on the principle of utility, he showed a much greater awareness of the potential obstacles to this approach in his earlier *Principles of Political Economy* (1848). In *On Liberty* he seems to reason thus: (1) each person is interested in her own happiness; (2) each is the best judge of how to achieve her own happiness; (3) each will try to achieve her own happiness; and (4) if each does so, the sum total of all these private efforts will be the greatest happiness of the greatest number (69–70, 72, 143, 151). In the *Principles of Political Economy*, however, Mill is conscious that (2) is quite doubtful, and cannot hold other than as a very general rule, which must admit of numerous "exceptions" (5:11:7–13). It is odd that Mill should later have forgotten this rather important point.

[4] Hayek 1971, 32, 34.

questions of moral value.[5] In his view, any such contention is an "illusion" pure and simple. The truth, he insists, is that Hume was right: reason is nothing more than a slave of the passions, a means of attaining ends that are set ultimately by our sensible natures. That is why, Hayek argues, we must eschew any attempt to organize political society around the pursuit of rationally discernable "common ends." We must instead allow each individual to pursue her own "particular ends," just because there are no other ends.

Hayek's position is skeptical, though he does not advertise it as such. Berlin's, on the other hand, is relativistic. He speaks of the "relativity of values," of their "subjective" nature, meanwhile disparaging the "old objectivistic thesis" that "there exists such a thing as an attainable . . . truth in the field of value judgments."[6] Berlin agrees with Hayek that there are no objective moral values for which we can claim "eternal validity."[7] Berlin and Hayek both believe this is why individual liberty is of such importance. When we come to understand, as Hayek would have it, that there are no common rational ends, only variable personal ends—or that all values are merely subjective and relative, as Berlin maintains—then we must conclude, both insist, that there is no higher good than the arbitrary or relative good each individual sets for herself. And so, Berlin and Hayek infer, we must fence off an area of individual liberty within which each person can be free to pursue her own purely subjective ends according to her own tastes.

The weakness of these views should be more or less apparent on first reading. Relativistic arguments have a tendency to be self-defeating.[8] If someone claims that "all truths are relative,"

---

[5] Hayek 1971, 32.
[6] Berlin 1969, li–lvi.
[7] Berlin 1969, 172.
[8] Useful critical discussions of relativism can be found in Putnam 1982, chaps. 5 and 6; see also Lyons, 15–35.

we need only remind him that if so, the truth of relativism must itself be only relative, in which case we may comfortably reject it by saying that it is "not true for us." A similar point can be made with respect to liberal defenses of individual freedom such as Hayek's and Berlin's, which rest on relativistic or skeptical assumptions about the rationality or objectivity of values. If there are no objective or rational values, then we are entitled to ask what makes individual ends, or individual choices, or individual freedom worth protecting. If Hayek's skepticism about moral rationality is well-founded, it may perhaps follow that there are no higher ends than rationally arbitrary individual ends. If these are the only ends there are, however, and if they are indeed morally arbitrary, it is unclear why they should be considered worth protecting at all, let alone why their protection should be the principal normative aim of political society.

Roughly the same questions arise with Berlin's relativism. How is it possible simultaneously to claim that there are no objective values, that all values are purely subjective, and yet that we ought always to hold personal liberty in such high regard as to make it one of the central pillars of political life?[9] We cannot consistently believe both that there are no objective moral values and that personal liberty is objectively valuable, something it makes sense to insist that people *should* always respect and preserve.

The long and short of it is that Hayek and Berlin make the same mistake. They both (1) deny that there are objective ends or values, and they both take this to mean (2) that the only ends or values worth preserving are the subjective ends and

---

[9] Sandel raises a similar issue about the liberal basis of individual freedom when he says that if all individual conceptions of the good are morally arbitrary, it is difficult to see why their protection should be a primary concern of justice, or indeed why justice itself should matter if it has no higher purpose than to protect the pursuit of such morally dubious goods (Sandel 1984, 161–62).

values of individuals. But the truth of the matter is that (1) undercuts rather than supports (2), since if there are no objective ends or values, neither can there be any rational or objective grounds for valuing individual ends or individual liberty. The lesson to be drawn from this is that liberals must avoid the temptation to base their arguments for personal liberty on relativistic or sceptical premises. The results will always be disappointing.

One of the chief merits of Kant's brand of liberalism is that it manages to avoid the pitfalls of relativism and skepticism without generating the kinds of problems that arise from utilitarian or consequentialist theories. Kant's justification of civil and political freedom is based, not on empirical claims to the effect that these liberties are utility maximizing; nor on skeptical or relativistic moral epistemologies that deny the objectivity of values; but rather on deontic principles, categorical imperatives, for which Kant claims universal validity at all times and in all circumstances. Kant is able to maintain that the protection of civil and political freedom is the primary normative function of political society because he believes that there are objective moral principles that impose duties to respect these freedoms, and which therefore also provide the basis for corresponding rights.

In Kant's moral theory the rights to civil and political freedom derive, as I indicated in Chapter 2, from the supreme principle of morality in the form of the principles of universal law, humanity, and autonomy. I shall not repeat my earlier explanations of how these principles serve to establish the moral necessity of civil and political freedom. Suffice it to say that, by grounding civil and political freedom in these a priori moral principles, Kant was able to do what liberals as diverse as Mill, Berlin, and Hayek have subsequently been unable to do: provide a firm, permanent, unwavering basis for the ideals of personal liberty and political self-determination, which are plainly part of the bedrock of our shared political culture.

Freedom, however, is not the only value that Kant believes political society is meant to promote. Altogether, civil society has three primary functions for Kant. Maximizing law-governed freedom is the first, but human beings have other rational ends besides freedom. Because human beings are embodied and thus have sensible needs, human reason, Kant insists, has a responsibility to attend to the sensible needs of humankind.[10] To exercise freedom human beings must live, and to live they must have their basic needs satisfied. Freedom as a purpose of civil society consequently presupposes a certain standard of well-being in the absence of which it is impossible to make effective use of freedom. In recognition of this, Kant argues that a rational social contract and a rational constitution must include a duty on the part of the state to provide for the needs of its subjects. This is not a duty of justice, for justice is concerned only with the ordering of individual freedom, not with human needs. The state's duty to provide for the needs of its citizens is instead a duty of benevolence or philanthropy. The mistake made by those who treat Kant as an advocate of the minimal state is to fail to see that Kant believes there is an ethical dimension to the responsibilities of the state alongside its obligation to ensure justice.

The third primary purpose of the state, for Kant, is teleological. Recall our earlier discussion of Kant's philosophy of history in Chapter 2. Nature's highest purpose for humankind is the development of all its rational capacities.[11] Civil society promotes this objective by providing a stable, law-governed social order within which individuals compete against each other to fulfill their varying personal ambitions, leading to the growth of art, science, and culture and the development of manifold human skills and talents. Civil society is thus the medium in which all human progress takes place. Initially, this

[10] KPV 61.
[11] IAG 18; KU 443–44.

progress takes the form of increasing instrumental and theoretical rationality. The growth of instrumental and theoretical rationality, however, enables human beings to gain control over their animal nature, to overcome the "tyranny" of sensible desires, and thereby to discover the "sovereignty" of reason.[12] Since reason is always "one and the same" faculty, varying only in its mode of employment, Kant is confident that once human rationality has developed in theoretical and instrumental forms, the flourishing of moral rationality must inevitably follow. By serving as an incubator of instrumental and theoretical rationality, the state therefore also serves to promote the development of moral rationality.

For Kant, then, the state has three principal functions and obligations: a duty of justice to ensure a condition of maximum law-governed freedom; a duty of benevolence to provide for the needs of it subjects; and a teleological responsibility to create the framework within which all forms of human rationality can flourish. In one sense, of course, these are all separate functions, but they also have an underlying unity. All are concerned ultimately with promoting freedom. The state's duty to provide for the needs of its subjects is, in effect, a duty to promote their capacity to pursue their own ends by ensuring a basic level of well-being without which the right to pursue one's own ends is nothing more than a formal and empty ideal, a chimera, an illusion. The state's teleological responsibility to foster the development of human rationality is likewise directed toward promoting freedom. Kant holds that the "final end" of creation is the full development of morally practical reason.[13] Inner freedom is negatively the will's capacity to resist the influence of sensible impulses, and positively the will's ability to determine itself in accordance with the demands of pure practical reason. The fullest development of morally practical reason is conse-

[12] KU 433.
[13] KU 435–36.

quently the fullest development of inner freedom. Since it is the historical function of civil society to foster the fullest development of human rationality in all its forms, it is also the historical function of civil society to promote inner freedom. In this way, all of the duties and responsibilities of the state converge on the idea of freedom.

Bibliography

Allison, Henry. 1983. *Kant's Transcendental Idealism.* New Haven: Yale University Press.

Althusius, J. A. [1603] 1965. *The Politics of Johannes Althusius.* Trans. F. S. Carney. Boston: Beacon Press.

Ansboro, John. 1973. "Kant's Limitations on Individual Freedom." *New Scholasticism* 47 (Winter): 88–99.

Arendt, Hannah. 1982. *Lectures on Kant's Political Philosophy.* Edited by Ronald Beiner. Chicago: University of Chicago Press.

Aris, Reinhold. 1965. *History of Political Thought in Germany from 1789 to 1815.* New York: Russell & Russell.

Aristotle, 1984. *The Complete Works of Aristotle,* vol. 2. Ed. J. Barnes, 2152–269. Princeton: Princeton University Press.

Aune, Bruce. 1979. *Kant's Theory of Morals.* Princeton: Princeton University Press.

Austin, John. 1885. *Lectures on Jurisprudence.* Edited by Robert Campbell. London: J. Murray.

Axinn, Sidney. 1971. "Kant, Authority and the French Revolution." *Journal of the History of Ideas* 32 (July–September): 423–32.

Baker, Keith Michael. 1975. *Condorcet: From Natural Philosophy to Social Mathematics.* Chicago: University of Chicago Press.

Barzun, Jacques. 1961. *Classic, Romantic, and Modern.* Chicago: University of Chicago Press.

Batscha, Zwi, ed. 1976. *Materialien zu Kants Rechtsphilosophie.* Frankfurt am Main: Suhrkamp Verlag.

Beattie, J. M. 1986. *Crime and the Courts in England, 1600–1800.* Princeton: Princeton University Press.

Beccaria, Cesare. [1764] 1986. *On Crimes and Punishments.* Translated by David Young. Indianapolis: Hackett.

Beck, Lewis White. 1960. *A Commentary on Kant's Critique of Practical Reason.* Chicago: University of Chicago Press.

———. 1965. "Kant's Two Conceptions of the Will in Their Political Context." In *Studies in the Philosophy of Kant,* 215–29. Indianapolis: Bobbs-Merrill.

———. 1971. "Kant and the Right of Revolution." *Journal of the History of Ideas* 32 (July–September): 411–22.

Bien, Gunther. 1976. "Revolution, Bürgerbegriff und Freiheit. Über die neuzeitliche Transformation der alteuropäischen Verfassungstheorie in politische Geschichtsphilosophie." In Batscha 1976, 77–101.

Berlin, Isaiah. 1969. "Two Concepts of Liberty." In *Four Essays on Liberty,* 118–72. Oxford: Oxford University Press.

Bodin, Jean. [1577] 1955. *Six Books of the Commonwealth.* Translated by M. J. Tooley. New York: Macmillan.

Booth, William J. 1986. *Interpreting the World: Kant's Philosophy of History and Politics.* Toronto: University of Toronto Press.

Burg, Peter. 1974. *Kant und die französische Revolution.* Berlin: Duncker & Humbolt.

Burke, Edmund. [1790] 1973. *Reflections on the Revolution in France.* New York: Anchor Books.

Cairns, H. 1949. *Legal Philosophy from Plato to Hegel.* Baltimore: Johns Hopkins University Press.

Cassirer, Ernst. 1945a. *The Question of Jean Jacques Rousseau.* Translated by Peter Gay. Bloomington: Indiana University Press.

———. 1945b. *Rousseau, Kant, Goethe.* Translated by James Gutman, Paul Oskar Kristellar, and John H. Randall, Jr. Princeton: Princeton University Press. Reprinted 1970.

———. 1968. *The Philosophy of the Enlightenment.* Translated by Fritz C. A. Koelln and James P. Pettegrove. Princeton: Princeton University Press. Reprinted 1979.

———. 1981. *Kant's Life and Thought.* New Haven: Yale University Press.

Cohen, Morris. 1950. *Reason and Law: Studies in Juristic Philosophy.* Glencoe, Ill.: Free Press.

Cohn, E. J. 1968. *A Manual of German Law*, vol. 3. London: British Institute of Comparative Law.

Collingwood, R. G. 1946. *The Idea of History*. Oxford: Oxford University Press. Reprinted 1975.

Cox, Archibald. 1976. *The Role of the Supreme Court in American Government*. New York: Oxford University Press.

———. 1987. *The Court and the Constitution*. Boston: Houghton Mifflin Company.

Dahl, Norman O. 1983. "Rational Desire." In Sartorius 1983, 261–71.

Denning, Alfred Lord. 1961. *Responsibility before the Law*. Jerusalem: Magnes Press.

d'Entrèves, A. P. 1952. *Natural Law: An Introduction to Legal Philosophy*.

Descartes, René. [1641] 1979. *Meditations on First Philosophy*. Translated by Donald Cress. Indianapolis: Hackett.

Devlin, Lord Patrick. 1965. *The Enforcement of Morals*. Oxford: Oxford University Press.

Dworkin, Ronald. 1978. *Taking Rights Seriously*, 81–130. Cambridge, Mass.: Harvard University Press.

———. 1986. *Law's Empire*. Cambridge, Mass.: Harvard University Press.

Edwards, J. L. 1955. *Mens Rea in Statutory Offences*. London: Macmillan.

Feinberg, Joel. 1983. "Legal Paternalism." In Sartorius 1983, 3–18.

———. 1984. *The Moral Limits of the Criminal Law*, vol. 1: *Harm to Others*. New York: Oxford University Press.

Fichte, J. G. [1889] 1970. *The Science of Rights*. Translated by A. E. Kroeger. New York: Harper & Row.

Flechter, George. 1987. "Law and Morality: A Kantian Perspective." *Columbia Law Review* 87 (April): 533–57.

Franklin, Julian. 1973. *Jean Bodin and the Rise of Absolutist Theory*. Cambridge: Cambridge University Press.

Friedrich, Carl J. 1958. *The Philosophy of Law in Historical Perspective*. Chicago: The University of Chicago Press.

———. 1968. *Constitutional Government and Democracy*. New York: Blaisdell Publishing.

Gay, Peter. 1969. *The Enlightenment: An Interpretation*. vol. 2. New York: W. W. Norton.

Gierke, Otto. 1957. *Natural Law and the Theory of Society*. Boston: Beacon Press.

Golding, M. P. Ed. 1966. *The Nature of Law*. New York: Random House.

Gray, J. C. 1972. *The Nature and Sources of the Law*. Gloucester, Mass.: Peter Smith.

Gray, John. 1988. *Liberalism*. Minneapolis: University of Minnesota Press.

Grcic, Joseph. 1986. "Kant on Revolution and Economic Inequality." *Kant-Studien* 77, 1: 447–57.

Green, T. H. 1986. *Lectures on the Principles of Political Obligation*. Edited by P. Harris and J. Morrow. Cambridge: Cambridge University Press.

Gregor, Mary. 1963. *Laws of Freedom. A Study of Kant's Method of Applying the Categorical Imperative in the* Metaphysik der Sitten. New York: Barnes and Noble.

Grey, Thomas. 1987. "Serpents and Doves: a Note on Kantian Legal Theory." *Columbia Law Review* 87 (April): 480–91.

Habermas, Jürgen. 1976. "Publizität als Prinzip der Vermittlung von Politik und Moral (Kant)." In Batscha 1976, 175–92.

Hare, R. M. 1981. *Moral Thinking: Its Levels, Method, and Point*. Oxford: Oxford University Press.

Hart, H. L. A. 1961. *The Concept of Law*. Oxford: Oxford University Press. Reprinted 1984.

———. 1968. *Punishment and Legal Responsibility*. Oxford: Clarendon Press. Reprinted 1982.

Hayek, Friedrich A. 1973. *Law, Legislation and Liberty*, vol. 1. Chicago: University of Chicago Press.

Henrich, Dieter. 1976. "Kant über die Revolution." in Batscha 1976, 359–65.

Hertz, F. 1975. *The German Public Mind in the Nineteenth Century*. London: Allen & Unwin.

Hinsley, F. H. 1986. *Sovereignty*. Cambridge: Cambridge University Press.

Hirschman, Albert O. 1977. *The Passions and the Interests: Political Arguments for Capitalism before its Triumph*. Princeton: Princeton University Press.

Hobbes, Thomas. [1651] 1968. *Leviathan*. Edited by C. B. MacPherson Harmondsworth, Middlesex: Penguin Books.

Hobhouse, L. T. 1911. *Liberalism*. Oxford: Oxford University Press. Reprinted 1964.

Hohfeld, Wesley N. 1964. *Fundamental Legal Conceptions, as Applied in Judicial Reasoning*. New Haven: Yale University Press.

Holborn, Hajo. 1982. *A History of Modern Germany 1648–1840*. Princeton: Princeton University Press.

Humboldt, Wilhelm von. [1852] 1969. *The Limits of State Action*. Translated and edited by J. W. Burrow. Cambridge: Cambridge University Press.

Hume, David. [1742] 1985. "Of the Original Contract." In *Essays Moral, Political and Literary*, 465–87. Edited by E. F. Miller. Indianapolis: Liberty Classics.

Jaspers, Karl. 1962. *Kant*. Translated by Ralph Mannheim. Edited by Hannah Arendt. New York: Harcourt, Brace & World.

Kelly, George A. 1972. *Idealism, Politics and History: Sources of Hegelian Thought*. Cambridge: Cambridge University Press.

Kern, Fritz. 1914. *Kingship and Law in the Middle Ages*, vol. 1, *The Divine Right of Kings and the Right of Resistance in the Early Middle Ages*. Translated by S. B. Chrimes. Oxford: Basil Blackwell. Reprinted 1948.

Kersting, Wolfgang 1984. *Wohlgeordnete Freiheit: Immanuel Kants Rechts-und Staatsphilosophie*. Berlin: Walter de Gruyter.

Korsgaard, Christine. 1987. "Kant's Formula of Humanity." *Kant-Studien* 77, 1:183–202.

Krieger, Leonard. 1965. *The Politics Of Discretion: Puffendorf and the Acceptance of Natural Law*. Chicago: University of Chicago Press.

Laski, Harold. 1951. *A Grammar of Politics*. London: George Allen & Unwin.

Leibniz, G. W. F. 1972. *The Political Writings of Leibniz*. Translated and edited by Patrick Riley. Cambridge: Cambridge University Press.

Locke, John. [1690] 1963. *Two Treatises of Government*. Edited by Peter Laslett. Cambridge: Cambridge University Press.

Lyons, David. 1970. "The Correlativity of Rights and Duties." *Nous* 4:45–57.

———. 1984. *Ethics and the Rule of Law*. Cambridge: Cambridge University Press.

Macpherson, C. B. 1978. *Property: Mainstream and Critical Positions*. Toronto: University of Toronto Press.

Maine, Henry. 1939. *Ancient Law*. Oxford: J. Murray.

Maritain, Jacques. "The Concept of Sovereignty." In *In Defense of Sovereignty*, edited by W. J. Stankiewicz, 41–64. London: Oxford University Press, 1969.

Marshall, Geoffrey. 1980. *Constitutional Theory*. Oxford: Oxford University Press.

Marx, Karl. 1913. *The German Ideology*. New York: International Publishers. Reprinted 1985.

Merkle, P. H. 1963. *The Origin of the West German Republic*. Oxford: Oxford University Press.

Merryman, J. H. 1985. *The Civil Law Tradition: An Introduction to the Legal Systems of Western Europe and Latin America*. Stanford: Stanford University Press.

Mill, John Stuart. [1854] 1984. *On Liberty*. Edited by Gertrude Himmglfarb. New York: Penguin Books.

——. [1848] 1987. *Principles of Political Economy*. Edited by Sir William Ashley. Fairfield, N.J.: August M. Kelly Publishers.

Miller, Arthur S. 1978. *The Supreme Court*. London: Greenwood Press.

Montesquieu, Baron de. [1748] 1949. *The Spirit of the Laws*. Translated by T. N. Nugent. New York: Macmillan & Co.

Morris, Clarence, ed. 1981. *The Great Legal Philosophers: Selected Readings in Jurisprudence*. Philadelphia: University of Pennsylvania Press.

Murphy, Jeffrey. 1970. *Kant: the Philosophy of Right*. London: Macmillan & Co.

Nell, Onora. See Onora O'Neill.

Nelson, M. V. 1967. *A Study of Judicial Review in Virginia*. New York: AMS Press.

Nicholas, Barry. 1962. *An Introduction to Roman Law*. Oxford: Clarendon Press. Reprinted. 1988.

Nicholson, Peter. 1975. "Kant on the Duty Never to Resist the Sovereign." *Ethics* 86, 3:214–30.

Nisbet, Robert. 1980. *History of the Idea of Progress*. New York: Basic Books.

Nozick, Robert. 1974. *Anarchy, State and Utopia*. New York: Basic Books.

O'Neill, Onora (Nell). 1975. *Acting on Principle: An Essay on Kantian Ethics*. New York: Columbia University Press. (Author's name Onora Nell at time of publication.)

——. 1986. "The Public Use of Reason." *Political Theory* 14, 4:523–51.

——. 1989. *Constructions of Reason: Explorations of Kant's Practical Philosophy*. Cambridge: Cambridge University Press.

Pateman, Carole. 1985. *The Problem of Political Obligation: A Critique of Liberal Theory*. Berkeley: University of California Press.

Paton, H. J. 1949. *The Categorical Imperative: A Study in Kant's Moral Theory.* Philadelphia: University of Pennsylvania Press. Reprinted 1971.

Plamenatz, J. 1963. *Man and Society,* vol. 1: *A Critical Examination of Some Important Social and Political Theories from Machiavelli to Marx.* London: Longmans. Reprinted 1965.

———. 1968. *Consent, Freedom and Political Obligation.* Oxford: Oxford University Press.

Plato, 1981. *Crito.* In *Five Dialogues: Euthyphro, Apology, Crito, Meno, Phaedo.* Translated by G. M. A. Grube. Indianapolis: Hackett.

Pogge, Thomas. 1988. "Kant's Theory of Justice." *Kant-Studien* 79, 4: 407–33.

Pound, Roscoe. 1954. *An Introduction to the Philosophy of Law.* New Haven: Yale University Press.

Putnam, Hilary. 1982. *Reason, Truth and History.* London: Cambridge University Press.

Rawls, John. 1971. *A Theory of Justice.* Cambridge, Mass.: Harvard University Press.

———. 1980. "Kantian Constructivism in Moral Theory." *Journal of Philosophy* 77, 9:515–72.

Reiss, Hans. 1956. "Kant and the Right of Rebellion." *Journal of the History of Ideas* 17, 2:179–92.

Riedel, Manfred. 1976. "Herrschaft und Gesellschaft. Zum Legitimationsproblem des Politischen in der Philosophie." In Batscha 1976, 125–50.

Riley, Patrick. 1983. *Kant's Political Philosophy.* Totowa, N. J.: Rowan & Littlefield.

Ritter, Gerhard. 1968. *Frederick the Great: A Historical Profile.* Berkeley: University of California Press. Reprinted 1974.

Ross, David. 1954. *Kant's Ethical Theory: A Commentary on the Grundlegung zur Metaphysik der Sitten.* Oxford: Oxford University Press.

Rossiter, Clinton, ed. 1964. *The Federalist Papers: Alexander Hamilton, James Madison, John Jay.* New York: New American Library.

Rousseau, Jean-Jacques. [1762] 1970. *The Social Contract.* Translated and edited by Lester Crocker. New York: Pocket Books.

———. [1835] 1980. *The Government of Poland.* Translated by W. Kendall. Indianapolis: Hacket.

———. [1755] 1986. *The First and Second Discourses together with the Replies to Critics and Essay on The Origin of Language.* Translated by Victor Gourevitch. New York: Harper & Row.

Ryan, Alan. 1984. *Property and Political Theory.* New York: Basil Blackwell.

Salmond, J. W. 1893.*The First Principles of Jurisprudence.* London: Stevens & Haynes.

Sandel, Michael. ed. 1984. *Liberalism and its Critics.* New York: New York University Press.

Saner, Hans. 1973. *Kant's Political Thought, Its Origins and Development.* Translated by E. B. Ashton. Chicago: University of Chicago Press.

Sartorius, Rolf. ed. 1983. *Paternalism.* Minneapolis: University of Minnesota Press.

Schilpp, Paul Arthur. 1938. *Kant's Pre-Critical Ethics.* Evanston, Il.: Northwestern University Press.

Setalvad, M. C. 1967. *The Indian Constitution.* Bombay: Bombay University Press.

Shklar, Judith. 1969. *Men and Citizens: A Study of Rousseau's Social Theory.* Cambridge: Cambridge University Press.

Sidgwick, Henry. [1874] 1981. *The Methods of Ethics,* 7th ed. Indianapolis: Hackett.

Skinner, Quentin. 1980. *The Foundations of Modern Political Thought,* vol. 2. Cambridge: Cambridge University Press.

Smith, Adam. [1776] 1976. *The Wealth of Nations.* Edited by Edwin Cannan. Chicago: University of Chicago Press.

———. [1759] 1982. *The Theory of Moral Sentiments.* Edited by D. D. Raphael and A. L. Macfie. Indianapolis: Liberty Classics.

Smith, J. C. 1965. *Criminal Law.* London: Butterworths.

Stafford, W. P. 1934. *A Hand Book of Equity.* Washington, D.C.: National Law Book Co.

Stephen, James Fitzjames. 1890. *Criminal Law of England.* New York: Macmillan & Co.

Strong, C. F. 1963. *A History of Modern Political Constitutions.* New York: Capricorn Books.

Thompson, J. M. 1985. *The French Revolution.* Oxford: Basil Blackwell.

Tribe, Laurence. 1985. *Constitutional Choices.* Cambridge Mass.: Harvard University Press.

Tuck, Richard. 1978. *Natural Rights Theories: Their Origin and Development.* Cambridge: Cambridge University Press.

van der Linden, Harry. 1988. *Kantian Ethics and Socialism*. Indianapolis: Hackett.

Vico, Giambattista. [1725] 1961. *The New Science of Giambattista Vico*. Translated by T. G. Bergin & H. Fisch. New York: Anchor Books.

Vorländer, Karl. 1977. *Immanuel Kant: Der Mann und das Werk*. Hamburg: Felix Meiner Verlag.

Watson, Alan. 1968. *Law of Property in the Later Roman Republic*. Oxford: Oxford University Press.

Wheare, K. C. 1962. *Modern Constitutions*. New York: Oxford University Press.

Williams, Howard. 1983. *Kant's Political Philosophy*. New York: St. Martin's Press.

Windeyer, W. J. V. 1973. *Some Aspects of Australian Constitutional Law*. Edmonton: University of Alberta, Institute of Law Research and Reform.

Wood, Allen. 1970. *Kant's Moral Religion*. Ithaca: Cornell University Press.

———. 1984. "Kant's Compatibalism." In *Self and Nature in Kant's Philosophy*, edited by Allen Wood, 73–101. Ithaca: Cornell University Press.

Wootton, David, ed. 1986. *Divine Right and Democracy: An Anthology of Political Writing in Stuart England*. Harmondsworth, Middlesex: Penguin Books.

Wynes, William A. 1970. *Legislative, Executive and Judicial Powers in Australia*. Sidney: Law Book Company.

Yovel, Yirmiyaha. 1980. *Kant and the Philosophy of History*. Princeton: Princeton University Press.

Index

Absolutism, 142–43, 144–45
American Constitution
  (1787), 145n
Anarchy argument, 158–59
Animality, 72–73, 75–76, 78–79,
  125–26. *See also* State of nature
Arendt, Hannah, 1
Aristotle, 35n, 69, 105
Augustine, Saint, 112
Aune, Bruce, 173, 174, 176n
Austin, John, 113, 114
Authoritarianism, 149–50
Autonomous laws, 60–61
Autonomy: and morality, 58–62,
  160–61; and political freedom,
  44–45, 58–62

Beck, Lewis White, 166–67, 169
Begging, 21
Beliefs, 90
Benevolence, 198–99; and coercion,
  177, 191–92; as function of civil
  society, 217; Kant's doubts about,
  197–98; and paternalism, 189–90,
  196; and preservation of general
  will, 179–80, 181, 201–2; and principle of humanity, 185–86; and
  publicity, 184; and rationality,
  199–200; *Rechtslehre* argument,
  179–80, 181, 184, 189, 192; vs.

rights, 183, 196; and social con-
  tract theory, 200–201, 202
Berlin, Isaiah, 213, 214, 215
Bestiality, 21
Bien, Gunther, 35n
Bodin, Jean, 145
Burke, Edmund, 38

Cassirer, Ernst, 84
Categorical imperatives, 52, 55; and
  autonomy, 58; and civil freedom,
  216; and consent, 23; and free
  choice, 8; and political obligation,
  150; and publicity, 182n; and supreme principle of morality, 50–51,
  53–54; and universal law of justice,
  12–13
Choice. *See* Free choice
Citizens. *See* Political freedom
Civil freedom, 13–14, 15–26, 210–11;
  and categorical imperatives, 216;
  and consent, 17, 23–26; of expression, 18–19; and happiness, 69–71;
  and infringement on freedom of
  others, 16–18; liberal defenses of,
  211–16; and negative freedom, 44,
  45; and paternalism, 15–16; and
  political freedom, 34, 212; principle of, 18; and principle of humanity, 63; and private property,

231

Library of Congress Cataloging-in-Publication Data

Rosen, Allen D. (Allen Duncan), 1952–
    Kant's theory of justice / Allen D. Rosen.
        p.   cm.
    Includes bibliographical references and index.
    ISBN 0-8014-2757-6 (alk. paper)
    1. Kant, Immanuel, 1724–1804—Political and social views.
2. Liberty.   3. State, The.   4. Social ethics.   I. Title.
JC181.K4R65   1993
320'.01—dc20
                                                    93-25807